# THE GALLIC WAR

# THE GALLIC WAR

DOVER THRIFT EDITIONS

Julius Caesar

Translated by
H. J. Edwards

DOVER PUBLICATIONS, INC.
MINEOLA, NEW YORK

# DOVER THRIFT EDITIONS

GENERAL EDITOR: MARY CAROLYN WALDREP
EDITOR OF THIS VOLUME: T. N. R. ROGERS

*Bibliographical Note*

This Dover edition, first published in 2006, is an unabridged republication of the translation first published (as part of a dual-language edition) by the Harvard University Press, Cambridge, Massachusetts, in 1917. For the sake of clarity, we have made minor changes to a few of the footnotes and have deleted references to the appendices in the Harvard edition.

*Library of Congress Cataloging-in-Publication Data*

Caesar, Julius.
[De bello gallico. English]
The Gallic war / Julius Caesar ; translated by H.J. Edwards.
    p. cm. — (Dover thrift editions)
"This Dover edition, first published in 2006, is an unabridged republication of the translation first published by the Harvard University Press, Cambridge, Massachusetts, in 1917."
Includes index.
ISBN-13: 978-0-486-45107-7 (pbk.)
ISBN-10: 0-486-45107-0 (pbk.)
    1. Gaul—History—Gallic Wars, 58–51 B.C. 2. Caesar, Julius—Military leadership. 3. Military history, Ancient. I. Edwards, H. J. (Henry John), 1869–1923. II. Title. III. Series.
DC62.C2E3813 2006
936.4—dc22

2006045433

Manufactured in the United States by LSC Communications
45107007    2018
www.doverpublications.com

# Contents

## Maps and Plans

# Introduction

## OUTLINE OF CAESAR'S LIFE

B.C.

100. Born on 12 July—the month subsequently called after him. Son of C. Julius Caesar and Aurelia.

86. Elected *flamen dialis* through his uncle, C. Marius.

84. Married (1) L. Cinna's daughter, Cornelia.

80. Won the "civic crown" of oak-leaves for saving a Roman's life at the storming of Mitylene.

78. Prosecuted Cn. Dolabella for extortion.

76. Captured by pirates.
Elected *tribunus militum*.

74. Raised a company of volunteers at Rhodes, and held Caria against Mithradates.

68. *Quaestor*: sent to Spain to settle the finances of the country.

67. Married (2) Pompeia, Pompey's cousin.
Helped to carry *Lex Gabinia,* giving Pompey command against the Mediterranean pirates.

66. Supported *Lex Manilia,* giving Pompey command against Mithradates.

65. *Aedile*: gave public games with great splendour.

63. Elected *Pontifex Maximus*.
Spoke in the Senate in the debate on the fellow-conspirators of Catiline.

62. *Praetor*: suspended by the Senate for opposition, but at once restored with an apology.

61. Governor, as *Propraetor,* of Further Spain: gained victories over the Lusitanians.

60. Formed with Pompey and Crassus "The First Triumvirate."

vii

B.C.

59.    *Consul* (I) with Bibulus. Appointed governor as *Proconsul,* of Gallia Cisalpina, Gallia Narbonensis (Provincia), and Illyricum, for five years—*i.e.* 1 March 59 to 28 February 54 B.C.

       Married (3) Calpurnia, daughter of L. Calpurnius Piso.

       Caesar's daughter Julia married to Pompey.

58–51.    Operations in Gaul, Germany, and Britain.

56.    Conference of the Triumvirs at Luca: Caesar's command to be prolonged for five years—*i.e.* to the end of February 49 B.C.

55.    Pompey and Crassus consuls.

54.    Death of Julia.

53.    Crassus killed in action against the Parthians at Carrhae.

51–50.    Disputes at Rome about Caesar's command and second consulship.

49.    Senate decreed that Caesar should disband his army: he crossed the Rubicon, which meant civil war.

       *Dictator* (I) for eleven days.

48.    *Consul* (II). Defeated Pompey at Pharsalus in Thessaly.

       *Dictator* (II) till end of 46 B.C.

47.    Murder of Pompey.

       Settlement of Egypt: Caesar nearly killed at Alexandria.

       Settlement of Asia Minor, after Caesar's victory at Zela (*"Veni, vidi, vici"*) against Pharnaces.

46.    *Consul* (III).

       War in North Africa: Caesar victorious at Thapsus over Scipio and the Pompeian army.

       *Dictator* (III) for ten years.

       Reforms in administration, and in the calendar.

45.    Sole *Consul* (IV). *Dictator.*

       War in Spain: Caesar victorious at Munda over the sons of Pompey (Gnaeus and Sextus) and their army.

       Caesar's triumphs. Further honours and offices: *Imperator* for life, *Consul* for the next ten years, *Dictator* and *Praefectus Morum* for life: *Pater Patriae.*

44.    *Dictator.*

       15 February (*Lupercalia*). Refused the crown.

       15 March (*Ides*) assassinated.

This tabulated outline may serve to indicate how Caesar leapt into prominence in 60 B.C., and spent nine good years in the business of conquering Gaul; and how the five years (49–44 B.C.) at the end were all that he had as a monarch. At forty, he had passed through the round of public offices, and was consul elect for 59 B.C.: he had shown himself a strong supporter of the people, in consistent opposition to the Senate: he had served his apprenticeship at the bar, and, as governor of Further Spain, he had commanded troops with success. In the "First Triumvirate" he was the moving spirit, though still, to the Roman world, it might seem that Pompey was the greatest of the three. Pompey had done wonders in Asia; but for all his successes, military and diplomatic, accepted grudgingly by the Senate, regarded jealously by the popular party, he found himself practically powerless on his return to Rome. In a spirit of true citizenship, he had disbanded his army; and with his army he lost the chance of sovereignty. Doubtless, before the return of Pompey, Caesar had realised that for him too the only path to power lay through conquests that should enlarge the Empire and open up fresh fields for Roman enterprise. Pompey had gone eastward, Caesar sought his fortune in the west. His uncle Marius had checked the stream of barbarian invasion in Transalpine and Cisalpine Gaul: danger was threatening again beyond the Alps, and Caesar saw that his duty and his opportunity lay there. A tribune of his own party, Vatinius, proposed his appointment as governor for five years of Cisalpine Gaul and Illyricum— the province adjoining Cisalpine Gaul at the north-east corner of the Adriatic: the Senate added Transalpine Gaul. Besides his *quaestor,* Caesar was to have ten *legati* to his staff: and four legions were assigned for his expeditionary force.

The order and connection of the campaigns in which Caesar conquered Gaul may be most easily understood by reading the summary of each book (pp. xv to xvii) with the maps of Gaul. After the defensive operations against the Helvetii and Ariovistus (Book I.) in the southeast, Caesar assumed the offensive. First the Belgae (Book II.) in the north, then the Veneti and the Aquitani (Book III.) in the west and south-west, were subdued: then, to prevent the intrusion of fresh support for the Gauls, the legions were sent across the Rhine and the Channel (Book IV.). A second expedition to Britain (Book V.) secured the northwest of Gaul against interference from oversea: but already there were ominous indications of troubles within—the massacre of two general officers with their troops; vehement attacks on the camps of two more. The operations of the next year (53 B.C.: Book VI.) were concerned with the northern tribes, and it was necessary to cross the Rhine once more. Book VII. is entirely taken up with the record of the great revolt of the Gauls under Vercingetorix, in which the central tribes, headed by the Arverni, and joined even by the Aedui, made a desperate but unsuccessful effort to rid themselves of Roman rule. At the beginning of Book

VIII. we are told that "all Gaul was subdued": but it would be truer to say (as in chapter 24) that "the most warlike nations were subdued," for there were still some centres of resistance, and some leaders of influence, to be overcome. The last chapters of the book show that in the year 50 B.C. all was quiet in Gaul: but in Italy events were moving rapidly and irresistibly towards civil war, and in January 49 Caesar crossed the Rubicon.

Generals are not born, but made—by study and experience. We can scarcely doubt that Caesar had added to a general study of war a more detailed knowledge of recent campaigns such as those of Sertorius, Lucullus, and Pompey. He had seen some service before the Gallic War: but to him, as to Oliver Cromwell, the opportunity of a large command came as it were by accident, after the fortieth year of age. The keynote of Caesar's generalship, as the Commentaries themselves frequently state, and everywhere imply, was speed, swiftness (*celeritas*). He was swift to calculate and decide, swift to move—and by movement to keep the initiative, to surprise the enemy and divide his strength; swift, in the hour of battle, to seize the tactical opportunity, to remedy the tactical mistake; swift always in pursuit, knowing full well that he only who pursues till he can go no further secures the full fruit of victory. Such speed in war as Caesar's was no gift of fortune: it depended on certain conditions in himself and his army. He had an energy which was invincible and irresistible: he had that courage which ignores fear or danger,[1] but which refuses to be foolhardy. In his expeditions he combined boldness and caution; he fought his battles not only of design, but as opportunity offered.[2] Strong himself in body, mind and character, he was still so human that he won and kept the affection of his officers and the devoted admiration of his men. As generous in praise as he was gentle in rebuke, as careful of his troops as he was careless of himself, eager to lead but unwilling to drive, seeing clearly and pursuing patiently the one great end through all the labyrinth of war—that is the picture of Caesar which this book reveals. To the faults of the men, even to the mistakes of his officers, he could be lenient: but to the real sins of a soldier—cowardice, mutiny, desertion—he showed no mercy. The discipline of Caesar was truly based on mutual understanding and self-respect; and his army grew to love him as a man and a soldier, and to believe in him as a leader, just as the British troops swore by "Corporal John," and the French adored "Le Petit Caporal." Like Marlborough and Napoleon, Caesar knew what the *moral* of an army means—knew how to create it, and to sustain it. So

---

[1] *cf.* Shakespeare, *Julius Caesar,* ii. 2:
        "Danger knows full well,
    That Caesar is more dangerous than he."
[2] *cf.* Suetonius, *Iulius,* c. 58.

trained, so led, troops will go anywhere and do anything: *possunt quia posse videntur.*

But moral superiority alone does not ensure success in war; soldiers are human, and armies cannot live or fight without supplies, nor move without transport. It is the mark of a good general that he appreciates and anticipates the material needs; and it is abundantly clear that Caesar's *celeritas* in the field was rendered possible only by the most careful and constant attention to all details of administration. Sir Arthur Wellesley, writing in 1803 of his own difficulties in command of a force in India, states the axiom for us; "The only mode by which we can inspire either our allies or our enemies with respect for our operations will be to shew them that the army can move with ease and celerity at all times and in all situations."[3] And the record of Caesar's legions in Gaul is no less remarkable for the works which they accomplished than for the battles which they won. With an amazing speed and versatility they built war-ships, transports, bridges, forts, siegeworks; and the master-mind of Caesar made itself felt always and everywhere, choosing special officers to superintend operations, keenly interested himself in the work, however technical,[4] expecting and commanding success, no matter how difficult the conditions.

In wars of conquest, such as were Caesar's campaigns in Gaul, the statesman is needed no less than the soldier, if the conquered peoples are to be reconciled to their new allegiance. Caesar was equal to the double task; indeed, in him the statesman and the soldier worked as one. With a truly imperial sagacity he set the government of Gaul beyond the Alps on so fair and firm a footing as to disarm resentment and turn enemies into loyal and useful subjects. The land of Gaul had peace almost unbroken for many years; the men of Gaul found their way into the service, both civil and military, of the Roman Empire, of which Caesar was now to become the lord and master. The Triumvirate, renewed in 56 B.C., had ceased to be when Crassus was killed in 53: the bond between Pompey and Caesar was weakened by the death of Julia in 54. Two rivals now were left; and the sword must settle which of them should survive and reign.

The manner in which Caesar's Commentaries on the Gallic War were published is an open question. It is held by some scholars that the first seven books were composed in the winter of 52–51 B.C., and published early in 51. Their publication at that season would undoubtedly have been of particular value, as an indication to the Roman people of

---

[3] Quoted in J. W. Fortescue's *History of the British Army*, vol. v. p. 8.

[4] The chapter (iv. 17) describing the first bridge over the Rhine is so technical in its terms that it may well have been written by an expert engineer—perhaps by Balbus himself, Caesar's *praefectus fabrum*.

Caesar's pre-eminence in strategy and statesmanship, and as a vindication to the Senate of his campaigns and conquests in defence of the Roman Empire. And there is a literary unity in these seven books which supports the theory of their simultaneous publication as volumes of a single work. But it does not necessarily follow that because they were published together they were composed at one time; and, in reading and translating them continuously, I have found myself unable to resist the impression that these books are in effect a popular edition, with introductions, notes, and digressions—in other words, a commentary—of the despatches (*epistulae*) sent by Caesar to the Senate at the end of each year of operations. There is no need to suppose, and to argue from differences of style in certain passages, that Caesar's Commentaries represent the actual words of reports and despatches received from general and staff officers: but he may well have used these as material for his own despatches, and incorporated passages from them *verbatim* in the Commentaries. The despatches to the Senate were extant when Suetonius wrote his life of Caesar[5]; and the biographer himself says that they were presented in the form of note-books, with pages duly numbered. The Commentaries—as the title implies—were regarded by Cicero[6] and Hirtius[7] as materials for the historian rather than as history proper.

By critics of his own and later days—Cicero, Asinius Pollio, Suetonius, Tacitus, Quintilian, Aulus Gellius—Caesar was considered a master of Latin speech. As an orator he was second to Cicero alone; and the literary style of the Commentaries, simple, straightforward, unadorned, found great favour with Cicero[8] himself. Even Asinius Pollio, characteristically finding fault with the inaccuracy of the Commentaries, which, as he thought, would have been revised by their author, has nothing to say against the style. The popular character of the work is seen in the occasional touches of rhetoric—excellent of their kind—and the rarity of technical details.

The text of the *de Bello Gallico* presents some difficulties, but it is in no sense, like the text of the *de Bello Civili*, a *crux criticorum*. The Manuscripts fall into two main groups, both of which are traceable to a common ancestor. In the first group (which contains only the *Bellum Gallicum*) the most important are **A** (at Amsterdam), of the ninth or tenth century, **B** and **M** (at Paris), of the ninth century and the eleventh century respectively, and **R** (at the Vatican), of the tenth century: in the second group

---

[5] Suetonius, *Iulius*, c. 56.
[6] *Brutus*, c. 75.
[7] Preface to the VIIIth Book of the *Gallic War*.
[8] *Brutus*, c. 75.

(which contains all the *Corpus Caesarianum*), **T** (at Paris), of the eleventh century, and **U** (at the Vatican), of the twelfth century. Nipperdey, who may still be regarded as chief among the critical editors of Caesar, based the text of his edition (1847) on the first group of MSS.: but the second has found considerable support among more recent scholars, notably H. Meusel. The text printed with the present translation rests on the recensions of Nipperdey and R. du Pontet (*Scriptorum Classicorum Bibliotheca Oxoniensis*): but in a few passages use has been made of corrections suggested by or through Dr. Rice Holmes in his critical edition of 1914.

The translation was made independently for the most part, and compared with those of Golding (1565), W. A. M'Devitte and W. S. Bohn (1851), T. Rice Holmes (1908), and F. P. Long (1911). In rendering military terms—officers, details of troops, formations, movements, and the like—it seemed best as a rule to give the nearest English equivalent.

# Analysis of the Books

## BOOK I. (58 B.C.)

## BOOK II. (57 B.C.)

## BOOK III. (57 and 56 B.C.)

# The Gallic War

# BOOK I

[1] Gaul is a whole divided into three parts, one of which is inhabited by the Belgae, another by the Aquitani, and a third by a people called in their own tongue Celtae, in the Latin Galli. All these are different one from another in language, institutions, and laws. The Galli (Gauls) are separated from the Aquitani by the river Garonne, from the Belgae by the Marne and the Seine. Of all these peoples the Belgae are the most courageous, because they are farthest removed from the culture and the civilization of the Province,[1] and least often visited by merchants introducing the commodities that make for effeminacy; and also because they are nearest to the Germans dwelling beyond the Rhine, with whom they are continually at war. For this cause the Helvetii also excel the rest of the Gauls in valour, because they are struggling in almost daily fights with the Germans, either endeavouring to keep them out of Gallic territory or waging an aggressive warfare in German territory. The separate part of the country which, as has been said, is occupied by the Gauls, starts from the river Rhone, and is bounded by the river Garonne, the Ocean, and the territory of the Belgae; moreover, on the side of the Sequani and the Helvetii, it touches the river Rhine; and its general trend is northward. The Belgae, beginning from the edge of the Gallic territory, reach to the lower part of the river Rhine, bearing towards the north and east. Aquitania, starting from the Garonne, reaches to the Pyrenees and to that part of the Ocean which is by Spain: its bearing is between west and north.

[2] Among the Helvetii the noblest man by far and the most wealthy was Orgetorix. In the consulship[2] of Marcus Messalla and Marcus Piso, his desire for the kingship led him to form a conspiracy of the nobility, and he persuaded the community to march out of their territory in full force, urging that as they excelled all in valour it was easy enough to

---

[1] *i.e.* the Roman province of *Gallia Narbonensis,* formed about 121 B.C.
[2] 61 B.C.

1

secure the sovereignty of all Gaul. In this he persuaded them the more easily, because the Helvetii are closely confined by the nature of their territory. On one side there is the river Rhine, exceeding broad and deep, which separates the Helvetian territory from the Germans; on another the Jura range, exceeding high, lying between the Sequani and the Helvetii; on the third, the Lake of Geneva and the river Rhone, which separates the Roman Province from the Helvetii. In such circumstances their range of movement was less extensive, and their chances of waging war on their neighbours were less easy; and on this account they were greatly distressed, for they were men that longed for war. Nay, they could not but consider that the territory they occupied—to an extent of 240 miles long and 180 broad—was all too narrow for their population and for their renown of courage in war.

[3] Swayed by these considerations and stirred by the influence of Orgetorix, they determined to collect what they needed for taking the field, to buy up as large a number as they could of draught-cattle and carts, to sow as much corn as possible so as to have a sufficient supply thereof on the march, and to establish peace and amity with the nearest communities. For the accomplishment of these objects they considered that two years were sufficient, and pledged themselves by an ordinance to take the field in the third year. For the accomplishment of these objects Orgetorix was chosen, and he took upon himself an embassage to the communities. In the course of his travels he persuaded Casticus, of the Sequani, son of Catamantaloedes, who had held for many years the kingship of the Sequani, and had been called by the Senate "the friend of the Roman people," to seize in his own state the kingship which his father had held before him; and Dumnorix also, of the Aedui, brother of Diviciacus, at that time holding the chieftaincy of the state and a great favourite with the common people, he persuaded to a like endeavour, and gave him his own daughter in marriage. He convinced them that it was easy enough to accomplish such endeavours, because he himself (so he said) was about to secure the sovereignty of his own state. There was no doubt, he observed, that the Helvetii were the most powerful tribe in all Gaul, and he gave a pledge that he would win them their kingdoms with his own resources and his own army. Swayed by this speech, they gave a mutual pledge, confirming it by oath; and they hoped that when they had seized their kingship they would be able, through the efforts of three most powerful and most steadfast tribes, to master the whole of Gaul.

[4] The design was revealed to the Helvetii by informers. In accordance with their custom they compelled Orgetorix to take his trial in bonds. If he were condemned, the penalty of being burnt alive was the consequence. On the day appointed for his trial Orgetorix gathered from

every quarter to the place of judgment all his retainers, to the number of some ten thousand men, and also assembled there all his clients and debtors, of whom he had a great number, and through their means escaped from taking his trial. The state, being incensed at this, essayed to secure its due rights by force of arms, and the magistrates were bringing together a number of men from the country parts, which Orgetorix died, not without suspicion, as the Helvetii think, of suicide.

[5] After his death the Helvetii essayed none the less to accomplish their determination to march forth from their borders. When at length they deemed that they were prepared for that purpose, they set fire to all their strongholds,[3] in number about twelve; their villages, in number about four hundred, and the rest of their private buildings; they burnt up all their corn save that which they were to carry with them, to the intent that by removing all hope of return homeward they might prove the readier to undergo any perils; and they commanded every man to take for himself from home a three months' provision of victuals. They persuaded their neighbours, the Rauraci, the Tulingi, and the Latobrigi, to adopt the same plan, burn up their strongholds and villages, and march out with them; and they received as partners of their alliance the Boii, who had been dwellers beyond the Rhine, but had crossed over into Noricum and attacked Noreia.

[6] There were two routes, and no more, by which they could leave their homeland. One lay through the territory of the Sequani, betwixt the Jura range and the river Rhone, a narrow route and a difficult, where carts could scarce be drawn in single file; with an exceeding high mountain overhanging it, so that a very few men might easily check them. The other route, through the Roman Province, was far more easy and convenient, forasmuch as the Rhone flows between the borders of the Helvetii and the Allobroges (who had lately been brought to peace[4]), and is in some places fordable. The last town of the Allobroges, the nearest to the borders of the Helvetii, is Geneva, from which a bridge stretches across to the Helvetii. These supposed that either they would persuade the Allobroges (deeming them not yet well disposed towards the Roman people), or would compel them perforce to suffer a passage through their borders. Having therefore provided all things for their departure, they named a day by which all should assemble upon the bank of the Rhone. The day was the 28th of March, in the consulship[5] of Lucius Piso and Aulus Gabinius.

[7] When Caesar was informed that they were endeavouring to march

---

[3] The word *oppidum*, which denotes "town," connotes a "stronghold" in the case of the Gauls.

[4] 60 B.C. The phrase is a euphemism for "subdued."

[5] 58 B.C.

through the Roman Province, he made speed to leave Rome, and has-tening to Further Gaul by as rapid stages as possible, arrived near Geneva. From the whole Province he requisitioned the largest possible number of troops (there was in Further Gaul no more than a single legion), and ordered the bridge at Geneva to be broken down. When the Helvetii learned of his coming, they sent as deputies to him the noblest men of the state. Nammeius and Verucloetius held the chief place in the depu-tation, with instructions to say that their purpose was to march through the Province without any mischief, because they had no other route; and they asked that they might have leave so to do of his good will. Remembering that the consul Lucius Cassius had been slain,[6] and his army routed and sent under the yoke, by the Helvetii, Caesar considered that no concession should be made; nor did he believe that men of unfriendly disposition, if granted an opportunity of marching through the Province, would refrain from outrage and mischief. However, to gain an interval for the assembly of the troops he had levied, he replied to the deputies that he would take a space of time for consideration: if they wished for anything, they were to return on the 13th of April.

[8] In the meanwhile he used the legion which he had with him, and the troops which had concentrated from the Province, to construct a continuous wall, sixteen feet high, and a trench, from the Lake of Geneva, which flows into the river Rhone, to the Jura range, which sep-arates the territory of the Sequani from the Helvetii, a distance of nine-teen miles. This work completed, he posted separate garrisons, in entrenched forts, in order that he might more easily be able to stop any attempt of the enemy to cross against his wish. When the day which he had appointed with the deputies arrived, and the deputies returned to him, he said that, following the custom and precedent of the Roman people, he could not grant anyone a passage through the Province; and he made it plain that he would stop any attempt to force the same. Disappointed of this hope, the Helvetii attempted, sometimes by day, more often by night, to break through, either by joining boats together and making a number of rafts, or by fording the Rhone where the depth of the stream was least. But they were checked by the line of the entrenchment and, as the troops concentrated rapidly, by missiles, and so abandoned the attempt.

[9] There remained one other line of route, through the borders of the Sequani, by which they could not march, on account of the narrow ways, without the consent of the Sequani. When they could not of their own motion persuade the Sequani, they sent deputies to Dumnorix the Aeduan, in order that they might attain their object through his inter-

---

[6] 107 B.C.

cession. Now Dumnorix had very great weight with the Sequani, for he was both popular and openhanded, and he was friendly to the Helvetii, because from that state he had taken the daughter of Orgetorix to wife; and, spurred by desire of the kingship, he was anxious for a revolution, and eager to have as many states as might be beholden to his own beneficence. Therefore he accepted the business, and prevailed on the Sequani to suffer the Helvetii to pass through their borders, and arranged that they should give hostages each to other—the Sequani, not to prevent the Helvetii from their march; the Helvetii, to pass through without mischief or outrage.

[10] The news was brought back to Caesar that the Helvetii were minded to march through the land of the Sequani and the Aedui into the borders of the Santones, which are not far removed from the borders of the Tolosates, a state in the Province. He perceived that this event would bring great danger upon the Province; for it would have a warlike tribe, unfriendly to the Roman people, as neighbours to a district which was at once unprotected and very rich in corn. For these reasons he set Titus Labienus, lieutenant-general, in command of the fortification which he had made, and himself hurried by forced marches into Italy. There he enrolled two legions, and brought out of winter quarters three that were wintering about Aquileia; and with these five legions made speed to march by the shortest route to Further Gaul, over the Alps. In that region the Ceutrones, the Graioceli, and the Caturiges, seizing points on the higher ground, essayed to stop the march of his army. They were repulsed in several actions; and on the seventh day he moved from Ocelum, the last station of Higher Gaul, into the borders of the Vocontii in Further Gaul. Thence he led his army into the borders of the Allobroges, and from thence into the country of the Segusiavi, the first tribe outside the Province, across the Rhone.

[11] By this time the Helvetii, having brought their own forces through the defiles and through the borders of the Sequani, had reached the borders of the Aedui, and were engaged in laying waste their lands. Unable to defend their persons and their property from the invaders, the Aedui sent deputies to Caesar to ask for aid. These pleaded that the Aedui had always deserved too well of the Roman people to merit the devastation of their lands, the removal of their children into slavery, and the capture of their towns, almost in sight of the Roman army. At the same time the Aedui Ambarri, close allies and kinsmen of the Aedui, informed Caesar that their lands had been laid waste, and that they could not easily safeguard their towns from the violence of the enemy. The Allobroges also, who had villages and settlements across the Rhone, fled to Caesar, affirming that they had nothing left to them save the bare ground. All these events drove Caesar to the decision that he must not

wait till the Helvetii, having wasted all the substance of the Roman allies, should penetrate into the land of the Santoni.

[12] There is a river Arar (Saône), which flows through the borders of the Aedui and the Sequani into the Rhone: its sluggishness is beyond belief, for the eye cannot determine in which direction the stream flows. This river the Helvetii proceeded to cross by rafts and boats fastened together. When Caesar's scouts informed him that three-quarters of the Helvetian forces had actually crossed, and that about a quarter remained on the near side of the river Saône, he left camp in the third watch with three legions and came up to the division of the enemy which had not yet crossed. He attacked them unawares when they were heavily loaded, and put a great number of them to the sword; the remainder betook themselves to flight and hid in the nearest woods. The name of the canton was the Tigurine; for the whole state of Helvetia is divided into four cantons. In the recollection of the last generation this canton had marched out alone from its homeland, and had slain the consul Lucius Cassius and sent his army under the yoke. And so, whether by accident or by the purpose of the immortal gods, the section of the Helvetian state which had brought so signal a calamity upon the Roman people was the first to pay the penalty in full. Therein Caesar avenged private as well as national outrages; for in the same battle with Cassius the Tigurini had slain Lucius Piso the general, grandfather of Lucius Piso, Caesar's father-in-law.

[13] This action over, he caused a bridge to be made over the Saône and sent his army across thereby, in order to pursue the remainder of the Helvetian forces. Alarmed at his sudden approach—for they perceived that the business of crossing the river, which they themselves had accomplished with the greatest difficulty in twenty days, had been despatched by Caesar in a single one—the Helvetii sent deputies to him. The leader of the deputation was Divico, who had been commander of the Helvetii in the campaign against Cassius. He treated with Caesar as follows: If the Roman people would make peace with the Helvetii, they would go whither and abide where Caesar should determine and desire; if on the other hand he should continue to visit them with war, he was advised to remember the earliest disaster of the Roman people and the ancient valour of the Helvetii. He had attacked one canton unawares, when those who had crossed the river could not bear assistance to their fellows; but that event must not induce him to rate his own valour highly or to despise them. The Helvetii had learnt from their parents and ancestors to fight their battles with courage, not with cunning nor reliance upon stratagem. Caesar therefore must not allow the place of their conference to derive renown or perpetuate remembrance by a disaster to the Roman people and the destruction of an army.

[14] To these remarks Caesar replied as follows: As he remembered

well the events which the Helvetian deputies had mentioned, he had therefore the less need to hesitate; and his indignation was the more vehement in proportion as the Roman people had not deserved the misfortune. If the Romans had been conscious of some outrage done, it would not have been hard to take precaution; but they had been misled, because they did not understand that they had done anything to cause them apprehension, and they thought that they should not feel apprehension without cause. And even if he were willing to forget an old affront, could he banish the memory of recent outrages—their attempts to march by force against his will through the Province, their ill-treatment of the Aedui, the Ambarri, the Allobroges? Their insolent boast of their own victory, their surprise that their outrages had gone on so long with impunity, pointed the same way[7]; for it was the wont of the immortal gods to grant a temporary prosperity and a longer impunity to make men whom they purposed to punish for their crime smart the more severely from a change of fortune. Yet, for all this, he would make peace with the Helvetii, if they would offer him hostages to show him that they would perform their promises, and if they would give satisfaction to the Aedui in respect of the outrages inflicted on them and their allies, and likewise to the Allobroges. Divico replied: It was the ancestral practice and the regular custom of the Helvetii to receive, not to offer, hostages; the Roman people was witness thereof. With this reply he departed.

[15] Next day the Helvetii moved their camp from that spot. Caesar did likewise, sending forward the whole of his cavalry, four thousand in number, which he had raised from the whole of the Province, from the Aedui, and from their allies, to observe in which direction the enemy were marching. The cavalry, following up the rearguard too eagerly, engaged in a combat on unfavourable ground with the cavalry of the Helvetii, and a few of ours fell. Elated by this engagement, because five hundred of their horsemen had routed so large a host of ours, the Helvetii began on occasion to make a bolder stand, and with their rearguard to provoke the Romans to a fight. Caesar kept his troops from fighting, accounting it sufficient for the present to prevent the enemy from plundering, foraging, and devastation. The march continued for about a fortnight with no more interval than five or six miles a day between the rearguard of the enemy and the vanguard of the Romans.

[16] Meanwhile Caesar was daily pressing the Aedui for the corn that they had promised as a state. For by reason of cold weather (since Gaul, as has been said above, lies under the northern heaven) not only were the

---

[7] i.e. to coming vengeance.

corn-crops in the fields unripe, but there was not even a sufficient supply of forage to be had. At the same time he was less able to use the corn-supply that he had brought up the river Saône in boats, because the Helvetii had diverted their march from the Saône, and he did not wish to lose touch with them. The Aedui put him off day after day, declaring that the corn was being collected, was being brought in, was at hand. He perceived that he was being put off too long, and that the day was close upon him whereon it was proper to issue the corn-ration to the troops: accordingly he summoned together the Aeduan chiefs, of whom he had a great number in his camp, among them Diviciacus and Liscus, who had the highest magistracy, called Vergobret[8] by the Aedui: the magistrate is elected annually, and holds the power of life and death over his fellow-countrymen. Caesar called them severely to account because they offered no relief in a time of stress, with the enemy close at hand, when corn could neither be purchased not taken from the fields. And just because he had undertaken the war largely in response to their entreaties, he complained the more severely of their desertion.

[17] Then, and not till then, the remarks of Caesar induced Liscus to reveal a fact concealed before. There were, he said, certain persons, of paramount influence with the common folk, and of more power in their private capacity than the actual magistrates. These persons, by seditious and insolent language, were intimidating the population against the collection of corn as required, on the plea that it was better for the Aedui, if they could not now enjoy the primacy of Gaul, to submit to the commands of Gauls rather than of Romans; for they did not doubt that, if the Romans overcame the Helvetii, they meant to deprive the Aedui of liberty, in common with the rest of Gaul. These, again, were the men, who informed the enemy of the Roman plans and all the doings of the camp; nor had he power to restrain them. Nay, more, he perceived with what risk he had acted in informing Caesar, under sheer force of necessity; and for that reason he had held his peace as long as he could.

[18] Caesar felt that Dumnorix, the brother of Diviciacus, was indicated in these remarks of Liscus; but as he would not have those matters threshed out in presence of a company, he speedily dismissed the meeting. He kept Liscus back, and questioned him separately on his statement in the assembly. Liscus now spoke with greater freedom and boldness. Caesar questioned others privately upon the same matters, and found that it was so—that Dumnorix was the man who, unequalled in boldness, and strong in the influence that his generosity gave him over the common folk, desired a revolution. For several years, it was said, he had

---

[8] *i.e.* dispenser of judgment.

contracted at a low price for the customs and all the rest of the Aeduan taxes, for the simple reason that when he made a bid none durst bid against him. By this means he had at once increased his own property and acquired ample resources for bribery; he maintained a considerable body of horse permanently at his own charges, and kept them about his person; not only in his own but even in neighbouring states his power was extensive. To secure this power he had given his mother in marriage to the noblest and most powerful man among the Bituriges, he had taken himself a wife from the Helvetii, and had married his half-sister and his female relations to men of other states. This connection made him a zealous supporter of the Helvetii; moreover, he hated Caesar and the Romans on his own account, because their arrival had diminished his power and restored his brother Diviciacus to his ancient place of influence and honour. If anything should happen to the Romans, he entertained the most confident hope of securing the kingship by means of the Helvetii: it was the empire of the Roman people which caused him to despair not only of the kingship, but even of the influence he now possessed. Caesar discovered also in the course of his questioning, as concerning the unsuccessful cavalry engagement of a few days before, that Dumnorix and his horsemen (he was commander of the body of horse sent by the Aedui to the aid of Caesar) had started the retreat, and that by their retreat the remainder of the horse had been stricken with panic.

[19] All this Caesar learnt, and to confirm these suspicions he had indisputable facts. Dumnorix had brought the Helvetii through the borders of the Sequani; he had caused hostages to be given between them; he had done all this not only without orders from his state or from Caesar, but even without the knowledge of either; he was now accused by the magistrate of the Aedui. Caesar deemed all this to be cause enough for him either to punish Dumnorix himself, or to command the state so to do. To all such procedure there was one objection, the knowledge that Diviciacus, the brother of Dumnorix, showed the utmost zeal for the Roman people, the utmost goodwill towards himself, in loyalty, in justice, in prudence alike remarkable; for Caesar apprehended that the punishment of Dumnorix might offend the feelings of Diviciacus. Therefore, before attempting anything in the matter, Caesar ordered Diviciacus to be summoned to his quarters, and, having removed the regular interpreters, conversed with him through the mouth of Gaius Valerius Procillus, a leading man in the Province of Gaul and his own intimate friend, in whom he had the utmost confidence upon all matters. Caesar related the remarks which had been uttered in his presence as concerning Dumnorix at the assembly of the Gauls, and showed what each person had said severally to him upon the same subject. He asked and urged that without offence to the feelings of Diviciacus he might

either hear his case himself and pass judgment upon him, or order the state so to do.

[20] With many tears Diviciacus embraced Caesar, and began to beseech him not to pass too severe a judgment upon his brother. "I know," said he, "that the reports are true, and no one is more pained thereat than I, for at a time when I had very great influence in my own state and in the rest of Gaul, and he very little, by reason of his youth, he owed his rise to me; and now he is using his resources and his strength not only to the diminution of my influence, but almost to my destruction. For all that, I feel the force of brotherly love and public opinion. That is to say, if too severe a fate befalls him at your hands, no one, seeing that I hold this place in your friendship, will opine that it has been done without *my* consent; and this will turn from me the feelings of all Gaul." While he was making this petition at greater length, and with tears, Caesar took him by the hand and consoled him, bidding him end his entreaty, and showing that his influence with Caesar was so great that he excused the injury to Rome and the vexation felt by himself, in consideration for the goodwill and the entreaties of Diviciacus. Then he summoned Dumnorix to his quarters, and in the presence of his brother he pointed out what he had to blame in him; he set forth what he himself perceived, and the complaints of the state; he warned him to avoid all occasions of suspicion for the future, and said that he excused the past in consideration for his brother Diviciacus. He posted sentinels over Dumnorix, so as to know what he did and with whom he spoke.

[21] On the same day his scouts informed him that the enemy had halted close under a height eight miles from the Roman camp. A party was sent to reconnoitre the height, and to see what kind of ascent a detour might afford: the report was that it was easy. Caesar ordered Titus Labienus, lieutenant-general and chief of the staff, to move in the third watch with two legions and the guides who knew the route, and to climb the topmost ridge of the height; and he showed him his own intention. He himself, starting in the fourth watch, marched speedily against the enemy by the same route which they had taken, sending forward the whole of the horse. Publius Considius, reputed a past master in the art of war, who had seen service in the army of Lucius Sulla and afterwards in that of Marcus Crassus, was sent forward with the scouts.

[22] At dawn Labienus was in possession of the summit of the height, and Caesar was no more than a mile and a half from the enemy's camp; and, as he learnt afterwards from prisoners, neither his own approach nor that of Labienus was discovered. At this moment Considius galloped back to him, saying that the mountain he had wished Labienus to seize

was in possession of the enemy: he knew it by the Gallic arms and badges. Caesar withdrew his own troops to the nearest hill, and formed line of battle. Labienus had instructions from Caesar not to join battle unless his own troops appeared near the enemy's camp, so that a simultaneous assault might be made upon the enemy from all sides; accordingly, having seized the height, he awaited the main body and refrained from engaging. At length, when the day was far spent, Caesar learnt from his scouts that the height was in possession of his own troops, and that the Helvetii had shifted their camp, and therefore that Considius in sheer panic had reported to him as seen that which he had not seen. On that day he followed the enemy at the customary interval, and pitched his camp three miles from theirs.

[23] On the morrow, as no more than two days remained before it was proper to issue the corn-ration to the troops, and as he was no more than eighteen miles from Bibracte, by far the largest and the best-provided of the Aeduan towns, he considered that he must attend to the corn-supply. He therefore turned his line of march away from the Helvetii, and made with all speed for Bibracte. The change was reported to the enemy by some deserters from Lucius Aemilius, a troop-leader of the Gallic horse. Now the Helvetii may have supposed that the Romans were moving away from them because of sheer panic, the more so because on the day before they had not joined battle after seizing the higher ground; or they may have believed that the Romans could be cut off from their corn-supply. Whichever the reason, they changed their plan, altered their route, and began to pursue and to annoy the Roman rearguard.

[24] As soon as he remarked this, Caesar withdrew his troops to the nearest hill, and sent the horse to check the enemy's charge. Meanwhile he himself drew up his four legions of veterans in triple line half-way up the hill: but he ordered the two legions which he had last enlisted in Nearer Gaul and all the auxiliary troops to be posted on the top of the ridge, so as to fill the hill-side entirely with men: in the meantime the packs were to be collected in one place, which was to be entrenched by the troops posted in line on the higher ground. The Helvetii followed with all their carts, and collected their baggage in one place: the fighting men, in a densely-crowded line, repulsed the Roman horse, then formed mass and moved up against our first line.

[25] Caesar first had his own horse and then those of all others sent out of sight, thus to equalise the danger of all and to take away hope of flight. Then after a speech to encourage his troops he joined battle. The legionaries, from the upper ground, easily broke the mass-formation of the enemy by a volley of javelins, and, when it was scattered, drew their swords and charged. The Gauls were greatly encumbered for the fight

because several of their shields would be pierced and fastened together by a single javelin-cast; and as the iron became bent, they could not pluck it forth, nor fight handily with the left arm encumbered. Therefore many of them preferred, after continued shaking of the arm,[9] to cast off the shield and so to fight bare-bodied. At length, worn out with wounds, they began to retreat, retiring towards a height about a mile away. They gained the height; and as the Romans followed up, the Boii and Tulingi, who with some fifteen thousand men brought up the rear and formed the rearguard, turned from their march to attack the Romans on the exposed[10] flank, and overlapped them. Remarking this, the Helvetii, who had retired to the height, began to press again and to renew the fight. The Romans wheeled, and advanced in two divisions, the first and second line to oppose the part of the enemy which had been defeated and driven off, the third to check the fresh assault.

[26] Thus the engagement became twofold, and the fight was fierce and long. When the enemy could no longer hold out against our attacks, one division continued to retire to the height, the other concentrated upon their baggage and carts. There was no rout, for throughout the action, though it lasted from the seventh hour to eventide, no one could have seen the back of an enemy. Even round the baggage the fight was continued far into the night, as the enemy had constructed a rampart of carts, and from the higher ground they continued to hurl missiles upon our advancing lines, while some of them kept discharging native pikes and darts from underneath the carts and wheels, wounding our men. However, after a long fight, our troops gained possession of the baggage and the camp, where the daughter of Orgetorix and one of his sons were taken prisoners. Some 130,000 persons survived the action, and marched continuously the whole of that night; the march was not interrupted for any part of the night, and three days after they reached the borders of the Lingones; for our own troops had not been able to pursue them, having halted for three days to tend their wounds and to bury the dead. Caesar despatched letters and messages to the Lingones, ordering them not to give assistance by corn or otherwise, and affirming that, if they gave such assistance, he would treat them in the same fashion as the Helvetii. He himself, after the three days' interval, began to follow them with all his forces.

[27] The Helvetii were compelled by lack of all provision to send deputies to him to treat of surrender. These found him on the march, and, throwing themselves at his feet, in suppliant tones besought peace

---

[9] *i.e.* to shake off the javelin.
[10] *i.e.* the right, unshielded side.

# THE BATTLE AGAINST THE HELVETII

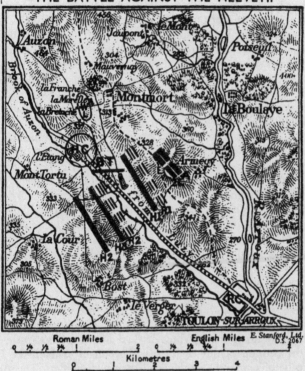

*Heights are indicated in metres above sea level.*

(*The map is reproduced from the French Survey dated 1853. There is little doubt that the battle took place on this ground, on which Colonel Stoffel discovered the entrenchment E. The positions of the opposing forces here shown are in general accordance with the theory of Colonel Bircher.*)

## NOTES

| | | |
|---|---|---|
| R C | Roman Camp. | |
| | Route of Roman Army northwards. | |
| | Route of Helvetii northwards. | |
| H C | Camp of Helvetii on morning of the battle. | |
| W L | Wagon laager, formed just before the battle. | |
| 2 L | The 2 new Legions | *occupying the whole hill and partly engaged in making E.* |
| A | Roman Auxiliaries | |
| E | Entrenchment to protect the men's packs. | |

| | |
|---|---|
| R 1 | 1st position of the 4 veteran Legions. |
| H 1 | 1st position of the Helvetii (advancing). |
| H 2 | 2nd position of the Helvetii (after retirement) |
| H 3 | 3rd position of the Helvetii (advancing). |
| B T | The Boii and Tulingi advancing against the exposed flank of R 2. |
| R 2 | 2nd position of the 4 Legions, with the 3rd line changing front to meet B T. |

with tears. He bade them await his arrival in their present station, and they obeyed. Upon arrival there Caesar demanded the surrender of hostages and arms, and of the slaves who had deserted to them. While these were sought out and collected together night intervened; and about six thousand men of the canton called Verbigene—it may be in sheer panic, lest after the surrender of their arms they might be put to the sword; or else they were tempted by the hope of escape, and the thought that in so vast a multitude of prisoners their own flight could be concealed or even unnoticed—left the Helvetian camp at nightfall and hastened to the Rhine and the borders of the Germans.

[28] So soon as Caesar came to know of this he commanded the inhabitants through whose borders they had marched to seek them out and bring them back, if they wished to clear themselves from complicity in his sight. When the runaways were brought back he treated them as enemies; all the remainder, upon delivery of hostages, arms, and deserters, he admitted to surrender. He commanded the Helvetii, Tulingi, and Latobrigi to return to their own borders, whence they had started; and as they had lost all their produce, and had no means at home of sustaining hunger, he required the Allobroges to give them a supply of corn. He also ordered them to restore with their own hands the towns and villages which they had burnt. His chief reason for so doing was that he did not wish the district which the Helvetii had left to be unoccupied, lest the excellence of the farmlands might tempt the Germans who dwell across the Rhine to cross from their own into the Helvetian borders, and so to become neighbours to the Province of Gaul and to the Allobroges. He granted the petition of the Aedui that they might establish the Boii, known to be of remarkable courage, in their own borders. The Aedui gave them farmlands, and afterwards admitted them to like measure of privilege and liberty with themselves.

[29] In the camp of the Helvetii were found, and brought to Caesar, records written out in Greek letters,[11] wherein was drawn up a nominal register showing what number of them had gone out from their homeland, who were able to bear arms, and also separately children, old men, and women. On all these counts the total showed 263,000 persons of the Helvetii, 36,000 of the Tulingi, 14,000 of the Latobrigi, 23,000 of the Rauraci, 32,000 of the Boii; of these there were about 92,000 able to bear arms. The grand total was about 368,000. Of those who returned home a census was taken in accordance with Caesar's command, and the number was found to be 110,000.

[30] Upon the conclusion of the Helvetian campaign deputies from

---

[11] Perhaps introduced through the Greek colony of Massilia (Marseilles): *cf.* VI. 14.

well-nigh the whole of Gaul, the chief men of the various states, assembled in Caesar's camp to congratulate him. They perceived, they said, that, although Caesar had by the campaign required satisfaction of the Helvetii for past outrages suffered by the Roman people at their hands, the result had been as beneficial to the land of Gaul as to the Roman people; for the Helvetii had left their homes at a time of exceeding prosperity with the express design of making war upon the whole of Gaul and obtaining an empire; they purposed from an ample field to select for their abode the spot which they judged to be the most convenient and the most productive in all Gaul, and to make the rest of the states tributary. The deputies asked that they might be allowed to announce—and that with Caesar's consent—a convention of all Gaul for a certain day, for they had certain petitions which, after general agreement, they wished to ask of him. Permission was given, and they appointed a day for the convention, pledging themselves by an oath that no man should publish its proceedings save the persons authorised by their general consent.

[31] The convention having been held and dissolved, the same chiefs of states as before returned to Caesar with a petition that they might be allowed to discuss with him apart, in private, the question of their own and the general welfare. The petition was granted, and they all threw themselves in tears at Caesar's feet, declaring that they were as anxious and as much concerned to prevent the publication of their utterances as to obtain their desires; for they saw that publication must expose them to the most cruel vengeance. Diviciacus the Aeduan spoke on their behalf. "In all Gaul," he said, "there are two parties; in one of them the Aedui have the primacy, in the other the Arverni. For many years there was a vehement struggle between the two for the dominion; then it came about that the Arverni and the Sequani summoned the Germans to their aid for a price. About fifteen thousand of them crossed the Rhine in the first instance; then, when those fierce barbarians had got a liking for the farmlands, the civilization, and the wealth of the Gauls, more were brought over, and at the present time there are about 120,000 of them in Gaul.

"With them the Aedui and their dependents have repeatedly fought in battle: defeat has brought great disaster, the loss of all our nobility, our senate, and our knights. It is these battles and disasters that have broken the men who by their own valour, and by the courtesy and the friendship of Rome, were formerly paramount in Gaul, and have obliged them to give as hostages to the Sequani the noblest men of the state, and to bind the state by oath not to require the return of the hostages, not to entreat the assistance of Rome, nor to refuse eternal submission to the sway and sovereignty of the Sequani. I am the one man of all the state of the Aedui upon whom it has not been possible to prevail to take the oath or give his children as hostages. It was for that reason that I fled from the state and came to the Senate at Rome to demand assistance, because I was the only man not bound by oath or hostages. But a worse fate has befallen the victorious Sequani than the conquered Aedui: Ariovistus, king of the Germans, has settled within their borders and seized a third part of their territory, the best in all Gaul; and now he orders them to evacuate another third, because a few months since 24,000 of the Harudes joined him, for whom he had to provide a settlement and a home. In a few years all the natives will have been driven forth from the borders of Gaul, and all the Germans will have crossed the Rhine; for there can be no comparison between the Gallic and the German territory, none between our usual scale of living and theirs. Having once conquered the forces of the Gauls in battle near Magetobriga, Ariovistus is exercising a proud and cruel tyranny, demanding as hostages the children of the greatest nobles, and perpetrating upon them all the direst forms of torture, if anything be not performed at his nod or at his pleasure. He is a passionate, a reckless barbarian: we can endure his tyrannies no longer. Unless some means of assistance is to be found in Caesar and in the Roman people, all the Gauls must needs do just what the Helvetii have done—emigrate, to seek another habitation, other abodes far from the Germans, and risk any fortune that may befall them. If these remarks of mine be reported to Ariovistus, I make no doubt that he will inflict the severest punishment on all the hostages in his keeping. You, Caesar, by your own and your army's influence, or by your late victory, or by the name of the Roman people, can prevent the crossing of a larger host of Germans over the Rhine, and defend the whole of Gaul from the outrage of Ariovistus."

[32] When Diviciacus had delivered this speech all who were present began with loud weeping to seek assistance from Caesar. He noticed, however, that of all the company the Sequani alone did not act like the rest, but with head downcast stared sullenly upon the ground. He asked them, wondering, what might be the cause thereof. The Sequani made no reply, but continued in the same sullen silence. When repeated questioning could extract not a word from them, Diviciacus the Aeduan made further reply. "The lot of the Sequani," he said, "is more pitiable, more grievous than that of the rest, inasmuch as they alone dare not even in secret make complaint or entreat assistance, dreading the cruelty of Ariovistus as much in his absence as if he were present before them. The rest, for all their suffering, have still a chance of escape; but the Sequani, who have admitted Ariovistus within their borders, and whose towns are all in his power, must needs endure any and every torture."

[33] When he had learnt this Caesar comforted the Gauls with his words, promising that he would concern himself with this matter: he

had, he said, great hope that by his good offices and his authority he would induce Ariovistus to put a stop to his outrages. With this speech he dissolved the convention. And straightway many considerations induced him to suppose that he must take thought and action in the matter. In the first place, he could see that the Aedui, often hailed by the Senate as brethren and kinsmen, were fast bound in slavery and subjection to the Germans, and he was aware that their hostages were with Ariovistus and the Sequani. This, considering the greatness of the Roman empire, he deemed to be an utter disgrace to himself and to the state. Next, he could see that the Germans were becoming gradually accustomed to cross over the Rhine, and that the arrival of a great host of them in Gaul was dangerous for the Roman people. Nor did he suppose that barbarians so fierce would stop short after seizing the whole of Gaul; but rather, like the Cimbri and Teutoni before them, they would break forth into the Province, and push on thence into Italy, especially as there was but the Rhone to separate the Sequani from the Roman Province. All this, he felt, must be faced without a moment's delay. As for Ariovistus himself, he had assumed such airs, such arrogance, that he seemed insufferable.

[34] He resolved, therefore, to send deputies to Ariovistus to request of him the choice of some half-way station between them for a parley, as it was his desire to discuss with him matters of state and of the highest importance to each of them. To the deputation Ariovistus made reply that if he had had need of aught from Caesar, he would have come to him, and if Caesar desired aught of him, he ought to come to him. Moreover, he did not venture without an army to come into those parts of Gaul which Caesar was occupying, and he could not concentrate his army without great exertion in the matter of supply. And he found himself wondering what business either Caesar or the Roman people might have in that Gaul which he had made his own by conquest in war.

[35] When this reply had been brought back to Caesar, he sent deputies again to him with the following message: Forasmuch as, after great kindness of treatment from Caesar himself and from the Roman people (for it was in Caesar's year of consulship[12] that he had been saluted as king and friend by the Senate), he expressed his thanks to Caesar and the Roman people by reluctance to accept the invitation to come to a parley and by thinking it needless to say or learn anything as touching their mutual concerns, Caesar's demand of him was, first, that he should not bring any further host of men across the Rhine into Gaul; second, that he should restore the hostages he held from the Aedui and grant the

---

[12] 59 B.C.

Sequani entire freedom to restore to the Aedui with his full consent the hostages they held; further, that he should not annoy the Aedui by outrage nor make war upon them and their allies. If he did as requested, Caesar and the Roman people would maintain a lasting kindness and friendship towards him. If Caesar's request were not granted, then, forasmuch as in the consulship[13] of Marcus Messalla and Marcus Piso the Senate had decided that the governor of the Province of Gaul should protect, as far as he could do so with advantage to the state, the Aedui and the other friends of the Roman people, Caesar would not disregard the outrages suffered by the Aedui.

[36] To this Ariovistus replied as follows: It was the right of war that conquerors dictated as they pleased to the conquered; and the Roman people also were accustomed to dictate to those whom they conquered, not according to the order of a third party, but according to their own choice. If he, for his part, did not ordain how the Roman people should exercise their own right, he ought not to be hindered by the Roman people in the enjoyment of his own right. The Aedui, having risked the fortune of war and having been overcome in a conflict of arms, had been made tributary to himself. Caesar was doing him a serious injury, for his advance was damaging his revenues. He would not restore their hostages to the Aedui, nor would he make war on them nor on their allies without cause, if they stood to their agreement and paid tribute yearly; if not, they would find it of no assistance whatever to be called "Brethren of the Roman people." As for Caesar's declaration that he would not disregard outrages suffered by the Aedui, no one had fought with Ariovistus save to his own destruction. He might join issue when he pleased: he would learn what invincible Germans, highly trained in arms, who in a period of fourteen years had never been beneath a roof, could accomplish by their valour.

[37] At the same hour in which this message was brought back to Caesar, deputies arrived from the Aedui and the Treveri. The Aedui came to complain that the Harudes, who had lately been brought over into Gaul, were devastating their borders, and that they themselves had not been able to purchase peace from Ariovistus even by the delivery of hostages. The Treveri reported that one hundred cantons of the Suebi had settled on the banks of the Rhine, and were attempting to cross the river, under the command of two brothers, Nasua and Cimberius. At this Caesar was exceedingly disquieted, and determined that he must make speed, for fear that, if the new company of Suebi joined the old forces of Ariovistus, resistance might be more difficult. Therefore he secured his

---

[13] 61 B.C.

corn-supply with all possible speed, and pushed on with forced marches to meet Ariovistus.

[38] He had advanced a three days' march when news was brought to him that Ariovistus with all his forces was pushing on to seize Vesontio (Besançon), the largest town of the Sequani, and had already advanced a three days' march from his own borders. Caesar considered that a great effort on his part was needed to prevent this occurrence. For there was in that town an abundant supply of all things needful for war, and the place was so well fortified by Nature as to afford great facilities for the conduct of a campaign. The river Dubis (Doubs), with a circuit that might have been traced by compasses, surrounds well-nigh the whole town: the remaining space of not more than sixteen hundred feet, where the river breaks off, is closed in by a height of great eminence, so placed that its foundations touch the river-bank on either side. This height is surrounded by a wall to form a citadel and join it with the town. It was to this place that Caesar pushed on with forced marches by night and day, and, seizing the town, posted a garrison in it.

[39] During a few days' halt near Vesontio for the provision of corn and other supplies, a panic arose from inquiries made by our troops and remarks uttered by Gauls and traders, who affirmed that the Germans were men of a mighty frame and an incredible valour and skill at arms; for they themselves (so they said) at meetings with the Germans had often been unable even to endure their look and the keenness of their eyes. So great was the panic, and so suddenly did it seize upon all the army, that it affected in serious fashion the intelligence and the courage of all ranks. It began first with the tribunes, the contingent-commanders, and the others who had followed Caesar from Rome to court his friendship, without any great experience in warfare. Advancing various reasons which, according to their own statement, obliged them to depart, some sought his permission to leave; some were compelled by very shame to stay, to avoid the suspicion of cowardice. They were unable to disguise their looks, or even at times to restrain their tears; they hid in their tents to complain of their own fate, or to lament in company with their friends the common danger. Everywhere throughout the camp there was signing of wills. By the cowardly utterances of such as these even men who had long experience in the field, soldiers, centurions, and cavalry commanders, were gradually affected. Those of them who desired to be thought less timid would declare that they were not afraid of the enemy, but feared the narrow defiles and the vast forests which lay between themselves and Ariovistus, or a possible failure of proper transport for the corn-supply. Some had even gone so far as to declare to Caesar that when he gave the order for camp to be shifted and standards advanced the soldiers would not obey, and by reason of cowardice would not move forward.

[40] Remarking this, he convened a council of war, and summoned thereto the centurions of all grades. Then indignantly he reprimanded them, first and foremost because they thought it their business to ask or to consider in which direction or with what purpose they were being led. "Ariovistus," he said, "in my own consulship sought most eagerly the friendship of the Roman people. Why should anyone conclude that he intends so recklessly to depart from his duty? For myself, I am persuaded that, when my demands are made known, and the fairness of my terms understood, Ariovistus will not reject the goodwill of myself or the Roman people. Even if, in a fit of rage and madness, he makes war, what, pray, have you to fear? Why do you despair of your own courage or of my competence? We have made trial of this foe in the time of our fathers, on the occasion when, in the defeat of the Cimbri[14] and Teutoni[15] by Gaius Marius, the army was deemed to have deserved no less praise than the commander himself. We have made further trial of late in Italy in the slave revolt,[16] and yet the slaves had the practice and training which they had learnt from us to give them some measure of support. You may judge from this what profit there is in a good courage, for the very men whom you had feared without cause during a long time, when they had no arms, you subsequently subdued, though they had taken up arms and won victories. Finally, these are the selfsame men with whom the Helvetii have had frequent encounters, and they have often subdued them, not only in Helvetian territory but also in Germany; yet the Helvetii have not proved a match for *our* army. If there be any who are concerned at the defeat and flight of the Gauls, they can discover for the asking that when the Gauls were worn out by the length of the campaign Ariovistus, who had kept himself for many months within his camp in the marshes, without giving a chance of encounter, attacked them suddenly when they had at last dispersed in despair of a battle, and conquered them rather by skill and stratagem than by courage. Even Ariovistus himself does not expect that our own armies can be caught by tactics for which there was a chance against unskilled barbarians. Those persons who ascribe their own cowardice to a pretended anxiety for the corn-supply or to the defiles on the route are guilty of presumption, for they appear either to despair of the commander's doing his duty or to instruct him in it. These matters are my own concern; corn is being supplied by the Sequani, the Leuci, the Lingones, and the corn-crops in the fields are already ripe; of the route you yourselves will shortly be able to judge. As for the statement that the soldiers will not obey orders nor

---

[14] 101 B.C.
[15] 102 B.C.
[16] 73–71 B.C.

move forward, I am not in the least concerned by that; in any cases where an army has not obeyed its general, either fortune has failed because of some actual blunder, or else some crime has been discovered and a charge of avarice has been brought home. My own blamelessness has been clearly seen throughout my life, my good fortune in the Helvetian campaign. Accordingly I intend to execute at once what I might have put off to a more distant day, and to break camp in the fourth watch of this next night, to the intent that I may perceive at once whether honour and duty, or cowardice, prevail in your minds. Even if no one else follows, I shall march with the Tenth Legion alone; I have no doubt of its allegiance, and it will furnish the commander-in-chief's escort." Caesar had shown special favour to this legion, and he had placed the greatest reliance in it because of its courage.

[41] By the delivery of this speech the spirit of all ranks was changed in a remarkable fashion; the greatest keenness and eagerness for active service was engendered, and the Tenth Legion was the first to express thanks to Caesar, through its tribunes, for the excellent opinion he had formed of it, and to affirm its complete readiness for active service. Then the remaining legions moved their tribunes and senior centurions to give satisfactory explanation to Caesar that they had felt neither doubt nor panic, and had regarded it as the commander's business, not their own, to decide the plan of campaign. Their explanation was accepted, and through Diviciacus (the one person in whom Caesar had absolute confidence) a route was found out to lead the army through open country, by a detour of more than fifty miles. In the fourth watch, as Caesar had said, the march began. On the seventh day of continuous marching the scouts reported that the forces of Ariovistus were four-and-twenty miles away from our own.

[42] When he learnt of Caesar's approach Ariovistus sent deputies to him to announce that he was now ready to do what Caesar had before demanded as touching a parley, because he had come nearer, and Ariovistus believed that he could comply without risk. Caesar did not reject the proposal, and he was inclined to think that Ariovistus was at length returning to a proper frame of mind, inasmuch as of his own motion he proffered what he had previously refused on request. Moreover, he began to have a good hope that, in consideration of the signal benefits conferred upon him by Caesar and the Roman people, Ariovistus would abandon his obstinacy when he knew Caesar's demands. A day—the fifth after that—was appointed for the parley. Meanwhile there was continual sending of deputies to and fro between them; and Ariovistus demanded that Caesar should bring no infantry with him to the parley, as he was afraid Caesar might surround him by treachery; let each party, therefore, come with an escort of horse; other-

wise he would not come at all. Caesar did not wish the parley to be broken off upon an excuse thus interposed; at the same time he could not venture to entrust his personal safety to Gallic horse. He decided, therefore, that the best plan was to take the horses from Gallic troopers and mount upon them soldiers of the Tenth Legion, in which he had absolute confidence; thus, if there were need of action, he would have an escort of the truest friends he could find. As the order was being carried out, one of the soldiers of the Tenth Legion remarked with some wit that Caesar was doing better than his promise; for he had promised to treat the Tenth Legion as the commander-in-chief's escort, and he was making new "cavalry"[17] of them.

[43] There was a large plain, and in it a mound of earth of considerable size. The place was about equally distant from the camps of Caesar and of Ariovistus. Thither, as agreed, they came for the parley. Caesar stationed the legion which he had brought on horseback two hundred paces from the mound. The horsemen of Ariovistus halted at an equal distance. Ariovistus demanded that they should parley on horseback, and that each should bring with him to the parley ten men besides himself. When they arrived at the spot Caesar began his speech by relating the benefits conferred upon Ariovistus by himself and by the Senate; the Senate had called him king and friend, and had sent gifts with a most lavish hand. This privilege, as he pointed out, had fallen to the lot of but few, and was usually granted in consideration of great personal services. Ariovistus, though he had no right to audience of the Senate, and no just cause of claim, had obtained the rewards in question by the favour and generosity of Caesar and of the Senate. He proceeded to show how long-established and how just were the reasons for a close relationship between Rome and the Aedui; the frequency and the distinction of the Senate's decrees in respect of them; the manner in which, even before they had sought the friendship of Rome, the Aedui had always held the primacy of all Gaul. It was the tradition of the Roman people to desire that its allies and friends should not only lose none of their possessions, but should enjoy increase of influence, dignity, and distinction; on the other hand, who, he asked, could endure that they should be despoiled of what they had brought with them to the friendship of the Roman people? He then made the same demands as those which he had given in his instruc-

---

[17] There is a certain irony in this. From the time of Marius onwards, the cavalry attached to a legion were usually foreign auxiliaries; so to transfer (*rescribere*) legionaries to the cavalry was not exactly a compliment. But there is probably an allusion also to the cavalry of earlier days, which was formed of noble and wealthy citizens, and to the Knights (*equites*), who at this time formed an influential party in Roman politics.

tions to the deputies—that is to say, Ariovistus must not make war on the Aedui or on their allies; he must restore the hostages; and if he could not send back home any part of the Germans, at any rate he must not suffer any more to cross the Rhine.

[44] To the demands of Caesar Ariovistus replied in brief, but he dilated at length upon his own good qualities. He had crossed the Rhine, he said, not of his own desire, but upon the request and summons of the Gauls; not without great hope of great rewards had he left home and kindred; the settlements he occupied in Gaul were granted by the natives, the hostages had been given with the consent of the natives; the tribute he took was by right of war, as customarily enforced by conquerors upon conquered. He had not made war upon the Gauls, but they upon him; all the states of Gaul had come to attack him and had set up their camp against him; all their forces had been beaten and overcome by him in a single action. If they wished to try the issue again, he was prepared to fight it out again; if they wished to enjoy peace, it was unjust to refuse the payment of tribute which of their own consent they had paid hitherto. The friendship of the Roman people ought to be a distinction and a security to him, not a hindrance; and he had sought it with that hope. If through the agency of the Roman people the tribute were to be remitted and the surrendered persons withdrawn, he would refuse the friendship of the Roman people no less heartily than he had sought it. As for the host of Germans that he was bringing over into Gaul, his object was to protect himself, not to attack Gaul; and the proof thereof was that he had not come except upon request, and that his warfare had been defensive, not offensive. He had come into Gaul before the Roman people. Never heretofore had an army of the Roman people left the borders of the Province of Gaul. What did Caesar mean? Why did he come into his sphere of occupation? This was his province of Gaul, as the other was the Roman. As it was not right to give way to him, if he made an attack on Roman territory, so likewise the Romans were unjust in obstructing him in his own jurisdiction. As for Caesar's statement that the Aedui were called "brothers," Ariovistus was not such a barbarian, not so ignorant of affairs as not to know that neither in the last campaign against the Allobroges had the Aedui rendered assistance to the Romans, nor in the disputes of the Aedui with himself and the Sequani had they enjoyed the assistance of the Roman people. He was bound to suspect, in spite of pretended friendship, that Caesar had an army in Gaul for the purpose of crushing him. Unless, therefore, Caesar departed and withdrew his army from this locality, he would regard him, not as a friend, but as an enemy. And if he put Caesar to death, he would gratify many nobles and leaders of the Roman people: this he knew for certain from themselves, by the messengers sent on behalf of all whose favour and

friendship he could purchase by Caesar's death. If, however, Caesar departed and resigned to him the uninterrupted occupation of Gaul, he would recompense him by a great reward, and would, without any exertion or risk on his part, execute any campaigns he might wish to be carried out.

[45] Caesar spoke at length for the purpose of showing why he could not give up the task in hand. His own practice, he said, and the practice of the Roman people did not suffer the abandonment of allies who had deserved so well, nor did he admit that Gaul belonged to Ariovistus rather than to the Roman people. The Arverni and the Ruteni had been subdued in a campaign by Quintus Fabius Maximus:[18] the Roman people had pardoned them, and had not formed them into a province nor imposed a tribute. If priority of time was to be the standard, then the sovereignty of the Roman people in Gaul had complete justification; if the decision of the Senate was to be observed, Gaul should be free, for after conquest of the country the Senate had willed that it should continue to observe its own laws.

[46] During the progress of the parley Caesar was informed that the horsemen of Ariovistus were approaching nearer the mound, riding up to our troops, and discharging stones and darts at them. Caesar made an end of speaking, and withdrawing to his own men, commanded them not to discharge a single dart against the enemy in reply. For, although he could see that a fight between the chosen legion and the horsemen would involve no danger, still he did not think proper, by so beating the enemy, to make possible the report that after pledge given they had been surrounded by him during a parley. As soon as the common soldiers learnt how arrogantly at the parley Ariovistus had forbidden all Gaul to the Romans, how his horsemen had attacked our troops, and how this action had broken off the parley, the army was inspired with far greater eagerness and enthusiasm for battle.

[47] Two days afterwards Ariovistus sent deputies to Caesar. He desired, he said, to discuss with him the matters which they had begun to discuss together but had not settled. Let him therefore again appoint a day for a parley, or, if he did not so wish, let him send to him one of his staff. Caesar thought there was no occasion for a parley, the more so as on the previous day the Germans could not be restrained from discharging darts upon our men. He thought it would be very dangerous to send one of his staff to him and so to expose a man to the ferocious Germans. The best plan seemed to be to send to him Gaius Valerius Procillus, son of Gaius Valerius Caburus. He was a young man of exemplary courage

---

[18] 121 B.C.

and courtesy, and his father had been presented with the citizenship by Gaius Valerius Flaccus. Caesar selected him because of his fidelity and his knowledge of the Gallic tongue (which from long practice Ariovistus could now use freely), and also because the Germans had in his case no reason for outrage; and with him he chose Marcus Mettius, who enjoyed the intimacy of Ariovistus. He gave them instructions that they should ascertain and bring back to him the views of Ariovistus. But when Ariovistus saw them near him in his camp he called aloud in the presence of his army, "Why come you to me? To spy?" When they tried to speak he prevented them and flung them into chains.

[48] On the same day he advanced and pitched his camp under a hillside six miles from Caesar's. The next day he led his forces past the camp of Caesar, and formed camp two miles beyond him, for the purpose of cutting Caesar off from the corn and supplies that were to be brought up from the borders of the Sequani and the Aedui. For five days in succession Caesar brought his own forces out in front of camp and kept them formed in line of battle, so that if Ariovistus wished to engage he might not lack the chance. On all these days Ariovistus kept his army in camp, but engaged daily in a cavalry encounter. The kind of fighting in which the Germans had trained themselves was as follows. There were six thousand horsemen, and as many footmen, as swift as they were brave, who had been chosen out of the whole force, one by each horseman for his personal protection. With them they worked in encounters; on them the horsemen would retire, and they would concentrate speedily if any serious difficulty arose; they would form round any trooper who fell from his horse severely wounded; and if it was necessary to advance farther in some direction or to retire more rapidly, their training made them so speedy that they could support themselves by the manes of the horses and keep up their pace.

[49] When Caesar observed that Ariovistus kept to his camp, to prevent further interruption of supplies he chose a suitable spot for a camp beyond that in which the Germans had pitched and about six hundred paces distant. Thither he marched in triple-line formation. The first and second line he ordered to keep under arms, the third to entrench a camp. The spot, as has been said, was about six hundred paces away from the enemy. Towards it Ariovistus sent some sixteen thousand light-armed troops with all the horse, as a force to frighten our men and to prevent their entrenching work. None the less Caesar kept to his previous decision, ordering two lines to drive back the enemy, the third to complete the work. When the camp was entrenched he left two legions there and a part of the auxiliaries; the remaining four he brought back to the larger camp.

[50] The next day, in accordance with his practice, Caesar moved out his forces from both camps, and, advancing a little from the larger camp,

he formed line to give the enemy a chance of battle. Perceiving that they did not even so come forth, he brought his army back to camp about noon. Then at last Ariovistus sent a part of his own forces to attack the lesser camp, and both sides fought in spirited fashion till eventide. At sunset, when many blows had been dealt and taken, Ariovistus led his forces back to camp. By questioning the prisoners why Ariovistus did not fight a decisive action, Caesar found out the reason. It was a custom among the Germans that their matrons should declare by lots[19] and divinations whether it was expedient or not to engage, and the matrons declared that heaven forbade the Germans to win a victory, if they fought an action before the new moon.

[51] On the next day Caesar left what he deemed a sufficient garrison for each camp; in front of the lesser camp, in full view of the enemy, he posted all the allied troops, intending to use them for a demonstration, because the total strength of his legionary troops was none too great in view of the enemy's numbers. He himself, with triple line deployed, advanced right up to the enemy's camp. Then at last, compelled by necessity, the Germans led their own forces out of camp and posted them at equal intervals according to their tribes, Harudes, Marcomani, Triboces, Vangiones, Nemetes, Sedusii, Suebi; and their whole line they set about with wagons and carts, to leave no hope in flight. Upon these they set their women, who with tears and outstretched hands entreated the men, as they marched out to fight, not to deliver them into Roman slavery.

[52] Caesar put the lieutenant-generals and the quartermaster-general[20] each in command of a legion, that every man might have their witness of his valour. He himself took station on the right wing, having noticed that the corresponding division of the enemy was the least steady, and joined battle. Our troops attacked the enemy so fiercely when the signal was given, and the enemy dashed forward so suddenly and swiftly, that there was no time to discharge javelins upon them. So javelins were thrown aside, and it was a sword-fight at close quarters. But the Germans, according to their custom, speedily formed mass, and received the sword-attack. Not a few of our soldiers were found brave enough to leap on to the masses of the enemy, tear the shields from their hands, and deal a wound from above. The left wing of the enemy's line was beaten and put to flight, but their right wing, by sheer weight of numbers, was pressing our line hard. Young Publius Crassus, commanding our cavalry, noticed this, and as he could move more freely than the officers who were occu-

---

[19] The *sortes* were pieces of wood marked with signs: see ch. 53 *infra*, and *cf.* Tacitus, *Germania* 10, and for these prophetic women *Germania* 8; *Histories* IV. 61.

[20] Here the *quaestor* commanded one legion, *legati* the other five.

pied in and about the line of battle, he sent the third line in support of our struggling troops.

[53] So the battle was restored, and all the enemy turned and ran: nor did they cease in their flight until they reached the river Rhine, some five[21] miles from that spot. There a very few, trusting to their strength, set themselves to swim across, or discovered boats and so won safety. Among these was Ariovistus, who found a skiff moored to the bank and escaped therein; all the rest our cavalry caught and slew. There were two wives of Ariovistus, one of Suebian nationality, whom he had brought with him from home; the other a woman of Noricum, sister to King Voccio, and sent by him to be married to Ariovistus in Gaul. Both wives perished in the rout; of his two daughters one was slain, and the other taken prisoner. Gaius Valerius Procillus, bound with a threefold chain, was being dragged by his keepers in the rout, when he chanced to meet Caesar himself pursuing the enemy with the cavalry. And indeed it brought Caesar no less pleasure than the victory itself, to see a most distinguished member of the Province of Gaul, his own close friend and guest, snatched from the hands of the enemy and restored to himself; and to feel that fortune had in no wise lessened, by the loss of his friend, his own great pleasure and gratification. Procillus said that in his own presence the lots had been thrice consulted to see whether he should be burnt to death at once or saved for another time: to the favour of the lots he owed his safety. Marcus Mettius also was discovered and brought back to Caesar.

[54] When the news of this battle was carried across the Rhine, the Suebi who had come to the banks of the river began to return homewards; and when the tribes which dwell next to the Rhine perceived their panic, they pursued and slew a great number of them. Two capital campaigns were thus finished in a single summer, and Caesar therefore withdrew his army a little earlier than the season required into winter cantonments among the Sequani, leaving Labienus in command thereof, while he himself set off for Hither Gaul to hold the assizes.[22]

---

[21] Dr. Rice Holmes suggests xv for v: or a mistake of the river Ill for the Rhine.

[22] A province was divided into districts (conventus), and for the administration of justice the governor visited these districts (conventus agere) at least once during his year of office.

# BOOK II

[1] While Caesar was wintering in Hither Gaul, as has been shown above, frequent rumours were brought to him, and despatches also from Labienus informed him, that all the Belgae (whom I have already described as a third of Gaul) were conspiring against Rome and giving hostages each to other. The causes of their conspiracy, it was said, were as follow. In the first place, they feared that when all Gaul was pacified[1] they might themselves be brought face to face with a Roman army; in the second, they were being stirred up by certain of the Gauls, who had either been unwilling that the Germans should stay longer in Gaul, and were now no less distressed that a Roman army should winter and establish itself in Gaul, or who for sheer fickleness and inconstancy were set upon a change of rule; in certain cases, too, the agitation was due to the fact that in Gaul the more powerful chiefs, and such as had the means to hire men, commonly endeavoured to make themselves kings, and this they could not so readily effect under our empire.

[2] These reports and despatches prompted Caesar to enrol two new legions in Hither Gaul, and at the beginning of summer he sent Quintus Pedius, lieutenant-general, to lead them into Inner[2] Gaul. He himself, as soon as there began to be a supply of forage, came to the army. He charged the Senones and the rest of the Gauls who were neighbours of the Belgae to find out what the latter were about and to keep him informed thereof. They all with one consent reported that bands were being collected, and an army assembled in one place. Then accordingly he determined that he must no longer hesitate about moving against them. He secured his corn-supply, struck his camp, and in about a fortnight reached the borders of the Belgae.

[3] He arrived there unexpectedly, and with more speed than anyone had looked for. The Remi, the Belgic tribe nearest to Gaul, sent as

---

[1] *i.e.* the Celtic portion of Gaul.
[2] *i.e.* Further Gaul.

deputies to him Iccius and Andecumborius, the first men of the community, to tell him that they surrendered themselves and all their stuff to the protection and power of Rome; that they had neither taken part with the rest of the Belgae, nor conspired against Rome; and that they were ready to give hostages, to do his commands, to receive him in their towns, and to assist him with corn and everything else. All the rest of the Belgae, they said, were under arms, and the Germans dwelling on the hither side of the Rhine had joined with them; and the infatuation of them all was so great that the Remi had not been able to dissuade even the Suessiones from taking part with them, though these were their own brethren and kinsfolk, observing the same law and ordinances, and sharing one government, one ruler with themselves.

[4] Caesar asked them what states were under arms, what was their size and their war-strength. He discovered that most of the Belgae were of German origin, and had been brought over the Rhine a long while ago, and had settled in their present abode by reason of the fruitfulness of the soil, having driven out the Gauls who inhabited the district. The Belgae, they said, were the only nation who, when all Gaul was harassed in the last generation, had prevented the Teutoni and Cimbri from entering within their borders; and for this cause they relied on the remembrance of those events to assume great authority and great airs in military matters. As concerning their numbers, the Remi affirmed that they had exact information in all particulars, because, as they were closely connected by relationship and intermarriage, they had learnt how large a contingent each chief had promised for the present campaign in the general council of the Belgae. Among these the Bellovaci had a predominant influence by courage, by authority, by numbers; they could furnish a hundred thousand men-at-arms, and of that number had promised sixty thousand picked men, demanding for themselves the command of the whole campaign. The Suessiones, the Remi said, were their own immediate neighbours; they occupied lands as extensive as they were productive. Among them, even within living memory, Diviciacus had been king, the most powerful man in the whole of Gaul, who had exercised sovereignty alike over a great part of these districts, and even over Britain. Galba was now king; to him, by reason of his justice and sagacity, the supreme charge of the campaign was delivered by general consent; he had twelve towns, and promised fifty thousand men-at-arms. An equal number were promised by the Nervii, accounted the fiercest among the Belgae, and dwelling farthest away; fifteen thousand by the Atrebates, ten by the Ambiani, five-and-twenty by the Morini, seven by the Menapii, ten by the Caleti, as many by the Veliocasses and the Viromandui, nineteen by the Aduatuci. The Condrusi, Eburones, Caeroesi, and Paemani (who are

indiscriminately called Germans), had promised, it was thought, some forty thousand men.

[5] Caesar addressed the Remi in a speech of generous encouragement; then he commanded their whole senate to assemble at his headquarters, and the children of their chieftains to be brought thither as hostages. All these commands were punctiliously and punctually performed. He made a powerful and a personal appeal to Diviciacus the Aeduan, showing him how important an advantage it was for the Roman state, and for the welfare of both parties, to keep the contingents of the enemy apart, so as to avoid the necessity of fighting at one time against so large a host. This could be done if the Aedui led their own forces into the borders of the Bellovaci and began to lay waste their lands. With these instructions he dismissed him. So soon as he perceived that all the forces of the Belgae had been concentrated and were coming against him, and learnt from the scouts he had sent and from the Remi that they were now not far distant, he made haste to lead his army across the river Axona (Aisne), which is upon the outermost borders of the Remi, and there pitched camp. By so doing, he had the banks of the river to protect one side of the camp, rendered his rear safe from the enemy, and made it possible for supplies to be brought up to him from the Remi and the rest of the states without danger. There was a bridge over the river; he set a guard there, and on the other side of the river he left Quintus Titurius Sabinus, lieutenant-general, with six cohorts. He ordered him to entrench a camp, with a rampart twelve feet high and a ditch eighteen feet broad.

[6] From this camp a town of the Remi called Bibrax was eight miles distant. The Belgae turned direct from their march to attack[3] this town with great violence. The defence was with difficulty maintained on that day. The Gauls and the Belgae use one method of attack. A host of men is set all round the ramparts, and when a rain of stones from all sides upon the wall has begun, and the wall is stripped of defenders, the attackers form a "tortoise,"[4] move up to the gates, and undercut the wall. This was easily done on the present occasion; for when so vast a host hurled stones and missiles, no man might stand firm on the wall. When night made an end of the assault, Iccius of the Remi, pre-eminent among his tribesmen in rank and favour, who was the officer in charge of the town at this time, and one of those who had come as deputies to Caesar to treat of peace, sent a report to him to the effect that unless a reinforcement were sent up to him he could no longer hold his position.

[7] Using again as guides the men who had come from Iccius to report,

---

[3] The Latin seems to mean "to assault direct from the march"—to storm a town by a *coup de main* without interrupting the main advance (*cf.* ch. 12 *infra*).

[4] *i.e.* lock their shields together over their heads.

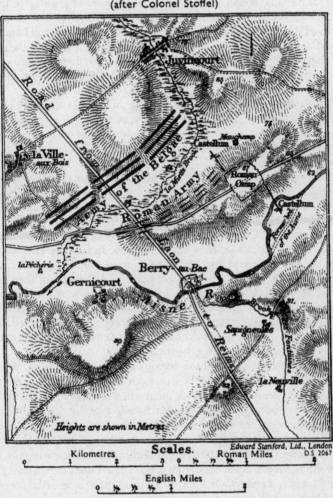

## THE BATTLE OF THE AISNE

### (after Colonel Stoffel)

Juvincourt

la Ville-aux-Bois

Castellum

Mauchamp

Roman Camp

Castellum

Road from Laon to the Army of the Belgae

Roman Army

la Miette Brook

la Pêchérie

Berry-au-Bac

Gernicourt

Aisne

Road to Reims

Brook

Fontaine

Sapigneules

la Neuville

*Heights are shown in Metres*

**Scales.**

Kilometres

Roman Miles

*Edward Stanford, Ltd., London*

D.S. 2067

English Miles

Caesar sent off to Bibrax in the middle of the night Numidian and Cretan archers and Balearic slingers, to reinforce the townsfolk. Their arrival brought the Remi not only hope of defence but heart for counter-attack, and for the same reason dissipated the enemy's hope of gaining the town. Therefore, halting for a short space near the town, they laid waste the lands of the Remi and set fire to all the hamlets and farm-buildings they could come nigh unto, and then with all their forces sped on to the camp of Caesar and pitched their own less than two miles from it. Their camp, as smoke and watch-fires showed, extended for more than eight miles in breadth.

[8] At first Caesar determined, because of the vast numbers of the enemy and their excellent reputation for valour, to avoid an engagement. By cavalry combats, however, he sought daily to prove what the valour of the enemy could do and what our men could dare. Then, perceiving that our men were not inferior, he chose a ground before the camp naturally suitable and appropriate for forming line of battle; for the hill where the camp had been pitched, standing up but a little from the plain, offered to the front as broad a space as a line deployed could occupy; on either flank it fell away, while in front by a gentle slope it came down gradually to the level of the plain. On either flank of that hill he dug at right angles[5] a protecting trench of about four hundred paces, and at the ends of the trenches he constructed forts and there posted his artillery, so that, when he had formed line, the enemy might not be able, because of their great superiority of numbers, to surround the Romans fighting on the flanks. This done, he left in camp the two legions he had last enrolled, that they might be brought up in support wherever needed, and he put the remaining six in line of battle before the camp. The enemy likewise had led their forces out of camp and drawn them up.

[9] Between our own and the enemy's army was a marsh of no great size. The enemy waited to see whether our men would cross it; but our men stood to arms, ready to attack them when in difficulties, should they be the first to attempt the crossing. Meanwhile a cavalry combat was taking place between the two lines. Neither army began to cross the marsh, and the cavalry combat tended to favour our side; so Caesar led his troops back to camp. The enemy hurried immediately from their station to the river Aisne, which, as has been shown, was behind our camp. There they found fords, and endeavoured to throw part of their forces across, intending if they could to storm the fort commanded by the lieutenant-general, Quintus Titurius, and break down the bridge; or, if they found that

---

[5] *i.e.* to his line.

impossible, to lay waste the lands of the Remi, which were of great service to us for the conduct of the campaign, and so to cut off our supplies.

[10] This was reported by Titurius, and Caesar led all the cavalry and the light-armed Numidians, slingers and archers, across the bridge, and hastened against the enemy. Fierce was the engagement fought there. Our troops attacked the enemy while in difficulties in the river, and slew a great number of them; the remainder, as they endeavoured with the utmost gallantry to cross over the bodies of their comrades, they drove back with a cloud of missiles; the first party, who were already across, the cavalry surrounded and slew. The enemy were now aware that they had been deceived in their hope of storming the town and of crossing the river, and saw that our men did not advance to unfavourable ground for the sake of a battle; moreover, their own corn-supply began to fail. They summoned a council, therefore, and decided that it was best for each man to return home, and to assemble from all quarters to the defence of the tribe into whose territory the Romans should first introduce their army, in order that they might fight in their own rather than in others' territory, and use native resources for their corn-supply. To this opinion they were brought, among the other reasons, by this particular consideration, that they had learnt of the approach of Diviciacus and the Aedui to the borders of the Bellovaci. The latter could not be induced to tarry longer, and thereby to fail in bringing assistance to their own tribe.

[11] This, then, being determined, they decamped in the second watch with great uproar and commotion, in no definite order, under no command, each seeking for himself the first place on the road, and hurrying to reach home, so that they made their departure seem like to a flight. Caesar learnt this at once through his scouts; and fearing an ambush, because he had not yet perceived the cause of their departure, he kept the army and the cavalry in camp. At break of day, when the information had been confirmed by reconnaissance, he sent forward all the cavalry to delay the rearguard. He appointed the lieutenant-generals Quintus Pedius and Lucius Aurunculeius Cotta to command the cavalry; and ordered the lieutenant-general Titus Labienus to follow in support with three legions. The cavalry attacked the rearguard, and, pursuing for many miles, they struck down a great host of them as they fled; for while the men at the end of the main column, which had been overtaken, stood at bay, bravely sustaining the attack of our troops, the men in front, thinking themselves clear of danger and restrained by no compulsion or command, broke ranks as soon as they heard the shouting, and all sought safety in flight. Thus without any danger our men slew as great a host of them as daytime allowed, and, ceasing at sunset, retired according to orders into camp.

[12] The next day, or ever the enemy could recover from their panic and rout, Caesar led the army into the borders of the Suessiones, next the

Remi, and making a forced march pressed on to the town of Noviodunum. He endeavoured to assault it direct from the march,[6] hearing that it was undefended; but, by reason of the breadth of its trench and the height of its wall he was not able to take it by storm, though there were few men to defend it. He entrenched his camp, therefore, and began to move up mantlets and to make ready the appliances needed for assault. Meanwhile all the host of the Suessiones returned from the rout and concentrated next night in the town. When the mantlets were speedily moved up to the town, a ramp cast up,[7] and towers constructed, the Gauls were prevailed on by the size of the siege-works, which they had not seen nor heard of before, and by the rapidity of the Romans, to send deputies to Caesar to treat of surrender; and upon the Remi interceding for their salvation, they obtained their request.

[13] The leading men of the state and the two sons of King Galba himself were accepted as hostages, and all arms were delivered up from the town; then Caesar admitted the Suessiones to surrender, and led the army into the territory of the Bellovaci. These had collected themselves and all their stuff in the town of Bratuspantium; and when Caesar with his army was about five miles from the place, all the older men came out of the town. They began to stretch out their hands to Caesar, and with loud voice to declare that they would come into his protection and power, and were making no armed effort against Rome. Likewise, when he was come up to the town and was pitching camp, the women and children, with hands outstretched from the wall, after their fashion, besought peace from the Romans.

[14] On their behalf Diviciacus (who, after the departure of the Belgae, had disbanded the forces of the Aedui and returned to Caesar) spake as follows: "The Bellovaci have always enjoyed the protection and friendship of the Aeduan state. They have been incited by their chiefs, who declared that the Aedui have been reduced to slavery by Caesar and are suffering every form of indignity and insult, both to revolt from the Aedui and to make war on the Roman people. The leaders of the plot, perceiving how great a disaster they have brought on the state, have fled to Britain. Not only the Bellovaci, but the Aedui also on their behalf, beseech you to show your wonted mercy and kindness towards them. By so doing you will enlarge the authority of the Aedui among all the Belgae, for it is by the succours and the resources of the Aedui that they have been used to sustain the burden of any wars that may have occurred."

[15] Caesar replied that for the respect he had towards Diviciacus and

---

[6] See note 3, page 30.
[7] Or, according to others, "earth was cast," *i.e.* into the fosse.

the Aedui he would receive them into his protection and save them alive. As their state was possessed of great authority among the Belgae and was largest in population, he demanded six hundred hostages. These were delivered, and all the arms were collected from the town. Then he left the place, and came into the borders of the Ambiani, who surrendered themselves and all their stuff without delay. Their next neighbours were the Nervii, and when Caesar inquired as touching the nature and character of these, he discovered as follows. Traders had no means of access unto them, for they allowed no wine nor any of the other appurtenances of luxury to be imported, because they supposed that their spirit was like to be enfeebled and their courage relaxed thereby. Fierce men they were, of a great courage, denouncing and accusing the rest of the Belgae for that they had surrendered to Rome and cast away the courage of their sires. For themselves they affirmed that they would send no deputies and accept no terms of peace.

[16] After a three days' march through their borders Caesar found out from prisoners that the river Sabis (Sambre) was not more than ten miles from his camp, and that across the river all the Nervii were in position, awaiting there the coming of the Romans, along with the Atrebates and the Viromandui, their neighbours (for the Nervii had persuaded both of these tribes to try with them the chance of war); further, that they were awaiting forces of the Aduatuci, already on the march, and that the women and all who by reason of age were deemed useless for battle had been collected together in a district to which there was no approach for an army by reason of the marshes.

[17] Upon this information Caesar sent forward scouts and centurions to choose a fit place for the camp. Now a considerable number of the surrendered Belgae and of the other Gauls were in the train of Caesar and marched with him; and certain of these, as was afterwards learnt from prisoners, having remarked the usual order of our army's march during those days, came by night to the Nervii and showed to them that between legion and legion a great quantity of baggage was interposed, and that it was an easy matter, when the first legion had reached camp and the rest were a great space away, to attack it while it was in heavy marching order; if it were driven back, and the baggage plundered, the rest would not dare to withstand. The plan proposed by those who brought the information was further assisted by an ancient practice of the Nervii. Having no strength in cavalry (for even to this day they care naught for that service, but all their power lies in the strength of their infantry), the easier to hamper the cavalry of their neighbours, whenever these made a raid on them, they cut into young saplings and bent them over, and thus by the thick horizontal growth of boughs, and by intertwining with them brambles and thorns, they contrived that these wall-like hedges should serve them

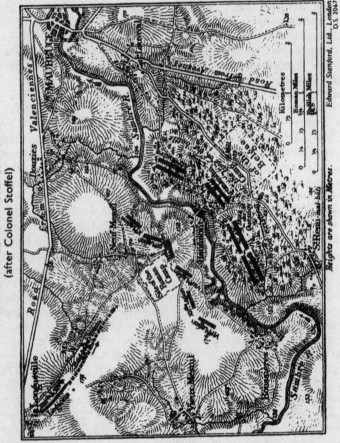

THE BATTLE OF THE SAMBRE
(after Colonel Stoffel)

Edward Stanford, Ltd., London
D.S. 2067

Heights are shown in Metres.

as fortifications which not only could not be penetrated, but not even seen through. As the route of our column was hampered by these abatis, the Nervii considered that the proposed plan should be tried.

[18] The character of the ground selected by our officers for the camp was as follows. There was a hill, inclining with uniform slope from its top to the river Sambre above mentioned. From the river-side there rose another hill of like slope, over against and confronting the other, open for about two hundred paces at its base, wooded in its upper half, so that it could not easily be seen through from without. Within those woods the enemy kept themselves in hiding. On open ground along the river a few cavalry posts were to be seen. The depth of the river was about three feet.

[19] Caesar had sent on the cavalry, and was following up with all his forces; but the arrangement and order of the column was different from the report given by the Belgae to the Nervii. For, as he was approaching an enemy, Caesar, according to his custom, was moving with six legions in light field order; after them he had placed the baggage of the whole army; then the two legions which had been last enrolled brought up the rear of the whole column and formed the baggage-guard. Our cavalry crossed the river along with the slingers and archers, and engaged the enemy's horsemen. The latter retired repeatedly upon their comrades in the woods, and, issuing thence, again charged our men; nor did our men dare to follow in pursuit farther than the extent of level open ground. Meanwhile the six legions first to arrive measured out the work, and began to entrench camp. The moment that the first baggage-detachments of our army were seen by the enemy, who were lurking hidden in the woods—the moment agreed upon among them for joining battle—they suddenly dashed forth in full force, having already in the woods ordered their line in regular ranks and encouraged one another for the conflict; and so charged down upon our cavalry. These were easily beaten and thrown into disorder, and with incredible speed the enemy rushed down to the river, so that almost at the same moment they were seen at the edge of the woods, in the river, and then at close quarters. Then with the same speed they hastened up-hill against our camp and the troops engaged in entrenching it.

[20] Caesar had everything to do at one moment—the flag to raise, as signal of a general call to arms; the trumpet-call to sound; the troops to recall from entrenching; the men to bring in who had gone somewhat farther afield in search of stuff for the ramp; the line to form; the troops to harangue; the signal to give. A great part of these duties was prevented by the shortness of the time and the advance of the enemy. The stress of the moment was relieved by two things: the knowledge and experience of the troops—for their training in previous battles

enabled them to appoint for themselves what was proper to be done as readily as others could have shown them—and the fact that Caesar had forbidden the several lieutenant-generals to leave the entrenching and their proper legions until the camp was fortified. These generals, seeing the nearness and the speed of the enemy, waited no more for a command from Caesar, but took on their own account what steps seemed to them proper.

[21] Caesar gave the necessary commands, and then ran down in a chance direction to harangue the troops, and came to the Tenth Legion. His harangue to the troops was no more than a charge to bear in mind their ancient valour, to be free from alarm, and bravely to withstand the onslaught of the enemy; then, as the enemy were no farther off than the range of a missile, he gave the signal to engage. He started off at once in the other direction to give like harangue, and found them fighting. The time was so short, the temper of the enemy so ready for conflict, that there was no space not only to fit badges in their places, but even to put on helmets and draw covers from shields. In whichever direction each man chanced to come in from the entrenching, whatever standard each first caught sight of, by that he stood, to lose no fighting time in seeking out his proper company.

[22] The army was drawn up rather as the character of the ground, the slope of the hill, and the exigency of the moment required than according to regular tactical formation. The legions were separated, and each was resisting the enemy in a different quarter; while the view to the front was interrupted, as above shown, by a barrier of very thick fences. Supports, therefore, could not be posted with certainty, nor could it be foreseen what would be needed anywhere, nor could all the commands be controlled by one man. Thus, with affairs in so grievous a difficulty, the issues of the day came likewise in varying sequence.

[23] The troops of the Ninth and the Tenth Legion, who had formed up on the left flank, discharged their pikes, and, as they possessed the higher ground, speedily drove the Atrebates (the section which happened to face them), into the river, breathless as they were with running and weakened with wounds; and, pursuing them with the sword as they endeavoured to cross, they slew a great part of them while in difficulties. They did not hesitate to cross the river themselves, and, advancing with the ground against them, when the enemy turned to resist, renewed the fight and put them to rout. Likewise in another quarter two detached legions, the Eleventh and the Eighth, having broken the Viromandui with whom they had engaged, left the higher ground, and continued the fight on the very banks of the river. But thereby—though on the right wing the Twelfth were stationed, and at no great distance from them the Seventh—almost all the front and the left face of the camp were laid

bare; and to this point[8] all the Nervii, led by Boduognatus, their commander-in-chief, pressed forward in a dense column, part of which began to envelop the legions on their exposed flank, part to attack the highest ground, where was the camp.

[24] At the same moment our cavalry and the light-armed infantry who had accompanied them, having been beaten back, as I related, by the first onslaught of the enemy, were retiring on to the camp, when they met the enemy face to face and again tried to flee in another direction. The sutlers too, who from the rear gate on the crest of the hill had remarked the passage of the river by our victorious troops, and had gone out to plunder, when they looked back and beheld the enemy moving about in our camp, betook themselves headlong to flight. At the same time there arose a confusion of shouting among the detachments coming up with the baggage-train, and they began to rush terror-stricken in all directions. All these events alarmed certain horsemen of the Treveri, whose reputation for valour among the Gauls is unique. Their state had sent them to Caesar as auxiliaries; but when they saw our camp filled with the host of the enemy, our legions hard pressed and almost surrounded in their grip, the sutlers, horsemen, slingers, Numidians, sundered, scattered, and fleeing in all directions, in despair of our fortunes they made haste for home, and reported to their state that the Romans were repulsed and overcome, and that the enemy had taken possession of their camp and baggage-train.

[25] After haranguing the Tenth Legion Caesar started for the right wing. There he beheld his troops hard driven, and the men of the Twelfth Legion, with their standards collected in one place, so closely packed that they hampered each other for fighting. All the centurions of the fourth cohort had been slain, and the standard-bearer likewise, and the standard was lost; almost all the centurions of the other cohorts were either wounded or killed, among them the chief centurion, Publius Sextius Baculus, bravest of the brave, who was overcome by many grievous wounds, so that he could no longer hold himself upright. The rest of the men were tiring, and some of the rearmost ranks, abandoning the fight, were retiring to avoid the missiles; the enemy were not ceasing to move upwards in front from the lower ground, and were pressing hard on either flank. The condition of affairs, as he saw, was critical indeed, and there was no support that could be sent up. Taking therefore a shield from the soldier of the rearmost ranks, as he himself was come thither without a shield, he went forward into the first line, and, calling on the centurions

---

[8] *i.e.* the exposed angle of the camp. Part of the Nervii attacked this, part tried to push round the right flank of the Twelfth and the Seventh. The two legions were thus in danger of being surrounded and cut off.

by name, and cheering on the rank and file, he bade them advance and extend the companies, that they might ply swords more easily. His coming brought hope to the troops and renewed their spirit; each man of his own accord, in sight of the commander-in-chief, desperate as his own case might be, was fain to do his utmost. So the onslaught of the enemy was checked a little.

[26] Perceiving that the Seventh Legion, which had formed up near at hand, was also harassed by the enemy, Caesar instructed the tribunes to close the legions gradually together, and then, wheeling, to advance against the enemy. This was done; and as one soldier supported another, and they did not fear that their rear would be surrounded by the enemy, they began to resist more boldly and to fight more bravely. Meanwhile the soldiers of the two legions which had acted as baggage-guard at the rear of the column heard news of the action. Pressing on with all speed, they became visible to the enemy on the crest of the hill; and Titus Labienus, having taken possession of the enemy's camp, and observed from the higher ground what was going forward in our own camp, sent the Tenth Legion to support our troops. When these learnt from the flight of cavalry and sutlers the state of affairs, and the grave danger in which the camp, the legions, and the commander-in-chief were placed, they spared not a tittle of their speed.

[27] Their arrival wrought a great change in the situation. Even such of our troops as had fallen under stress of wounds propped themselves against their shields and renewed the fight; then the sutlers, seeing the panic of the enemy, met their armed assault even without arms; finally, the cavalry, to obliterate by valour the disgrace of their flight, fought at every point in the effort to surpass the legionaries. The enemy, however, even when their hope of safety was at an end, displayed a prodigious courage. When their front ranks had fallen, the next stood on the prostrate forms and fought from them; when these were cast down, and the corpses were piled up in heaps, the survivors, standing as it were upon a mound, hurled darts on our troops, or caught and returned our pikes. Not without reason, therefore, was it to be concluded that these were men of a great courage, who had dared to cross a very broad river, to climb very high banks, and to press up over most unfavourable ground. These were tasks of the utmost difficulty, but greatness of courage had made them easy.

[28] This engagement brought the name and nation of the Nervii almost to utter destruction. Upon report of the battle, the older men, who, as above mentioned, had been gathered with the women and children in the creeks and marshes, supposed that there was nothing to hinder the victors, nothing to save the vanquished; and so, with the consent of all the survivors, they sent deputies to Caesar and surrendered to him. In relating the disaster which had come upon their state, they declared

that from six hundred senators they had been reduced to three, and from sixty thousand to barely five hundred that could bear arms. To show himself merciful towards their pitiful suppliance, Caesar was most careful for their preservation; he bade them keep their own territory and towns, and commanded their neighbours to restrain themselves and their dependents from outrage and injury.

[29] The Aduatuci, of whom I have written above, were coming with all their forces to the assistance of the Nervii, but upon report of this battle they left their march and returned home; and, abandoning all their towns and forts, they gathered all their stuff in one stronghold, which was admirably fortified by Nature. On every side of its circumference it looked down over the steepest rocks, and on one side only was left a gently sloping approach, not more than two hundred feet in breadth. This place they had fortified with a double wall of great height, and at this time they were setting stones of great weight and sharpened beams upon the wall. The tribe was descended from the Cimbri and Teutoni, who, upon their march into our Province and Italy, set down such of their stock and stuff as they could not drive or carry with them on the near (*i.e.* west) side of the Rhine, and left six thousand men of their company therewith as guard and garrison. This party, after the destruction of the others, were harassed for many years by their neighbours, and fought sometimes on the offensive, sometimes on the defensive; then by general agreement among them peace was made, and they chose this place to be their habitation.

[30] And now, upon the first arrival of our army, they made frequent sallies from the stronghold, and engaged in petty encounters with our troops. Afterwards, when they had round them a fortified rampart of fifteen thousand feet in circumference, with forts at close interval, they kept within the town. When our mantlets had been pushed up and a ramp constructed, and they saw a tower set up in the distance, they first of all laughed at us from the wall, and loudly railed upon us for erecting so great an engine at so great a distance. By what handiwork, said they, by what strength could men, especially of so puny a stature (for, as a rule, our stature, short by comparison with their own huge physique, is despised of the Gauls), hope to set so heavy a tower on the wall?

[31] But when they saw that it was moving and approaching the walls, they were alarmed at the novel and extraordinary sight, and sent deputies to Caesar to treat of peace, who spake after this fashion: They supposed that the Romans did not wage war without divine aid, inasmuch as they could move forward at so great a speed engines of so great a height; they therefore submitted themselves and all they had to the power of Rome. In one matter only did they seek indulgence: that if haply of his mercy and kindness, whereof they heard from others, Caesar decided to save the

Aduatuci alive, he would not despoil them of their arms. Almost all their neighbours were at enmity with them and envied their courage; and from such, if they delivered up their arms, they could not defend themselves. If they were to be brought into such case, it were better for them to suffer any fortune at the hand of Rome than to be tortured and slain by men among whom they were accustomed to hold mastery.

[32] To this Caesar replied that he would save their state alive rather because it was his custom than for any desert on their part, if they surrendered before the battering-ram touched the wall; but there could be no terms of surrender save upon delivery of arms. He would do, he said, what he had done in the case of the Nervii, and command the neighbours to do no outrage to the surrendered subjects of Rome. They reported this to their tribesmen, and agreed to perform his commands. A great quantity of arms was cast from the wall into the trench which was before the town, so that the heaps of weapons were well-nigh level with the top of the wall and the height of the ramp; and for all this about a third part, as was afterwards seen, was concealed and kept back in the town. So they threw open their gates, and on that day enjoyed the benefit of peace.

[33] At eventide Caesar ordered the gates to be closed and the troops to leave the town, in order that the townsfolk might suffer no outrage at their hands in the night. In the belief that after the surrender our troops would withdraw their posts or would at least look after them less carefully, the townsfolk, it appeared, had previously formed a plan. Part of them had the weapons which they had kept back and concealed, part had shields made of bark or plaited osiers and hastily (as the shortness of time necessitated) spread over with hides. In the third watch they made a sudden sally from the town in full force, on the side where the ascent to our fieldworks seemed least steep. Speedily, as Caesar had ordered beforehand, the signal was given by flares, and the detachments from the nearest forts doubled in to the point. The enemy fought fiercely, as was to be expected of brave men in desperate case, where all hope of safety lay in valour alone, contending on unfavourable ground against troops who could hurl missiles at them from rampart and towers. Some four thousand men were slain, and the rest were flung back into the town. On the morrow the gates were broken open, for there was no more defence, and our troops were sent in; then Caesar sold as one lot the booty of the town. The purchasers furnished a return to him of three-and-fifty thousand persons.

[34] At the same season Publius Crassus, whom he had despatched with one legion against the Veneti, Venelli, Osismi, Curiosolitae, Esubii, Aulerci, and Redones, the maritime states which border upon the Ocean, reported that all these states had been brought into subjection to the power of Rome.

[35] These achievements brought peace throughout Gaul, and so

mighty a report of this campaign was carried to the natives that deputies were sent to Caesar from the tribes dwelling across the Rhine, to promise that they would give hostages and do his commands. As Caesar was for hastening to Italy and Illyricum, he bade these deputations return to him at the beginning of the next summer. As soon as the legions had been withdrawn to winter quarters among the Carnutes, the Andes, the Turones, and such states as were near the scenes of the recent campaign, he himself set out for Italy. And for those achievements, upon receipt of Caesar's despatches, a fifteen days' thanksgiving was decreed, an honour that had previously fallen to no man.

# BOOK III

[1] When he was starting for Italy, Caesar sent Servius Galba with the Twelfth Legion and a detachment of cavalry to the district of the Nantuates, Veragri, and Seduni, which reaches from the borders of the Allobroges, from the Lake of Geneva, and from the river Rhone to the summits of the Alps. The reason for sending him was that he wished to open up a route[1] through the Alps by which traders had been accustomed to travel, but at great risk and on payment of great tolls; and Caesar gave him permission to station his legion in this locality for the winter, if he thought it necessary. A certain number of successful engagements were fought; several of the enemy's forts were taken by storm; then deputies were sent to Galba from all sides, hostages given, and peace made. So Galba decided to station two cohorts in the district of the Nantuates, and to winter himself with the remaining cohorts of the legion in a hamlet of the Veragri called Octodurus. It is set in a valley, with no great space of level about it, and shut in all round by very lofty mountains. As the hamlet was divided in two by a river, Galba granted one part of it to the Gauls, and assigned the other, which the Gauls evacuated, to his cohorts to winter in. He fortified the place with rampart and trench.

[2] Several days had passed in winter quarters, and Galba had given orders for corn to be brought in from the neighbourhood, when on a sudden his scouts informed him that in the night every soul had withdrawn from that part of the hamlet which he had granted to the Gauls, and that the heights overhanging were occupied by an enormous host of Seduni and Veragri. Several causes had contributed to make the Gauls suddenly adopt the plan of renewing the war and crushing the legion. In the first place, they despised the small numbers of a legion, from which, never at full establishment, two cohorts had been withdrawn, and a considerable number of private soldiers sent off to seek supplies. In the sec-

---

[1] *i.e.* over the Great St. Bernard.

44

ond place, they supposed that, because of the disadvantage of position, since they themselves would charge down from the heights into the valley and hurl their missiles, not even their first onset could be withstood. Moreover, they were indignant that their children had been taken away from them under the title of hostages; and they were convinced that the Romans were endeavouring to seize the peaks of the Alps and to add those districts to their neighbouring Province, not only for the sake of the routes, but to secure a permanent occupation.

[3] This was the information received by Galba. Now he knew that the construction and entrenchment of the winter quarters were not fully completed, and that no adequate provision had been made for corn and supplies in general, because he had come to the conclusion that, as surrender had been made and hostages received, no warlike development was to be apprehended. He therefore summoned with speed a council of war, and proceeded to ask for expressions of opinion. The danger that had arisen was as serious as it was sudden and unexpected, and indeed by this time almost all the higher ground was seen to be packed with a host of armed men, while, with the communications interrupted, reinforcements could not be attempted nor supplies brought up. In the council, therefore, the chance of safety was almost despaired of, and not a few opinions were expressed in favour of abandoning the baggage, making a sortie, and striving to win safety by the same routes which had brought them thither. None the less, the majority decided to reserve this expedient to the final emergency, and meanwhile to await the issue and defend the camp.

[4] After a short interval—so short that it scarcely allowed time to complete the dispositions and arrangements determined upon—the enemy, upon a signal given, charged down from all sides, and hurled volleys of stones and javelins against the rampart. At first the Roman troops repelled them gallantly with strength unimpaired, and discharged not a missile in vain from their higher station;[2] and if any part of the camp was stripped of defenders and seemed to be hard pressed, they sped thither to render assistance. But they were at a disadvantage, because when any of the enemy, wearied by the long continuance of the battle, retired from the fighting line, others with strength unimpaired would step into their places; but nothing of the kind could be done by the Romans on account of their scantiness of numbers, and not only had a wearied man no chance of retiring from the battle, but not even a wounded man could leave the spot where he had been posted and look after himself.

[5] The fighting actually went on for more than six hours on end, and

---

[2] i.e. from the "command" of the rampart.

not only the strength but the missiles of the Romans were failing; the enemy were pressing on more fiercely, and beginning, as our energies slackened, to break down the rampart and fill in the trench. At this juncture Publius Sextius Baculus, the senior centurion (whom we have mentioned[3] as disabled by several wounds in the battle with the Nervii), and with him Gaius Volusenus, a military tribune, a man of great sagacity and courage, hastened to Galba, and informed him that the only hope of safety was to try the last expedient in making a sortie. Galba accordingly summoned the centurions, and speedily instructed the troops to make a short pause in the fighting, and merely to intercept the missiles discharged against them, and to refresh themselves after their effort; then, upon a given signal, to burst from the camp and place all hope of safety in courage.

[6] They did as they were bid; and suddenly from all the gates a sortie was made, leaving the enemy no chance of learning what was afoot, nor of rallying. So there was a complete change of fortune; the Romans surrounded on every side and slew the multitude which had come in hope of capturing the camp, and of more than thirty thousand men (for that was known to be the number of the natives who came against the camp) more than a third were slain, while the rest were driven in headlong flight, and not suffered to stand fast even on the higher ground. Thus all the forces of the enemy were routed, and the Romans, stripping off the arms of the slain, retired to their own entrenched camp. This battle over, Galba declined to try fortune too often: he remembered that there was a great difference between the purpose of his coming into winter quarters and the state of things which he had found, and he was very greatly concerned by the lack of corn and supplies. Accordingly, on the next day he caused all the buildings of that hamlet to be burnt, and made haste to return to the Province; and, as there was no enemy to hinder him or delay his march, he brought the legion safely into the territory of the Nantuates, and then into that of the Allobroges, and there wintered.

[7] After these events Caesar had every reason to suppose that Gaul was at peace again, for the Belgae were defeated, the Germans driven out, and the Seduni in the Alpine region conquered; therefore after the beginning of winter he had set out for Illyricum, desiring to visit the tribes there also and to become acquainted with the country. But at this point war broke out suddenly in Gaul, of which the cause was as follows. Publius Crassus the younger with the Seventh Legion had been wintering by the Ocean in the country of the Andes. As there was a lack of corn in those parts, he despatched several commandants and tribunes into the neighbouring states to seek it. Of these officers Titus Terrasidius was sent among the

---

[3] II. 25.

Esubii, Marcus Trebius Gallus among the Curiosolites, Quintus Velanius with Titus Silius among the Veneti.

[8] These Veneti exercise by far the most extensive authority over all the sea-coast in those districts, for they have numerous ships, in which it is their custom to sail to Britain, and they excel the rest in the theory and practice of navigation. As the sea is very boisterous, and open, with but a few harbours here and there which they hold themselves, they have as tributaries almost all those whose custom is to sail that sea. It was the Veneti who took the first step, by detaining Silius and Velanius, supposing that through them they should recover their own hostages whom they had given to Crassus. Their authority induced their neighbours—for the Gauls are sudden and spasmodic in their designs—to detain Trebius and Terrasidius for the same reason, and, rapidly despatching deputies among their chiefs, they bound themselves by mutual oath to do nothing save by common consent, and to abide together the single issue of their destiny. Moreover, they urged the remaining states to choose rather to abide in the liberty received from their ancestors than to endure Roman slavery. The whole sea-coast was rapidly won to their opinion, and they despatched a deputation in common to Publius Crassus, bidding him restore their hostages if he would receive back his own officers.

[9] Caesar was informed by Crassus concerning these matters, and, as he himself was at some distance, he ordered men-of-war to be built meanwhile on the river Loire, which flows into the Ocean, rowers to be drafted from the Province, seamen and steersmen to be got together. These requirements were rapidly executed, and so soon as the season allowed he himself hastened to join the army. The Veneti and likewise the rest of the states were informed of Caesar's coming, and at the same time they perceived the magnitude of their offence—they had detained and cast into prison deputies, men whose title had ever been sacred and inviolable among all nations. Therefore, as the danger was great, they began to prepare for war on a corresponding scale, and especially to provide naval equipment, and the more hopefully because they relied much on the nature of the country. They knew that on land the roads were intersected by estuaries, that our navigation was hampered by ignorance of the locality and by the scarcity of harbours, and they trusted that the Roman armies would be unable to remain long in their neighbourhood by reason of the lack of corn. Moreover, they felt that, even though everything should turn out contrary to expectation, they were predominant in sea-power, while the Romans had no supply of ships, no knowledge of the shoals, harbours, or islands in the region where they were about to wage war; and they[4]

_____
[4] The Veneti.

could see that navigation on a land-locked sea was quite different from navigation on an Ocean very vast and open. Therefore, having adopted this plan, they fortified their towns, gathered corn thither from the fields, and assembled as many ships as possible in Venetia, where it was known that Caesar would begin the campaign. As allies for the war they took to themselves the Osismi, the Lexovii, the Namnetes, the Ambiliati, the Morini, the Diablintes, and the Menapii; and they sent to fetch auxiliaries from Britain, which lies opposite those regions.

[10] The difficulties of the campaign were such as we have shown above; but, nevertheless, many considerations moved Caesar to undertake it. Such were the outrageous detention of Roman knights, the renewal of war after surrender, the revolt after hostages given, the conspiracy of so many states—and, above all, the fear that if this district were not dealt with the other nations might suppose they had the same liberty. He knew well enough that almost all the Gauls were bent on revolution, and could be recklessly and rapidly aroused to war; he knew also that all men are naturally bent on liberty, and hate the state of slavery. And therefore he deemed it proper to divide his army and disperse it at wider intervals before more states could join the conspiracy.

[11] Accordingly he despatched Titus Labienus, lieutenant-general, with the cavalry to the territory of the Treveri, who live next the river Rhine. His instructions were to visit the Remi and the rest of the Belgae, and to keep them loyal, and to hold back the Germans, who were said to have been summoned by the Belgae to their assistance, in case they should endeavour to force the passage of the river by boats. Publius Crassus, with twelve cohorts from the legions and a large detachment of cavalry, was ordered to start for Aquitania, to prevent the despatch of auxiliaries from the tribes there into Gaul, and the junction of the two great nations. Quintus Titurius Sabinus, lieutenant-general, was despatched with three legions to the territory of the Venelli, the Curiosolites, and the Lexovii, to keep that force away from the rest. Decimus Brutus the younger was put in command of the fleet, and of the Gallic ships already ordered to assemble from the territory of the Pictones, the Santoni, and the others now pacified, and was ordered to start as soon as possible for the country of the Veneti, whither Caesar himself hastened with the land force.

[12] The positions of the strongholds were generally of one kind. They were set at the end of tongues and promontories, so as to allow no approach on foot, when the tide had rushed in from the sea—which regularly happens every twelve hours—nor in ships, because when the tide ebbed again the ships would be damaged in shoal water. Both circumstances, therefore, hindered the assault of the strongholds; and, whenever the natives were in fact overcome by huge siege-works—that is to say, when the sea had been set back by a massive mole built up level to the

town-walls—and so began to despair of their fortunes, they would bring close inshore a large number of ships, of which they possessed an unlimited supply, and take off all their stuff and retire to the nearest strongholds, there to defend themselves again with the same advantages of position. They pursued these tactics for a great part of the summer the more easily because our own ships were detained by foul weather, and because the difficulty of navigation on a vast and open sea, with strong tides and few—nay, scarcely any—harbours, was extreme.

[13] Not so the ships of the Gauls, for they were built and equipped in the following fashion. Their keels were considerably more flat than those of our own ships, that they might more easily weather shoals and ebb-tide. Their prows were very lofty, and their sterns were similarly adapted to meet the force of waves and storms. The ships were made entirely of oak, to endure any violence and buffeting. The cross-pieces were beams a foot thick, fastened with iron nails as thick as a thumb. The anchors were attached by iron chains instead of cables. Skins and pieces of leather finely finished were used instead of sails, either because the natives had no supply of flax and no knowledge of its use, or, more probably, because they thought that the mighty ocean-storms and hurricanes could not be ridden out, nor the mighty burden of their ships conveniently controlled, by means of sails. When our own fleet encountered these ships it proved its superiority only in speed and oarsmanship; in all other respects, having regard to the locality and the force of the tempests, the others were more suitable and adaptable. For our ships could not damage them with the ram (they were so stoutly built), nor, by reason of their height, was it easy to hurl a pike, and for the same reason they were less readily gripped by grapnels. Moreover, when the wind began to rage and they ran before it, they endured the storm more easily, and rested in shoals more safely, with no fear of rocks or crags if left by the tide; whereas our own vessels could not but dread the possibility of all these chances.

[14] Caesar had taken several towns by assault, when he perceived that all his labour availed nothing, since the flight of the enemy could not be checked by the capture of towns, nor damage done to them; accordingly he determined to await the fleet. It assembled in due course, and so soon as it was sighted by the enemy about two hundred and twenty of their ships, fully prepared and provided with every kind of equipment, sailed out of harbour and took station opposite ours. Brutus, who commanded the fleet, and his tribunes and centurions in charge of single ships, were by no means certain what to do or what plan of battle they were to pursue. For our commanders knew the enemy could not be damaged by the ram; while, even when turrets were set up on board, the lofty sterns of the native ships commanded even these, so that from the lower level missiles could not be hurled properly, while those discharged by the Gauls gained

a heavier impact. One device our men had prepared to great advantage—sharp-pointed hooks let in and fastened to long poles, in shape not unlike siege-hooks. When by these contrivances the halyards which fastened the yards to the masts were caught and drawn taut, the ship was rowed hard ahead and they were snapped short. With the halyards cut, the yards of necessity fell down; and as all the hope of the Gallic ships lay in their sails and tackle, when those were torn away all chance of using their ships was taken away also. The rest of the conflict was a question of courage, in which our own troops easily had the advantage—the more so because the engagement took place in sight of Caesar and of the whole army, so that no exploit a little more gallant than the rest could escape notice. The army, in fact, was occupying all the hills and higher ground from which there was a near view down upon the sea.

[15] When the yards had been torn down as described, and each ship was surrounded by two or three, the troops strove with the utmost force to climb on to the enemy's ships. When several of them had been boarded, the natives saw what was toward; and, as they could think of no device to meet it, they hastened to seek safety in flight. And they had headed all their vessels down the wind, when suddenly a calm so complete and absolute came on that they could not stir from the spot. This circumstance was in the highest degree fortunate for the settlement of the business, for our troops pursued and boarded the vessels one by one, with the result that of all the number very few, when night came on, reached the land. The battle, indeed, lasted from about the fourth hour to sunset.

[16] This engagement finished the campaign against the Veneti and the whole sea-coast. For, on the one hand, all the fighting men, nay, all the older men who had any sagacity or distinction, had there assembled; on the other, they had collected in one place every single ship they had anywhere; and after such losses[5] the rest of their men had no point to retire to, no means of defending the towns. Accordingly they surrendered themselves and all they had to Caesar. He decided that their punishment must be the more severe in order that the privilege of deputies might be more carefully preserved by the natives for the future. He therefore put the whole of their senate to the sword, and sold the rest of the men as slaves.

[17] During these events in the land of the Veneti Quintus Titurius Sabinus, with the force received from Caesar, reached the borders of the Venelli. Their chief, Viridovix, held the supreme command of all the revolted states, from which he had raised an army, and large levies[6] besides.

---

[5] *i.e.* of both men and ships.
[6] *i.e.* of irregular forces.

Further, in the last few days the Aulerci, Eburovices, and the Lexovii, after putting their senate to death because they refused to approve the war, closed their gates and joined Viridovix. Moreover, from every corner of Gaul a great host of desperadoes and brigands had gathered, whom the hope of plunder and the passion for war seduced from the daily toil of agriculture. Sabinus confined himself to camp, in a spot suited for any emergency. Viridovix had encamped against him two miles away, and daily led out his forces to give him a chance of fighting, so that at last Sabinus not only incurred the contempt of the enemy, but was assailed by occasional reproaches even of the Roman troops; indeed, he created so strong an impression of cowardice that at length the enemy ventured to come up to the rampart of the camp. He pursued these tactics because he deemed it improper for a lieutenant-general to fight an engagement with so large a host of the enemy, especially in the absence of his commander-in-chief, unless on favourable ground or on some opportunity offered.

[18] When this impression of timidity had been confirmed, he chose out a fit man and a cunning, one of the Gauls whom he had with him as auxiliaries. He induced him by great rewards and promises to go over to the enemy, and instructed him in what he would have done. When the pretended deserter had reached the enemy, he set before them the timidity of the Romans, explained to them how Caesar himself was in straits and hard pressed by the Veneti, and told them that no later than next night Sabinus was to lead his army secretly out of his camp and to set out to the assistance of Caesar. Upon hearing this, they all cried with one consent that the chance of successful achievement should not be lost—that they should march upon the camp. Many considerations encouraged the Gauls to this course: the hesitation of Sabinus during the previous days, the confirmation given by the deserter, the lack of victuals (for which they had made too careless a provision), the hope inspired by the Venetian war, and the general readiness of men to believe what they wish. With these thoughts to spur them on, they would not suffer Viridovix and the rest of the leaders to leave the council until they had their permission to take up arms and press on to the camp. Rejoicing at the permission given as though at victory assured, they collected faggots and brushwood to fill up the trenches of the Romans and marched on the camp.

[19] The position of the camp was on high ground, with a gradual slope from the bottom of about a mile. Hither the Gauls hastened at great speed to give the Romans the least possible time to assemble and to arm; and they arrived out of breath. Sabinus exhorted his troops, and gave the signal which they longed for. The enemy were hampered by reason of the burdens which they were carrying, and he ordered a sudden sortie to be made from two gates. The order was executed with the advantage of ground; the enemy were inexperienced and fatigued, the Romans coura-

geous and schooled by previous engagements. The result was that without standing even one of our attacks the Gauls immediately turned and
ran. Hampered as they were, our troops pursued them with strength
unimpaired and slew a great number of them; the rest our cavalry chased
and caught, and left but a few, who had got clear away from the rout. So
it chanced that in the same hour Sabinus learnt of the naval battle, and
Caesar of Sabinus' victory; and all the states at once surrendered to
Sabinus. For while the temper of the Gauls is eager and ready to undertake a campaign, their purpose is feeble and in no way steadfast to endure
disasters.

[20] About the same time Publius Crassus had reached Aquitania, a
district which, as has been said before, for extent of territory and number
of inhabitants is to be reckoned as a third part of Gaul. He understood
that he was to conduct a campaign in the localities where a few years
before Lucius Valerius Praeconinus, the lieutenant-general, had been
defeated and slain, and from which the proconsul Lucius Mallius had
escaped with the loss of his baggage; he understood, therefore, that he
must exercise no common care. Accordingly he provided a supply of
corn, he collected auxiliaries and cavalry, and he further called up singly
many brave men from Toulouse and Narbonne, communities of the
Province of Gaul adjacent to the regions concerned; he then marched his
army into the borders of the Sotiates. Hearing of his approach, the
Sotiates collected a large force, with cavalry, in which lay their chief
strength, and attacked our column on the march. First of all they engaged
in a cavalry combat; then, when their cavalry were beaten, and ours pursued, they suddenly unmasked their infantry force, which they had posted
in ambush in a valley. The infantry attacked our scattered horsemen and
renewed the fight.

[21] The battle was long and fierce. The Sotiates, with the confidence
of previous victories, felt that upon their own courage depended the
safety of all Aquitania: the Romans were eager to have it seen what they
could accomplish under a young leader without the commander-in-chief
and the rest of the legions. At last, however, after heavy casualties the
enemy fled from the field. A large number of them were slain; and then
Crassus turned direct from his march and began to attack the stronghold
of the Sotiates. When they offered a brave resistance he brought up
mantlets and towers.[7] The enemy at one time attempted a sortie, at
another pushed mines as far as the ramp and the mantlets—and in min-
ing the Aquitani are by far the most experienced of men, because in many
localities among them there are copper-mines and diggings. When they

---

[7] See illustrations on page 151.

perceived that by reason of the efficiency of our troops no advantage was to be gained by these expedients, they sent deputies to Crassus and besought him to accept their surrender.

[22] Their request was granted, and they proceeded to deliver up their arms as ordered. Then, while the attention of all our troops was engaged upon that business, Adiatunnus, the commander-in-chief, took action from another quarter of the town with six hundred devotees, whom they call vassals. The rule of these men is that in life they enjoy all benefits with the comrades to whose friendship they have committed themselves, while if any violent fate befalls their fellows, they either endure the same misfortune along with them or take their own lives; and no one yet in the memory of man has been found to refuse death, after the slaughter of the comrade to whose friendship he had devoted himself. With these men Adiatunnus tried to make a sortie; but a shout was raised on that side of the entrenchment, the troops ran to arms, and a sharp engagement was fought there. Adiatunnus was driven back into the town; but, for all that, he begged and obtained from Crassus the same terms of surrender as at first.

[23] After receiving arms and hostages Crassus set his march for the borders of the Vocates and the Tarusates. At this juncture the natives, alarmed by the information that a town fortified alike by natural position and by the hand of man had been carried within a few days of his arrival, began to send deputies about in every direction, to conspire together, to deliver hostages each to other, and to make ready a force. They even sent deputies to those states of Nearer Spain which border on Aquitania, inviting succours and leaders from thence. Upon their arrival they attempted the campaign with great prestige and a great host of men. And as their leaders for the same they selected men who had served for the whole period with Quintus Sertorius and were believed to be past masters of war. These leaders, in Roman fashion, set to work to take up positions, to entrench a camp, and to cut off our supplies. Crassus remarked that his own force by reason of its slender numbers could not easily be split up, while the enemy could range at will, beset the roads, and yet leave sufficient garrison for their camp; and that for this reason his corn and supplies were less conveniently brought up, while the numbers of the enemy daily increased: he therefore considered that he must not delay to fight a decisive battle. He referred the question to a council of war; and, perceiving that all were agreed, he appointed the following day for the battle.

[24] At dawn he brought out all his force and formed double line, with the auxiliaries massed in the centre; then he waited to see what plan the enemy would adopt. Although they considered that they could fight an action safely by reason of their numbers and their past glory in war and the smallness of the Roman force, they still thought it safer to close the

roads and cut off supplies, and so to secure victory without bloodshed. And further, if through lack of corn the Romans began to retire, they had it in mind to attack them when they were encumbered in column by the weight of their packs, so that their spirit would be weaker. This plan was approved by their leaders; therefore, when the Roman force was brought out, they kept in camp. Crassus perceived this; and, inasmuch as the enemy by their hesitation had created an impression of timidity and increased the eagerness of our soldiers for action, and a general protest was heard against longer delay before an advance on the camp, he harangued his troops, and then amid general enthusiasm he pressed on to the enemy's camp.

[25] Arrived there, some proceeded to fill up the trenches, others by many volleys of missiles to clear the defenders from the rampart and fortifications, while the auxiliaries, in whom Crassus had no great confidence for actual fighting, by handing up stones and missiles and carrying sods to make a ramp, gave the appearance and impression of fighting troops. Meanwhile the enemy, for their part, fought in no irresolute or cowardly fashion, and their missiles discharged from a higher level fell to some purpose. A party of cavalry, however, having moved round the enemy's camp, reported to Crassus that it was not fortified with the same care on the rear side, and might easily be approached there.

[26] Crassus exhorted the cavalry commanders to incite their men by great rewards and promises, and showed what he would have done. In accordance with his orders they led out the cohorts which had been left to guard the camp and were unwearied by exertion; and, having led them a long way round, so as not to be seen from the enemy's camp, they rapidly reached the fortifications above mentioned while the eyes and attention of all were set on the actual fight. They threw down the fortifications, and established themselves in the enemy's camp before they could be clearly seen by them or their action perceived. But when shouting was heard in that quarter the Romans, with strength renewed, began, as is frequent and usual where there is hope of victory, to assault the more vigorously. The enemy, surrounded on all sides and in utter despair, hastened to lower themselves over the fortifications and to seek safety in flight. The cavalry chased them over plains wholly without shelter; and of fifty thousand, the number known to have assembled from Aquitania and the Cantabrian country, they had left scarce a quarter when they returned to camp late at night.

[27] Upon hearing of this battle the greatest part of Aquitania surrendered to Crassus, and of its own motion sent hostages, among whom were representatives of the Tarbelli, Bigerriones, Ptianii, Vocates, Tarusates, Elusates, Gates, Ausci, Garumni, Sibuzates, Cocosates. A few of the most distant tribes, trusting in the season, as winter was at hand, omitted to do this.

[28] In the general pacification of Gaul the Morini and Menapii remained under arms, and had never sent deputies to Caesar to treat for peace. About this same time, therefore, although the summer was almost over, he led his army against them, believing that the campaign could be speedily completed. These tribes, however, started upon the campaign with tactics quite different from the rest of the Gauls. For, perceiving that the most powerful tribes which had fought an action had been beaten and vanquished, and possessing continuous forests and marshes, they conveyed themselves and all their stuff thither. Caesar reached the outskirts of these forests, and determined to entrench a camp, having in the meanwhile seen nothing of the enemy. When, however, our men were scattered at work, the enemy suddenly dashed out of all parts of the forest and charged our troops. These speedily took up arms, and drove the enemy back into the forests: a considerable number of them were slain, but as the Romans pursued too far in almost impassable places they lost a few of their own side.

[29] In the days then remaining Caesar set to work to cut down the forests, and, to prevent any flank attack on troops unarmed and unprepared, he placed all the timber felled on the side towards the enemy, and also piled it as a rampart on both flanks. With incredible rapidity a great space was cleared in a few days, until the enemy's cattle and the rearward of their baggage were in our keeping, while they themselves sought the denser forests. But then such storms ensued that the work was of necessity interrupted, and the continual rains made it impossible to keep the troops longer under canvas. Accordingly, after laying waste all the fields of the enemy, and burning villages and farm-buildings, Caesar brought back his army, and placed it in winter quarters among the Aulerci, the Lexovii, and the rest of the states which had recently waged war.

# BOOK IV

[1] In the following winter—the year in which Gnaeus Pompeius and Marcus Crassus were consuls[1]—the Usipetes from Germany, and likewise the Tencteri, crossed the Rhine with a large host of men, not far from the sea into which it flows. The reason for their crossing was that for several years they had been much harassed by the Suebi, who pressed on them by force of arms and prevented them from husbandry. The Suebi are by far the largest and the most warlike nation among the Germans. It is said that they have a hundred cantons, from each of which they draw one thousand armed men yearly for the purpose of war outside their borders. The remainder, who have stayed at home, support themselves and the absent warriors; and again, in turn, are under arms the following year, while the others remain at home. By this means neither husbandry nor the theory and practice of war is interrupted. They have no private or separate holding of land, nor are they allowed to abide longer than a year in one place for their habitation. They make not much use of corn for food, but chiefly of milk and of cattle, and are much engaged in hunting; and this, owing to the nature of the food, the regular exercise, and the freedom of life—for from boyhood up they are not schooled in a sense of duty or discipline, and do nothing whatever against their wish— nurses their strength and makes men of immense bodily stature. Moreover, they have regularly trained themselves to wear nothing, even in the coldest localities, except skins, the scantiness of which leaves a great part of the body bare, and they bathe in the rivers.

[2] They give access to traders rather to secure purchasers for what they have captured in war than to satisfy any craving for imports. And, in fact, the Germans do not import for their use draught-horses, in which the Gauls take the keenest delight, procuring them at great expense; but they take their home-bred animals, inferior and ill-favoured, and by regular exercising they render them capable of the utmost exertion. In cavalry

---

[1] 55 B.C.

56

combats they often leap from their horses and fight on foot, having trained their horses to remain in the same spot, and retiring rapidly upon them at need; and their tradition regards nothing as more disgraceful or more indolent than the use of saddles. And so, however few in number, they dare approach any party, however large, of saddle-horsemen. They suffer no importation of wine whatever, believing that men are thereby rendered soft and womanish for the endurance of hardship.

[3] As a nation, they count it the highest praise to have the land on their borders untenanted over as wide a tract as may be, for this signifies, they think, that a great number of states cannot withstand their force. Thus it is said that on one side for about six hundred miles from the territory of the Suebi the land is untenanted. On the other side the Ubii come nearest, a state which was once extensive and prosperous, according to German standards. Its inhabitants are somewhat more civilised than the other folk of the same race, because their borders touch the Rhine and traders visit them frequently, and, further, because the Ubii themselves by close neighbourhood have grown accustomed to Gallic fashions. Upon this people the Suebi had made frequent attempts in many wars, but had proved unable to drive them from their territory because the state was populous and powerful: however, they made the Ubii tributary to themselves, and greatly diminished their strength and importance.

[4] The Usipetes and the Tencteri, mentioned above, were in the same case. For several years they withstood the force of the Suebi, but at last they were driven out of their lands, and after wandering for three years in many districts of Germany they reached the Rhine. The localities thereabout were inhabited by the Menapii, who possessed lands, buildings, and villages on both banks of the river; but, being alarmed by the approach of so great a host, they removed from the buildings which they had possessed beyond the river, and, setting garrisons at intervals on the near side of the Rhine, sought to prevent the Germans from crossing. The Germans tried every expedient, but when they found that they could neither force their way because of their lack of vessels nor cross privily because of the Menapian piquets, they pretended to retire to their own homes and districts. They proceeded for a three days' journey, and then returned; and their cavalry, having completed the whole of this distance in a single night, caught the Menapii uninformed and unawares, for, having learnt through their scouts of the departure of the Germans, they had moved back without fear over the Rhine into their own villages. So they were put to the sword and their vessels seized; then the Germans crossed the river before the section of the Menapii on the near side of the Rhine could learn of it, seized all their buildings, and for the remainder of the winter sustained themselves on the supplies of the Menapii.

[5] Caesar was informed of these events; and fearing the fickleness of the Gauls, because they are capricious in forming designs and intent for the most part on change, he considered that no trust should be reposed in them. It is indeed a regular habit of the Gauls to compel travellers to halt, even against their will, and to ascertain what each of them may have heard or learnt upon every subject; and in the towns the common folk surround traders, compelling them to declare from what districts they come and what they have learnt there. Such stories and hearsay often induce them to form plans upon vital questions of which they must forthwith repent; for they are the slaves of uncertain rumours, and most men reply to them in fictions made to their taste.

[6] Caesar was aware of this their habit, and, for fear that otherwise he might have to face a more serious campaign, set out for the army earlier than was his wont. When he reached headquarters he learnt that his suspicions had been realised; deputations had been sent by some states to the Germans, inviting them to leave the Rhine, and promising to furnish all things demanded of them. The hope thus inspired encouraged the Germans to range more widely, and they had already reached the borders of the Eburones and the Condrusi, dependents of the Treveri. Thereupon Caesar summoned the chiefs of Gaul from their homes; but, thinking it best to conceal the information in his possession, he comforted and encouraged them, and, having made requisition of cavalry, determined to make war on the Germans.

[7] Having secured his corn-supply and selected his cavalry, he began to march into the localities in which the Germans were reported to be. When he was a few days' march away deputies arrived from them, whose address was to the following effect: The Germans did not take the first step in making war on the Roman people, nor yet, if provoked, did they refuse the conflict of arms, for it was the ancestral custom of the Germans to resist anyone who made war upon them, and not to beg off. They declared, however, that they had come against their will, being driven out of their homes: if the Romans would have their goodwill, they might find their friendship useful. Let the Romans either grant them lands, or suffer them to hold the lands their arms had acquired. They yielded to the Suebi alone, to whom even the immortal gods could not be equal; on earth at any rate there was no one else whom they could not conquer.

[8] To this Caesar replied as seemed good; but the conclusion of his speech was as follows: He could have no friendship with them, if they remained in Gaul. On the one hand, it was not just that men who had not been able to defend their own territories should seize those of others; on the other hand, there was no land in Gaul which could be granted without injustice, especially to so numerous a host. However, they had

permission, if they pleased, to settle in the territories of the Ubii, whose deputies were in his camp, complaining of the outrages of the Suebi and seeking his assistance: he would give orders to the Ubii to this effect.

[9] The envoys said that they would report this to their people and, after deliberation upon the matter, return to Caesar in three days: they asked him not to move his camp nearer in the meanwhile. Caesar replied that he could not even grant that request. He knew, in fact, that they had sent a large detachment of cavalry some days before to the country of the Ambivariti across the Meuse, to get booty and corn: he supposed that they were waiting for this cavalry, and for that reason sought to interpose delay.

[10] The Meuse flows from the range of the Vosges, in the territory of the Lingones, and, receiving from the Rhine a certain tributary called the Waal, forms the island of the Batavi; then, no more than eighty miles from the Ocean, it flows into the Rhine. The Rhine rises in the land of the Lepontii, who inhabit the Alps; in a long, swift course it runs through the territories of the Nantuates, Helvetii, Sequani, Mediomatrices, Triboci, and Treveri, and on its approach to the Ocean divides into several streams, forming many large islands (a great number of which are inhabited by fierce barbaric tribes, believed in some instances to live on fish and birds' eggs); then by many mouths it flows into the Ocean.

[11] When Caesar was no more than twelve miles away from the enemy, the deputies returned to him as agreed: they met him on the march, and besought him earnestly not to advance further. When their request was not granted, they asked him to send forward to the cavalry in advance of his column and to prevent them from engaging, and to grant themselves an opportunity of sending deputies into the land of the Ubii. They put forward the hope that, if the chiefs and the senate of the Ubii pledged their faith on oath, they (the Germans) would accept the terms which Caesar offered; and they asked him to give them an interval of three days to settle these affairs. Caesar supposed that all these pleas had the same object as before, to secure by a three days' interval the return of their absent cavalry; however, he said that on that day he would advance no further than four miles, in order to get water. He instructed them to meet him there next day with as large a number as they could, in order that he might take cognisance of their demands. Meanwhile he sent instructions to the commanders who had gone forward with all the cavalry not to provoke the enemy to an engagement, and, if provoked themselves, to hold their ground until he himself with the army had come up nearer.

[12] The enemy had no more than eight hundred cavalry, for the party which was gone across the Meuse to get corn was not yet returned. Our own men, five thousand strong, had nothing to fear, for the deputies of

the Germans had left Caesar but a short while before, having asked for a truce that day. However, directly they saw our cavalry, the enemy charged, and speedily threw our men into confusion. When our men turned to resist, the enemy, according to their custom, dismounted, and, by stabbing our horses and bringing down many of our troopers to the ground, they put the rest to rout, and indeed drove them in such panic that they did not desist from flight until they were come in sight of our column. In that engagement were slain seventy-four of our cavalry, and among them the gallant Piso of Aquitania, the scion of a most distinguished line, whose grandfather had held the sovereignty in his own state, and had been saluted as Friend by the Roman Senate. Piso went to the assistance of his brother, who had been cut off by the enemy, and rescued him from danger, but was thrown himself, his horse having been wounded. He resisted most gallantly as long as he could; then he was surrounded, and fell after receiving many wounds. His brother, who had escaped from the fight, saw him fall from a distance; then spurred his horse, flung himself upon the enemy, and was slain.

[13] After this engagement was over, Caesar felt that he ought no longer to receive deputies nor to accept conditions from tribes which had sought for peace by guile and treachery; and then had actually begun war. Further, he judged it the height of madness to wait till the enemy's forces should be increased and their cavalry returned. Knowing as he did the fickleness of the Gauls, he apprehended how much influence the enemy had already acquired over them by a single engagement; and he considered that no time to form plans should be given them. Thus determined, he communicated to the lieutenant-generals and the quartermaster-general his purpose not to lose a day in giving battle. Then, most fortunately, a certain thing occurred. The next morning, as treacherous and as hypocritical as ever, a large company of Germans, which included all the principal and senior men, came to his quarters, with a double object—to clear themselves (so they alleged) for engaging in a battle the day before, contrary to the agreement and to their own request therein, and also by deceit to get what they could in respect of the truce. Caesar rejoiced that they were delivered into his hand, and ordered them to be detained; then in person he led all his troops out of camp, commanding the cavalry, which he judged to be shaken by the recent engagement, to follow in the rear.

[14] Triple line of columns[2] was formed, and the eight-mile march was so speedily accomplished that Caesar reached the enemy's camp before the Germans could have any inkling of what was toward. They

---

[2] The army advanced, not in column of route, but in line of columns, ready to form up into line of battle. *Cf.* VIII. 8.

were struck with sudden panic by everything—by the rapidity of our approach, the absence of their own chiefs; and, as no time was given them to think, or to take up arms, they were too much taken aback to decide which was best—to lead their forces against the enemy, to defend the camp, or to seek safety by flight. When their alarm was betrayed by the uproar and bustle, our troops, stung by the treachery of the day before, burst into the camp. In the camp those who were able speedily to take up arms resisted the Romans for a while, and fought among the carts and baggage-wagons; the remainder, a crowd of women and children (for the Germans had left home and crossed the Rhine with all their belongings), began to flee in all directions, and Caesar despatched the cavalry in pursuit.

[15] Hearing the noise in rear, and seeing their own folk slain, the Germans threw away their arms, abandoned their war-standards, and burst out of the camp. When they reached the junction of the Meuse and the Rhine, they gave up hope of escaping further; a large number were already slain, and the rest hurled themselves into the river, there to perish, overcome by terror, by exhaustion, by the force of the stream. The Romans, with not a man lost and but few wounded, freed from the fear of a stupendous war—with an enemy whose numbers had been 430,000 souls—returned to camp. Caesar gave to the Germans detained in camp permission to depart; but they, fearing punishments and tortures at the hand of the Gauls whose land they had harassed, said that they would stay in his company, and he gave them liberty so to do.

[16] The German campaign thus finished, Caesar decided for many reasons that he must cross the Rhine. The most cogent reason was that, as he saw the Germans so easily induced to enter Gaul, he wished to make them fearful in turn for their own fortunes, by showing them that a Roman army could and durst cross the Rhine. Moreover, that section of the cavalry of the Usipetes and Tencteri which, as I have mentioned above, had crossed the Meuse to get booty and corn, and had taken no part in the battle, had now, after the rout of their countrymen, withdrawn across the Rhine into the territory of the Sugambri, and joined them. To them Caesar sent envoys to demand the surrender of the men who had made war upon himself and Gaul. They replied that the Rhine marked the limit of the Roman empire: if he thought it unfair that the Germans should cross into Gaul against his will, why did he claim any imperial power across the Rhine?

The Ubii, on the other hand, the only tribe beyond the Rhine which had sent deputies to Caesar, made friendly terms, and given hostages, earnestly besought him to assist them, as they were grievously hard pressed by the Suebi; or, if the urgent concerns of state prevented that, only to transport his army across the Rhine: that would suffice for their present help and future hope. So great, they said, even among the farthest tribes of Germany was the renown and reputation of his army, after the defeat of Ariovistus and the success of this last action, that their own safety was secure in the prestige and the friendship of Rome. They promised a large supply of boats for the transport of his army.

[17] For the reasons above mentioned Caesar had decided to cross the Rhine; but he deemed it scarcely safe, and ruled it unworthy of his own and the Romans' dignity, to cross in boats. And so, although he was confronted with the greatest difficulty in making a bridge, by reason of the breadth, the rapidity, and the depth of the river, he still thought that he must make that effort, or else not take his army across. He proceeded to construct a bridge on the following plan.[3] He caused pairs of balks eighteen inches thick, sharpened a little way from the base and measured to suit the depths of the river, to be coupled together at an interval of two feet. These he lowered into the river by means of rafts, and set fast, and drove home by rammers; not, like piles, straight up and down, but leaning forward at a uniform slope, so that they inclined in the direction of the stream. Opposite to these, again, were planted two balks coupled in the same fashion, at a distance of forty feet from base to base of each pair, slanted against the force and onrush of the stream. These pairs of balks had two-foot transoms let into them atop, filling the interval at which they were coupled, and were kept apart by a pair of braces on the outer side at each end. So, as they were held apart and contrariwise clamped together, the stability of the structure was so great and its character such that, the greater the force and thrust of the water, the tighter were the balks held in lock. These trestles[4] were interconnected by timber laid over at right angles, and floored with long poles and wattlework. And further, piles were driven in aslant on the side facing down stream, thrust out below like a buttress and close joined with the whole structure, so as to take the force of the stream; and others likewise at a little distance above the bridge, so that if trunks of trees, or vessels, were launched by the natives to break down the structure, these fenders might lessen the force of such shocks, and prevent them from damaging the bridge.

[18] The whole work was completed in ten days from that on which the collecting of timber began, and the army was taken across. Leaving a strong post at either end of the bridge, Caesar pressed on into the territory of the Sugambri. Meanwhile from several states deputies came to him, to whose request for peace and friendship he replied in generous

---

[3] See page 63. The bridge is believed to have been thrown across between Andernach and Coblenz.

[4] *i.e.* each set of balks and transoms.

# SECTION OF A TRESTLE

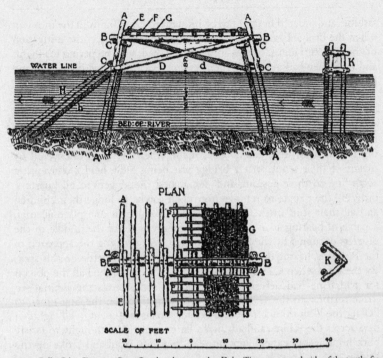

## PLAN

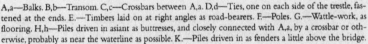

SCALE OF FEET

A,a—Balks. B,b—Transom. C,c—Crossbars between A,a. D,d—Ties, one on each side of the trestle, fastened at the ends. E.—Timbers laid on at right angles as road-bearers. F.—Poles. G.—Wattle-work, as flooring. H,h—Piles driven in asiant as buttresses, and closely connected with A,a, by a crossbar or otherwise, probably as near the waterline as possible. K.—Piles driven in as fenders a little above the bridge.

## THE BRIDGE OVER THE RHINE (iv. 17)

The present breadth of the Rhine at Coblenz is about 400 yards; the depth thereabout varies from 5 to 25 feet. In the section given 16 feet is taken as an average depth. The width of roadway shown is 36 feet. The space (40 feet) between the pairs of balks (A,a) is reckoned along the waterline—*i.e.* the lowest visible part. If it were reckoned along the river-bed, it would mean that the successive pairs of balks would incline inwards at different angles as the bridge approached mid-stream from each bank: for it is not to be supposed that the width of the roadway varied. We are not told at what angle the balks inclined, nor at what height above the water-line the transoms were, nor how far each pier or trestle was from the next. It is highly probable that, in a military bridge of this kind, for the sake of rapidity in construction, a uniform profile was followed for the part of each pier or trestle visible above the water-line.

It is not clear what is meant by the *fibulae* mentioned by Caesar. Some authorities have thought that these are the diagonal ties (D,d), which are certainly required for the stability of the bridge, and which are probably implied by the phrase *quibus disclusis aique in contrariam partem revinctis.* The triangle formed by balk, transom, and tie resembles the shape, and performs the function, of a brooch (*fibula*). Other authorities hold that the *fibulae* were iron "dogs" (—), driven in to clamp each transom to its two pairs of balks at the points of juncture.

fashion, and ordered hostages to be brought to him. But from the moment when the bridge began to be constructed the Sugambri, at the instigation of the Tencteri and Usipetes among them, had been preparing for flight; and now they had evacuated their territory, carried off all their stuff, and hidden themselves in the remote part of the forests.

[19] Caesar tarried for a few days in their territory, until he had burnt all the villages and buildings, and cut down the corn-crops. Then he withdrew into the territory of the Ubii; and, after a promise of his help to them, if they were hard pressed by the Suebi, he received the following information from them. The Suebi, when they had discovered by means of their scouts that a bridge was being built, held a convention according to their custom, and despatched messengers to all quarters, ordering the people to remove from their towns, to lodge their children and all their stuff in the woods, and to assemble in one place all men capable of bearing arms. The place chosen was about the middle of the districts occupied by the Suebi; here they were awaiting the approach of the Romans, having determined to fight the decisive battle on this spot. By the time when Caesar learnt this he had accomplished all the objects for which he had determined to lead his army across the Rhine—to strike terror into the Germans, to take vengeance on the Sugambri, to deliver the Ubii from a state of blockade. So, having spent in all eighteen days across the Rhine, and advanced far enough, as he thought, to satisfy both honour and expediency, he withdrew into Gaul and broke up the bridge.

[20] Only a small part of the summer was left, and in these regions, as all Gaul has a northerly aspect, the winters are early; but for all this Caesar was intent upon starting for Britain. He understood that in almost all the Gallic campaigns succours had been furnished for our enemy from that quarter; and he supposed that, if the season left no time for actual campaigning, it would still be of great advantage to him merely to have entered the island, observed the character of the natives, and obtained some knowledge of the localities, the harbours, and the landing-places; for almost all these matters were unknown to the Gauls. In fact, nobody except traders journeys thither without good cause; and even traders know nothing except the sea-coast and the districts opposite Gaul. Therefore, although he summoned to his quarters traders from all parts, he could discover neither the size of the island, nor the number or the strength of the tribes inhabiting it, nor their manner of warfare, nor the ordinances they observed, nor the harbours suitable for a number of large ships.

[21] To gain such knowledge before he made the venture, Caesar thought Gaius Volusenus a proper person to send on in advance with a ship of war. His orders were to spy out everything and to return to him at once. He himself with all his forces started for the territory of the

Morini, from which was the shortest passage across to Britain. He commanded the general concentration here of ships from the neighbouring districts, and of the fleet which he had built in the previous summer for the Venetian campaign. Meanwhile his purpose had become known and had been reported through traders to the Britons, and deputies came to him from several states in the island with promises to give hostages and to accept the empire of Rome. He heard them, and made them a generous promise, encouraging them to keep their word; then he sent them back home, and along with them he sent Commius, whom he himself, after subduing the Atrebates, had made king over them. Caesar approved his courage and discretion, and believed him loyal to himself; and his influence was reckoned to be of great account in those parts.[5] Him he commanded to visit what states he could, to exhort them to seek the protection of Rome, and to announce his own speedy advent thither. Volusenus observed all the country so far as was possible for an officer who did not dare to disembark and entrust himself to the rough natives, and on the fifth day returned to Caesar, and reported his observations in Britain.

[22] While Caesar tarried where he was to fit out his ships, deputies came to him from a great part of the Morini to make excuse for their policy of the previous season, when in their barbarism and ignorance of our usage they had made war against Rome, and to promise that they would carry out his commands. Caesar thought this overture exceedingly opportune. He did not wish to leave an enemy in his rear, nor had he a chance of carrying out a campaign because of the lateness of the season; nor did he think the settlement of such trivialities should take precedence of Britain. He therefore ordered them to furnish a large number of hostages; and when they brought these he received them under his protection. When about eighty transports—enough, in his opinion, to carry two legions across—had been collected and concentrated, he distributed all the ships of war he had over between his quartermaster-general, lieutenant-generals, and commandants. To the total stated eighteen transports should be added, which were detained eight miles off by the wind, and prevented from entering the port of concentration;[6] these he allotted to the cavalry. The rest of the army he handed over to Quintus Titurius Sabinus and Lucius Aurunculeius Cotta, lieutenant-generals, to be led against the Menapii and against those cantons of the Morini from which no deputies had come to him. He commanded Publius Sulpicius Rufus, lieutenant-general, with a garrison he considered sufficient, to hold the port.

---

[5] i.e. in Britain.
[6] Probably Boulogne.

[23] These arrangements made, he caught a spell of fair weather for sailing, and weighed anchor about the third watch: he ordered the cavalry to proceed to the further harbour,[7] embark, and follow him. They took somewhat too long to despatch the business; he himself reached Britain about the fourth hour of the day, and there beheld the armed forces of the enemy displayed on all the cliffs.[8] Such was the nature of the ground, so steep the heights which banked the sea, that a missile could be hurled from the higher levels on to the shore. Thinking this place to be by no means suitable for disembarkation, he waited at anchor till the ninth hour for the rest of the flotilla to assemble there. Meanwhile he summoned together the lieutenant-generals and tribunes, to inform them what he had learnt from Volusenus, and what he wished to be done; and he warned them that, to meet the requirements of tactics and particularly of navigation—with its liability to movements as rapid as they were irregular—they must do everything in the nick of time at a hint from him. He then dismissed them; and catching at one and the same moment a favourable wind and tide, he gave the signal, and weighed anchor, and, moving on about seven miles from that spot, he grounded his ships where the shore was even and open.[9]

[24] The natives, however, perceived the design of the Romans. So they sent forward their cavalry and charioteers—an arm which it is their regular custom to employ in fights—and, following up with the rest of their forces, they sought to prevent our troops from disembarking. Disembarkation was a matter of extreme difficulty, for the following reasons. The ships, on account of their size, could not be run ashore, except in deep water; the troops—though they did not know the ground, had not their hands free, and were loaded with the great and grievous weight of their arms—had nevertheless at one and the same time to leap down from the vessels, to stand firm in the waves, and to fight the enemy. The enemy, on the other hand, had all their limbs free, and knew the ground exceeding well; and either standing on dry land or advancing a little way into the water, they boldly hurled their missiles, or spurred on their horses, which were trained to it. Frightened by all this, and wholly inexperienced in this sort of fighting, our troops did not press on with the same fire and force as they were accustomed to show in land engagements.

[25] When Caesar remarked this, he commanded the ships of war (which were less familiar in appearance to the natives, and could move

---

[7] Probably Ambleteuse.
[8] About Dover.
[9] Probably between Walmer and Deal.

more freely at need) to remove a little from the transports, to row at
speed, and to bring up on the exposed flank of the enemy; and thence
to drive and clear them off with slings, arrows, and artillery. This movement proved of great service to our troops; for the natives, frightened by
the shape of the ships, the motion of the oars, and the unfamiliar type of
the artillery, came to a halt, and retired, but only for a little space. And
then, while our troops still hung back, chiefly on account of the depth
of sea, the eagle-bearer of the Tenth Legion, after a prayer to heaven to
bless the legion by his act, cried: "Leap down, soldiers, unless you wish
to betray your eagle to the enemy; it shall be told that I at any rate did
my duty to my country and my general." When he had said this with a
loud voice, he cast himself forth from the ship, and began to bear the
eagle against the enemy. Then our troops exhorted one another not to
allow so dire a disgrace, and leapt down from the ship with one accord.
And when the troops on the nearest ships saw them, they likewise followed on, and drew near to the enemy.

[26] The fighting was fierce on both sides. Our troops, however,
because they could not keep rank, nor stand firm, nor follow their proper
standards—for any man from any ship attached himself to whatever standard he chanced upon—were in considerable disorder. But the enemy
knew all the shallows, and as soon as they had observed from the shore a
party of soldiers disembarking one by one from a ship, they spurred on
their horses and attacked them while they were in difficulties, many surrounding few, while others hurled missiles into a whole party from the
exposed[10] flank. Caesar noticed this; and causing the boats of the war-
ships, and likewise the scout-vessels, to be manned with soldiers, he sent
them to support any parties whom he had observed to be in distress. The
moment our men stood firm on dry land, they charged with all their
comrades close behind, and put the enemy to rout; but they could not
pursue very far, because the cavalry had not been able to hold on their
course and make the island. This one thing was lacking to complete the
wonted success of Caesar.

[27] So the enemy were overcome in the fight; and as soon as they had
recovered from the rout they at once sent deputies to Caesar to treat for
peace, promising that they would give hostages and do what he commanded. Together with these deputies came Commius the Atrebatian,
who, as shown above, had been sent forward by Caesar into Britain.
When Commius disembarked and delivered Caesar's messages to the
Britons in the character of an ambassador, they had seized him and
thrown him into chains; but now, after the fight, they sent him back. In

---

[10] *i.e.* the right, or unshielded, side.

their entreaty for peace they cast the blame of the misdeed upon the multitude, and sought pardon in consideration of their ignorance. Caesar complained that, though of their own motion they had sent deputies on to the Continent to seek peace from him, they had now begun war on him without cause; but he agreed to pardon their ignorance, and required hostages. Part of these they gave at once, part they said they would summon from the more distant parts and give in a few days. Meanwhile they ordered their own folk to get back to their fields; and the chiefs began to assemble from every quarter, and to deliver themselves and their states to Caesar.

[28] Peace was thus established. Four days after the arrival in Britain the eighteen ships above mentioned, which had embarked the cavalry, weighed anchor, in a gentle breeze, from the upper[11] port. When they were nearing Britain, and in view of the camp, so fierce a storm suddenly arose that none of them could hold on its course; some were carried back to the selfsame port whence they had started, others were driven away, with great peril to themselves, to the lower, that is, to the more westerly, part of the island. None the less, they cast anchor; but when they began to fill with the waves they were obliged to stand out to sea in a night of foul weather, and made for the Continent.

[29] That same night, as it chanced, the moon was full, the day of the month which usually makes the highest tides in the Ocean, a fact unknown to our men. Therefore the tide was found to have filled the warships, in which Caesar had caused his army to be conveyed across, and which he had drawn up on dry land; and at the same time the storm was buffeting the transports, which were made fast to anchors. Nor had our troops any chance of handling them or helping. Several ships went to pieces; and the others, by loss of cordage, anchors, and the rest of their tackle, were rendered useless for sailing. This, as was inevitable, caused great dismay throughout the army. For there were no other ships to carry them back; everything needful for the repair of ships was lacking; and, as it was generally understood that the army was to winter in Gaul, no corn had been provided in these parts against the winter.

[30] When they became aware of this, the British chiefs who had assembled at Caesar's headquarters after the fight took counsel together. As they knew that the Romans lacked cavalry, ships, and corn, and perceived the scantiness of the army from the smallness of the camp (it was straitened even more by the fact that Caesar had brought the legions over without baggage), they thought that the best thing to do was to renew the war, cut off our corn and other supplies, and prolong the business

---

[11] *i.e.* the more northerly: see ch. 23 and note 9.

into the winter; for they were confident that when the present force was overcome or cut off from return no one thereafter would cross over into Britain to make war upon them. Therefore they conspired together anew, and, departing a few at a time from the camp, they began secretly to draw in their followers from the fields.

[31] Although Caesar had not yet learnt their designs, yet the misfortune of his ships and the fact that the chiefs had broken off the surrender of hostages led him to suspect that events would turn out as they did; and therefore he prepared means to meet any emergency. He collected corn daily from the fields into the camp, and he utilised the timber and bronze of the ships which had been most severely damaged to repair the rest, and ordered the necessary gear for that purpose to be brought from the Continent. The work was most zealously carried out by the troops; and thus, though twelve ships had been lost, he was able to render the rest tolerably seaworthy.

[32] Meanwhile one legion, called the Seventh, had been sent as usual to collect corn; nor as yet had any suspicion of hostilities intervened, since part of the people remained in the fields, and part were actually frequent visitors to the camp. Then the outposts on duty before the gates of the camp reported to Caesar that a greater dust than usual was to be seen in that quarter to which the legion had marched. Caesar suspected the truth—that some fresh design had been started by the natives—and ordered the cohorts which were on outpost to proceed with him to the quarter in question, two of the others to relieve them on outpost, and the rest to arm and follow him immediately. When he had advanced some little way from the camp, he found that his troops were being hard pressed by the enemy and were holding their ground with difficulty: the legion was crowded together, while missiles were being hurled from all sides. The fact was that when the corn had been cut from the rest of the neighbourhood one part remained, and the enemy, supposing that our troops would come hither, had hidden by night in the woods; then, when the men were scattered and, having grounded arms, were engaged in cutting corn, they had suddenly attacked them. They had killed a few, throwing the rest into confusion before they could form up, and at the same time surrounding them with horsemen and chariots.

[33] Their manner of fighting from chariots is as follows. First of all they drive in all directions and hurl missiles, and so by the mere terror that the teams inspire and by the noise of the wheels they generally throw ranks into confusion. When they have worked their way in between the troops of cavalry, they leap down from the chariots and fight on foot. Meanwhile the charioteers retire gradually from the combat, and dispose the chariots in such fashion that, if the warriors are hard pressed by the host of the enemy, they may have a ready means of retirement to

their own side. Thus they show in action the mobility of cavalry and the stability of infantry; and by daily use and practice they become so accomplished that they are ready to gallop their teams down the steepest of slopes without loss of control, to check and turn them in a moment, to run along the pole, stand on the yoke, and then, quick as lightning, to dart back into the chariot.

[34] When our troops were thrown into confusion in this fashion by the novel character of the fighting, Caesar brought assistance in the very nick of time; for his arrival caused the enemy to halt, and enabled our men to recover from their fear. This done, he deemed the moment unsuitable for provoking and engaging in a combat; he therefore stood to his own ground and, after a brief interval, led the legions back to camp. In the course of these events all our troops were busily occupied, and the natives who remained in the fields withdrew. Then for several days on end storms ensued, severe enough to keep our men in camp and to prevent the enemy from fighting. Meanwhile the natives despatched messengers in every direction, to tell of the scanty numbers of our troops and to show how great a chance was given of getting booty and of liberating themselves for ever by driving the Romans out of their camp. By this means they speedily collected a great host of footmen and horsemen, and came on towards the camp.

[35] Caesar saw that the result would be the same as on the previous days—that the enemy, if repulsed, would use their speed to escape from danger; nevertheless, as he had got about thirty horsemen, whom Commius, the Atrebatian before mentioned, had brought over with him, he formed the legions in line before the camp. When battle was joined the enemy, unable to endure for long the attack of our troops, turned and fled. The Romans followed after, as far as their speed and strength enabled, and slew not a few of them; then, after setting on fire all buildings far and wide, they retired to camp.

[36] On the same day deputies sent by the enemy came to Caesar to treat of peace. For them Caesar doubled the number of hostages previously commanded, and ordered them to be brought to the Continent, because the equinox was close at hand, and with a damaged flotilla he did not think it right to subject his crossing to the hazard of winter storms. He himself, taking advantage of a spell of fair weather, weighed anchor a little after midnight, and all the ships came safe to the Continent; but two of the transports were unable to make the same port as the rest, and were carried a little lower down the coast.

[37] When about three hundred men had been landed from these vessels and were marching rapidly to camp, the Morini, who had been left by Caesar in a state of peace when he set out for Britain, were fired by the hope of booty, and surrounded the troops, at first with no very large

number of their own folk, bidding them lay down their arms if they did not wish to be killed. The Romans formed square and defended themselves, and at the noise of shouting some six thousand men speedily came about them. Upon report of this Caesar sent the whole of the cavalry from the camp to assist his men. Meanwhile our troops withstood the enemy's assault, and fought with the greatest gallantry for more than four hours: they received but a few wounds, and slew a good many of the enemy. Howbeit, as soon as our cavalry came in sight, the enemy threw down their arms and fled, and a great number of them were slain.

[38] The next day Caesar sent Titus Labienus, the lieutenant-general, with the legions which he had brought back from Britain, against the Morini, who had renewed hostilities. The enemy had no place of retreat, by reason of the dryness of the marshes, their refuge in the previous year; almost all of them, therefore, came and surrendered to Labienus. As for Quintus Titurius and Lucius Cotta, the lieutenant-generals who had led legions into the territory of the Menapii, they did not return to Caesar until they had laid waste all the fields of the natives, cut down the corn-crops, and burnt the buildings, because the Menapii had all hidden in their densest forests. Then Caesar established the winter quarters of all the legions in Belgic territory. Thither no more than two of the British states sent hostages; the remainder omitted to do so. And for these achievements, upon receipt of Caesar's despatches, the Senate decreed a public thanksgiving of twenty days.

# BOOK V

[1] Lucius Domitius and Appius Claudius were still consuls[1] when Caesar, on the eve of his departure from winter quarters to go to Italy, as it was his practice every year to do, ordered the lieutenant-generals in charge of the legions to have as many ships as possible built during the winter, and the old fleet repaired. He set forth the plan and pattern of the new ships. For speed of loading and for purposes of beaching he would build them somewhat lower than those which we are accustomed to use on our own sea[2]—and the more so because he had learnt that by reason of the frequent turns of the tides the waves off Gaul were generally smaller. For the transport of cargo, and of the numerous draught-animals, he would have the ships somewhat broader than those we use on the other seas. All of them he ordered to be fitted for oars as well as sails, to which end their lowness of build helped much. The necessary tackle for the equipment of the ships he commanded to be brought out of Spain. When he had concluded the assizes[3] of Hither Gaul he himself set out for Illyricum, for he learnt that the Pirustae were devastating by raids the portion of the Province nearest them. When he was come thither he made a levy of troops upon the states, and commanded them to assemble at a certain spot. Upon report of this the Pirustae sent deputies to him to declare that none of those raids had been the result of any public decision, and they affirmed that they were ready by every means to give satisfaction for the outrages. Accepting their statement, Caesar made requisition of hostages and commanded them to be brought in by a certain day; failing this, he affirmed that he would visit the state with war. The hostages were brought in by the day, as ordered; and Caesar appointed arbitrators as between state and state to assess the damages and determine the penalty.

---

[1] 54 B.C.
[2] The Mediterranean.
[3] See note 22, page 27.

72

[2] When these matters were settled and the assizes concluded he returned to Hither Gaul, and thence set out for the army. When he was come thither he went round all the winter quarters, and learnt that by the exemplary energy of the soldiers, and in spite of the utmost lack of all necessaries, about six hundred ships of the type set forth above and twenty-eight men-of-war had been built, and lacked but little to make them ready for launching in a few days. Caesar warmly commended the troops and the officers who had been in charge of the work; he gave his instructions, and commanded all the ships to assemble at the Itian port,[4] from which, as he was informed, was the most convenient passage to Britain, a transit of about thirty miles from the Continent. He left such troops as he thought sufficient for this business; and himself, with four legions marching light and eight hundred horse, set out for the borders of the Treveri, because this tribe came not to the councils nor obeyed his command, and, according to report, was stirring up the Germans beyond the Rhine.

[3] Their state is by far the most powerful in cavalry of all the Gauls, and possesses great forces of infantry; and, as above set forth, it touches the Rhine. Two men in the state were striving together for the chieftaincy, Indutiomarus and Cingetorix. The latter of these, directly he was informed of the coming of Caesar and his legions, came to him, affirming that he and all his followers would abide in loyalty and not forsake their friendship with Rome; moreover, he showed what was afoot among the Treveri. Indutiomarus, on the other hand, began to raise horse and foot, and to prepare for war, as soon as he had hidden away those whose age made them unfit for service, in the Forest of Ardennes, which is of great size, stretching right through the territory of the Treveri, from the river Rhine to the border of the Remi. But some of the chiefs of the Treveri, actuated by their friendship for Cingetorix, and at the same time alarmed at the coming of our army, came to Caesar and began to make requests of him as touching their own private interests, since it was not in their power, they said, to take measures in the interests of the state.[5] Then Indutiomarus feared that he might be deserted by one and all, and sent deputies to Caesar. He urged that in his reluctance to leave his own folk and to come to Caesar his object was to keep the state the more easily to its allegiance, lest, if the whole of the nobility left them, the common people might go astray through ignorance. As a result, he said, the state was in his power, and, if Caesar allowed, he would come to his headquarters and commit the fortunes of himself and of the state to his protection.

---

[4] Probably Boulogne: cf. IV. 22.

[5] i.e. openly in the general assembly to urge coming to terms with Caesar.

[4] Caesar knew very well the purpose of these remarks, and the circumstance which was discouraging Indutiomarus from his deliberate design; nevertheless, that he might not be obliged to waste the summer among the Treveri, when everything was prepared for the campaign in Britain, he commanded Indutiomarus to come to him with two hundred hostages. When these were brought in, among them his son and all his relatives, whom Caesar had summoned by name, he comforted[6] Indutiomarus and exhorted him to abide in loyalty. Nevertheless he assembled at his headquarters the chiefs of the Treveri, and won them over severally for Cingetorix. He was aware that Cingetorix deserved this of him, but he deemed it also of great importance that the authority of one whose signal goodwill towards himself he had fully proved should be as strong as possible among his own folk. This action Indutiomarus took grievously to heart, for he saw that his own influence among his people was being diminished; and though he had previously felt hostility towards us, his indignation now burst far more vehemently into flame.

[5] When these matters had been settled Caesar proceeded with the legions to the Itian port. There he was informed that sixty ships, which had been built in the country of the Meldi, had been driven back by the weather so that they could not hold on their course, and had therefore returned to their starting-point. The rest he found ready for sailing and equipped in all respects. A body of cavalry from all Gaul, four thousand strong, assembled at the same spot, together with chiefs from every state. A very few of the latter, whose loyalty towards himself he had proved, he had decided to leave in Gaul, taking the rest with him by way of hostages, because he feared a rising in Gaul during his own absence.

[6] Among the others there was Dumnorix of the Aedui, of whom we have spoken before.[7] Caesar had determined to keep Dumnorix in particular with him, because he knew him to be bent on revolution, bent on sovereignty, a man of great courage and of great weight among the Gauls. Moreover, in the council of the Aedui Dumnorix had said that Caesar meant to offer him the kingship of the state; and while the Aedui took the saying grievously to heart, they did not dare to send envoys to Caesar either to repudiate or deprecate his purpose. Caesar had learnt this fact from his own partisans. Dumnorix at first by every kind of entreaty pressed his petition to be left in Gaul, affirming now that he was unused to a voyage and feared the sea, now that he was hindered on religious grounds.[8] Then, when he saw that leave was inexorably refused, and all

---

[6] *i.e.* assured him that no harm should befall the hostages or himself.

[7] I. 18–20.

[8] *Cf.* I. 50.

hope of obtaining it was taken away, he began to stir up the Gallic chieftains, drawing them aside severally and exhorting them to stay on the Continent. And he sought to frighten them by expressing apprehension that there was some reason for stripping Gaul of all her nobility: that it was Caesar's design to transport to Britain and there slaughter all whom he feared to put to death in the sight of Gaul. To the rest he pledged his word, and demanded of them an oath that they would execute by common consent whatever they judged to be for the advantage of Gaul. These plots were reported to Caesar by several persons.

[7] Upon this information Caesar was disposed to think, in view of the great importance he attached to the Aedui, that Dumnorix should be repressed and discouraged by all possible means, and at the same time, as his infatuation was obviously going too far, that precaution should be taken against his being able to do any damage to himself and the Roman state. And therefore, as he was delayed at that spot for some five-and-twenty days, because a north-west wind (prevalent for a great part of every season in those localities) prevented his sailing, he endeavoured to keep Dumnorix to his allegiance, but none the less to learn all his designs. At length fair weather came, and he ordered foot and horse to embark. But when all were thus preoccupied, Dumnorix, along with certain troopers of the Aedui, was minded to leave camp and depart for home. Caesar knew not of this; but upon report thereof he countermanded the sailing and put off everything, and then despatched a large detachment of cavalry to follow him up, with orders to hale him back, and, if he offered force or refused to obey, to put him to death; for he supposed that a man who had disregarded his command before his face would do nothing right-minded behind his back. And indeed when Dumnorix was summoned to return he sought to resist and to defend himself by force, entreating the help of his followers and crying repeatedly that he was a free man and of a free state. The pursuers, as they were ordered, surrounded the man and despatched him; but the troopers of the Aedui all returned to Caesar.

[8] When this was done Labienus was left on the Continent with three legions and two thousand horse, and with instructions to guard the ports, to ensure the corn-supply, to keep himself informed of events in Gaul, and to make plans as occasion and circumstance should require. The commander-in-chief, with five legions and a contingent of horse equal to that left on the Continent, weighed anchor about sunset, and proceeded under a gentle south-west wind. But about midnight the wind failed, and he did not make the course: he was carried on too far by the tide, and at sunrise he sighted Britain left afar on the port side. Then once more he followed the turn of the tide, and strove by rowing to make that part of the island where (as he had learnt in the previous sum-

mer) was the best place of disembarkation. And herein was the spirit of the troops much to be commended, who, in the heavily built transports, by uninterrupted effort of rowing kept level with the men-of-war. The whole fleet reached the shore of Britain about midday, but no enemy was to be seen there. They had, indeed, as Caesar learnt afterwards from prisoners, assembled there in large companies; but, alarmed at the host of ships, of which, counting those of the previous year and the private vessels which individuals had built for their own convenience, over eight hundred had been seen at once, they had withdrawn from the shore and concealed themselves on the high ground.

[9] The army was landed and a place suitable for the camp was chosen. When Caesar had learnt from prisoners where the enemy's forces had taken post, he left ten cohorts and three hundred horse by the seashore to guard the fleet; then, starting in the third watch, he pressed on to meet the enemy, having the less fear for the fleet because he was leaving it at anchor on a sandy, open shore; and he appointed Quintus Atrius to command the troops guarding the ships. He himself, advancing about twelve miles in the night, came in sight of the enemy's forces. They advanced their cavalry and chariots from the higher ground to a river,[9] and sought to check our troops and to engage. Driven back by our horse, they concealed themselves in the woods: there they had got a position excellently fortified by nature as well as by handiwork, which, as it would seem, had been prepared before for a war among themselves; for all the entries had been barred by a great number of felled trees. The enemy came out of the woods to fight in small groups, and sought to prevent our troops from entering the fortifications. But the men of the Seventh Legion formed a "tortoise,"[10] and threw up a ramp against the fortifications, and so took the position, driving the enemy out of the woods at the cost of a few men wounded. Caesar forbade them to pursue the fugitives very far, because he did not know the character of the country, and also because a great part of the day was spent, and he wished to leave time for the entrenchment of the camp.

[10] In the morning of the next day he divided the foot and the horse in three detachments, and sent them as flying columns to pursue the fugitives. When these had advanced a good long march and the rearguards were just in sight, troopers came from Quintus Atrius to Caesar to report that a violent storm had arisen in the previous night, and that nearly all the ships had been damaged and cast up on shore, as the anchors and cables would not hold, and the seamen and steersmen could

---

[9] The Great Stour.
[10] See page 30, note 4.

not face the force of the storm: and so the collision of ships had caused serious damage.

[11] Upon receipt of this intelligence Caesar commanded the legions and the cavalry to be recalled, and to keep off attacks on the line of march, while he himself returned to the fleet. With his own eyes he saw almost exactly what he had learnt from the messengers and despatches: some forty vessels indeed were lost, but it appeared that the rest could be repaired with great trouble. He therefore picked out artificers from the legions, and ordered others to be fetched from the Continent; and wrote to Labienus to construct as many ships as possible by the help of the legions he had with him. For himself he determined that, although the task involved much labour and effort, it was still the best plan to have all the ships beached and connected with the camp by a single entrenchment. Upon this business he spent about ten days, allowing no interruption even at night-time in the work of the troops. When the ships had been beached and the camp thoroughly well entrenched, he left the same forces as before to guard the ships: he himself then set out for the point whence he had returned. When he was come thither he found that still greater forces of the Britons had assembled there from every direction, and that by common consent they had entrusted the supreme command and conduct of the campaign to Cassivellaunus, whose territories are divided from the maritime states by the river called Thames, about eighty miles from the sea. Hitherto there had been continuous wars between this chief and the other states; but our arrival had moved the Britons to appoint him commander-in-chief for the conduct of the whole campaign.

[12] The inland part of Britain is inhabited by tribes declared in their own tradition to be indigenous to the island, the maritime part by tribes that migrated at an earlier time from Belgium to seek booty by invasion. Nearly all of these latter are called after the names of the states from which they sprang when they went to Britain; and after the invasion they abode there and began to till the fields. The population is innumerable, the farm-buildings are found very close together, being very like those of the Gauls; and there is great store of cattle. They use either bronze, or gold coins, or instead of coined money tallies of iron, of a certain standard of weight. In the midland districts of Britain tin is produced, in the maritime iron, but of that there is only a small supply; the bronze they use is imported. There is timber of every kind, as in Gaul, save beech and pine. They account it wrong to eat of hare, fowl, and goose; but these they keep for pastime or pleasure. The climate is more temperate than in Gaul, the cold seasons more moderate.

[13] The natural shape of the island is triangular, and one side lies opposite to Gaul. Of this side one angle, which is in Kent (where almost

all the ships from Gaul come in to land), faces the east, the lower angle faces south. This side stretches about five hundred miles. The second side bears towards Spain and the west, in which direction lies Ireland, smaller by one half, as it is thought, than Britain; the sea-passage is of equal length to that from Gaul to Britain. Here in mid-channel is an island called Man; in addition, several small islands are supposed to lie close to land, as touching which some have written that in midwinter night there lasts for thirty whole days. We could discover nothing about this by inquiries; but, by exact water measurements,[11] we observed that the nights were shorter than on the Continent. The length of this side, according to the belief of the natives, is seven hundred miles. The third side bears northwards, and has no land confronting it; the angle, however, of that side faces on the whole towards Germany. The side is supposed to be eight hundred miles long. Thus the whole island is two thousand miles in circumference.

[14] Of all the Britons the inhabitants of Kent, an entirely maritime district, are by far the most civilised, differing but little from the Gallic manner of life. Of the inlanders most do not sow corn, but live on milk and flesh and clothe themselves in skins. All the Britons, indeed, dye themselves with woad, which produces a blue colour, and makes their appearance in battle more terrible. They wear long hair, and shave every part of the body save the head and the upper lip. Groups of ten or twelve men have wives together in common, and particularly brothers along with brothers, and fathers with sons; but the children born of the unions are reckoned to belong to the particular house to which the maiden was first conducted.

[15] The horsemen and charioteers of the enemy engaged in fierce conflict with our cavalry on the march, with the result, however, that our troops proved their superiority in all respects, and drove them into the woods and highlands; but, pursuing too eagerly after slaying several of the enemy, they lost some of their own number. After an interval, however, when our troops were off their guard and engaged in entrenching the camp, the enemy suddenly dashed out from the woods, and charging the detachments on outpost duty in advance of the camp, they fought fiercely. And though Caesar sent up two cohorts in support—and those the first cohorts of two legions—and the two detachments had taken post with a very slight interval between them, the enemy most gallantly broke through in the middle (as our troops were disconcerted by the novel kind of fighting), and retired safely from the field. On that day a tribune, Quintus Laberius Durus, was

---

[11] *i.e.* measurements made with a water-clock, *clepsydra.*

killed. The enemy were driven back when more cohorts had been sent up.

[16] The action took place in front of the camp and under the eyes of all; and it was clear that in all such fighting our infantry, by reason of their heavy armament, since they could neither pursue a retiring enemy nor venture far from the standards,[12] were but poorly fitted for an enemy of this kind. It was clear, again, that our cavalry fought with great risk, because the enemy often retired of deliberate purpose, and, when they had separated our horse a little from the legions, leapt down from their chariots and fought on foot to our disadvantage. Their cavalry tactics, however, threatened us with exactly the same danger in retirement or pursuit.[13] Add to this that the enemy never fought in close array, but in small parties with wide intervals; and had detachments posted at regular stations, so that one party covered another in turn, and fresh, unspent warriors took the place of the battle-weary.

[17] Next day the enemy took post on the hills, at a distance from the camp, and began to show themselves in small parties and to assail our horsemen, though more feebly than on the day before. But at noon, when Caesar had sent three legions and all the cavalry with Gaius Trebonius, the lieutenant-general, to get forage, the enemy swooped suddenly from all directions upon the foraging parties, with such vigour that they did not stop short of the legions drawn up for battle. Our troops charged them fiercely and drove them back, and did not bring the pursuit to an end until the cavalry, relying on the support of the legions they saw behind them, drove the enemy headlong and slew a great number of them, giving them no chance to rally or stand fast, nor to leap down from their chariots. After this rout the succours which had assembled from all quarters took their departure; and never afterwards did the enemy engage us at their full strength.

[18] Having obtained knowledge of their plans, Caesar led his army into the borders of Cassivellaunus as far as the river Thames, which can be crossed at one place only on foot, and that with difficulty. When he was come thither he remarked that on the other bank of the river a great force of the enemy was drawn up. The bank was fortified with a fringe of sharp projecting stakes, and stakes of the same kind fixed under water were concealed by the stream. When he had learnt these details from prisoners and deserters, Caesar sent the cavalry in advance and ordered

---

[12] *i.e.* because they were armed for fighting only in close formation.
[13] The skilful co-operation between the British chariot-fighters and cavalry placed the Roman cavalry at a disadvantage at every turn of the fight. For the tactics of the chariot-fighters see IV. 33. Many editors bracket this sentence as spurious.

the legions to follow up instantly. But the troops moved with such speed and such spirit, although they had only their heads above water, that the enemy could not withstand the assault of legions and cavalry, but abandoned the banks and betook themselves to flight.

[19] When Cassivellaunus, as above set forth, had relinquished all hope of a struggle, and disbanded the greater part of his force, with the remainder—about four thousand charioteers—he kept our marches under observation, and, withdrawing a little from the route, concealed himself in entangled positions among the woods. In whatever districts he had learnt that we intended to march he drove all cattle and human beings from the fields into the woods; then, whenever our cavalry dashed out over the fields to plunder and devastate more freely, he sent out charioteers from the woods by every road and path, engaging our cavalry to their great danger, and preventing them by the fear thus caused from ranging farther afield. The only course left to Caesar was to allow no party to remove very far from the main column of the legions, and to do as much harm to the enemy in laying waste the fields and in conflagrations as the marching powers of the legionaries could accomplish.

[20] In the meantime the Trinobantes, the strongest state, perhaps, in those parts—the state from which young Mandubracius, in quest of the protection of Caesar, had come to him on the mainland of Gaul: his own father had held the kingship in the state, but had been slain by Cassivellaunus, when he himself had escaped death by flight—sent deputies to Caesar, promising to surrender to him and to do his commands, and beseeching him to protect Mandubracius from outrage at the hands of Cassivellaunus, and to send him to their state as ruler and sovereign lord. Caesar required of them forty hostages, and corn for the army, and sent Mandubracius to them. They speedily did his commands, and sent hostages to the number required, and corn.

[21] When the Trinobantes had been placed under protection and secured from all outrage at the hands of the troops, the Cenimagni, the Segontiaci, the Ancalites, the Bibroci, and the Cassi sent deputations and surrendered to Caesar. From them he learnt that the stronghold of Cassivellaunus was not far from thence, fenced by woods and marshes; and that he had assembled there a considerable quantity of men and cattle. Now the Britons call it a stronghold when they have fortified a thickset woodland with rampart and trench, and thither it is their custom to collect, to avoid a hostile inroad. For this spot Caesar now started with the legions: he found it thoroughly fortified by nature and by handiwork, but none the less he made a vigorous assault from two sides. The enemy tarried for a space, but did not stand the assault of our troops, and broke away from another side of the stronghold. A great quantity of cattle was

found there; and many of the enemy were caught in the act of fleeing and put to death.

[22] While these events were proceeding thereabout, Cassivellaunus sent messages to Kent, a country by the sea, as above set forth,[14] over whose four districts Cingetorix, Carvilius, Taximagulus, and Segovax ruled as kings, and commanded them to collect all their forces for a sudden attempt and assault upon the naval camp. But when they were come to the camp the Romans made a sortie and slew many of them, capturing also Lugotorix, a commander of noble station; and then withdrew the detachment without loss. Upon report of this engagement Cassivellaunus was constrained, by the numerous defeats he had suffered, by the devastation of his borders, and chiefly by his alarm at the revolt of the states, to send deputies to Caesar and treat for peace, by the help of Commius the Atrebatian. Caesar had determined to winter on the Continent, in view of sudden commotions in Gaul; and as he had little of the summer left, and was aware that it might easily be spun out to no purpose, he made requisition of hostages, and determined what tribute Britain should pay yearly to Rome. He straitly charged Cassivellaunus to do no hurt to Mandubracius or the Trinobantes.

[23] As soon as the hostages were received he led the army back to the sea, and found the ships repaired. When they had been launched he decided, as he had a great number of prisoners, and some ships had perished in the storm, to convey the army back by two journeys. And eventually, of all that number of ships and in all those voyages, not a single ship carrying troops in this or the previous year was missing. But of the ships sent back empty to him from the Continent—both those which had disembarked troops on the first journey, and the second fleet which Labienus had caused to be built,[15] to the number of sixty—very few made the rendezvous; almost all the rest were driven back. Caesar waited some time for these in vain; then, fearing he might be precluded from sailing by the season, as the equinox was nigh at hand, he packed the troops of necessity more closely together; a complete calm ensued, and he weighed anchor at the beginning of the second watch, and at dawn touched land and brought all the ships safely to port.

[24] The ships were beached, and a council of the Gauls was held at Samarobriva (Amiens). Then, as the corn-crop had been scantier that year in Gaul on account of droughts, Caesar was forced to dispose the army in winter quarters in a different fashion from that of previous years, distributing the legions over a larger number of states. One of the legions

[14] Ch. 14. supra.
[15] See ch. 11.

he gave to Gaius Fabius, the lieutenant-general, to be led into the country of the Morini, a second to Quintus Cicero for the Nervii, a third to Lucius Roscius for the Esubii; a fourth, with Titus Labienus in command, he ordered to winter among the Remi on the border of the Treveri. Three he stationed among the Belgae: in command of them he set Marcus Crassus, the quartermaster-general, and Lucius Munatius Plancus and Gaius Trebonius, lieutenant-generals. One legion, the most recently enrolled north of the Po, with five cohorts, he sent into the country of the Eburones, of which the chief part lies between the Meuse and the Rhine; the tribe was under the rule of Ambiorix and Catuvolcus. He ordered Quintus Titurius Sabinus and Lucius Aurunculeius Cotta, lieutenant-generals, to command those detachments. With the legions distributed after this fashion, he supposed that he could easiest remedy any shortage of corn-supply. And yet the winter quarters of all the legions, save that which he had assigned to Lucius Roscius to be led into the most quiet and peaceful district, were within a range of one hundred miles. He himself meanwhile determined to wait in Gaul until he should have information that the legions were at their stations and the cantonments entrenched.

[25] There was among the Carnutes one Tasgetius, a man of the highest lineage, whose ancestors had held the kingship in their state. To him, in consideration for his character and his goodwill towards himself—for in all the campaigns he had profited by his remarkable energy—Caesar had restored the position of his ancestors. He had now reigned for two years and more, when his enemies, with the open approval of many persons in the state, put him to death. The matter was reported to Caesar, who, apprehending—as a considerable number of persons were concerned—that the state might revolt at the prompting of the regicides, ordered Lucius Plancus to move speedily with his legion from Belgium far into the country of the Carnutes and there to winter, and to seize and send to him the persons by whose instrumentality he knew that Tasgetius had been put to death. Meanwhile he received information from all the lieutenant-generals and the quartermaster-general, to whom he had assigned the legions, that winter quarters had been reached and each station duly entrenched for the same.

[26] In about a fortnight after the troops had moved into winter quarters, disorder and revolt suddenly began. It originated with Ambiorix and Catuvolcus, who, after attending Sabinus and Cotta upon the borders of their kingdom, and bringing in corn to the cantonments, were induced by messages from Indutiomarus of the Treveri to stir up their own folk. They overwhelmed of a sudden the detachments gathering wood, and with a large force came to assault the camp. Our troops speedily took up arms and mounted the rampart; and a party of Spanish horse

sent out on one flank secured us the advantage in a cavalry engagement, upon which the enemy, despairing of success, withdrew their men from the assault. Then, according to their national usage, they called loudly for some one of our number to go forth for a parley, affirming that they had something to say for the interest of both parties, whereby they trusted to be able to reduce the matters in dispute.

[27] Gaius Arpineius, a Roman knight, a friend of Quintus Titurius, and Quintus Junius, a Spaniard, who had previously been accustomed to go to and fro upon Caesar's errands to Ambiorix, were sent to them for the purpose of a parley. Before them Ambiorix spake as follows. He admitted that he was very greatly indebted to Caesar for his good offices towards himself; for it was by Caesar's instrumentality that he had been set free from the tribute which he had been accustomed to pay to his neighbours the Aduatuci, and by Caesar's action that a son and a nephew, sent to the Aduatuci as hostages, and kept in their country in slavery and bondage, had been sent back to him. He declared that his action in assaulting the camp had been the result, not of judgment or intention on his part, but of compulsion on the part of his state; and that the conditions of his own sovereignty were such that the people had as much authority over him as he himself over the people. The state, moreover, had gone to war because it had not been able to resist the sudden conspiracy of the Gauls. He could easily prove that by the insignificance of his own position;[16] for he was not so ignorant of affairs as to believe that by his own forces the Roman people could be overcome. No, there was common consent among the Gauls: this was the day appointed for assaulting all the cantonments of Caesar, so that one legion might not be able to come to the support of another. It would not have been easy for Gauls to refuse Gauls, especially when they considered that the design they had entered on was for the recovery of their common freedom. And now, having satisfied the Gauls as far as the claim of his country required, he had regard to his duty in response to the good offices of Caesar; and he warned, he prayed Titurius, as in private duty bound, to take measures for his own and his soldiers' safety. A great company of Germans had been hired, and had crossed the Rhine; in two days it would be at hand. It was for the Romans themselves to consider whether they would choose to bring the troops out of cantonments before neighbours could know of it, and to march them either to Cicero or to Labienus, one of whom was about fifty miles from them, the other a little

---

[16] The argument appears to be: "I was compelled by my state, against my better judgment, to attack you. Left to myself, I should never have supposed that any forces of mine could defeat the Romans."

farther. He promised them, and confirmed it with an oath, that he would grant them safe passage through his borders. In so doing, he said, he was consulting the interests of his state, by relieving it of the burden of cantonments, and was making a return to Caesar according to his merits. After delivering this address Ambiorix departed.

[28] Arpineius and Junius reported what they heard to the lieutenant-generals. The latter were alarmed by the sudden news, and, though the statement was made by an enemy, they nevertheless considered that it must not be disregarded. One thing especially stirred their anxiety—it was scarcely credible that the Eburones, an undistinguished and insignificant state, had dared of their own motion to make war on Rome. They accordingly submitted the question to a council of war, and a great dispute arose among them. Lucius Aurunculeius, with several tribunes and centurions of the first grade, thought that nothing should be done rashly, and no departure from winter quarters made without Caesar's order. They sought to show that even German forces, no matter how numerous, could be withstood by entrenched cantonments; there was proof of it in the fact that they had most gallantly withstood the first charge of the enemy, and had actually dealt them many wounds. They were not hard pressed for corn; meanwhile reinforcements would reach them alike from the nearest cantonments and from Caesar. In fine, what was more senseless or more discreditable than to take the advice of an enemy in deciding supreme issues?

[29] Against this Titurius vociferated that it would be too late to act when larger bodies of the enemy, with Germans in addition, had come up, or when some disaster had been experienced in the cantonments next their own. There was short time, he said, for deliberation. He believed that Caesar had started for Italy; otherwise the Carnutes would not have conceived the design of murdering Tasgetius, nor, with Caesar present, would the Eburones now have come against the camp with so profound a contempt for us. He had regard, not to the suggestion of the enemy, but to fact. The Rhine was close at hand; the Germans were highly indignant at the death of Ariovistus and our previous victories; Gaul was incensed at all the insults experienced since it was brought in subjection to the authority of Rome, and at the extinction of its earlier renown in war. In fine, who could persuade himself that Ambiorix had engaged in such a design without sure cause? His own view made for safety in either event: if nothing very serious occurred, they would reach the next legion without danger; if the whole of Gaul were at one with the Germans, the sole chance of safety lay in speedy action. And to what was the plan of Cotta, and those who disagreed with himself, to lead? There might be no present danger in it, but there was certainly famine to fear from a prolonged siege.

[30] After this discussion of the alternatives Cotta and the senior centurions vehemently opposed Sabinus, who exclaimed—and with a louder voice than usual, so that a great number of the soldiers might hear—"Have your way, if you please. I am not the man to feel the most serious alarm of any of you at the danger of death. The troops will understand. If anything very serious comes to pass, they will require an account from yourself; for, if you allowed them, they would by the day after to-morrow have joined forces with the nearest cantonments, and would abide the event of war along with the rest, instead of perishing by sword or famine, far removed and isolated from their comrades."

[31] The council rose, and the officers laid hold on the two generals and prayed them not utterly to endanger the issue by their own obstinacy in disagreement. There was no difficulty, whether they stayed or marched, if only all shared and approved one plan; in disagreement, on the contrary, they saw no safety. The matter continued in dispute till midnight. At last Cotta was induced to yield, and the view of Sabinus prevailed. It was announced that the troops would march at dawn. The rest of the night was spent without sleep, for each soldier was looking over his effects, to see what he could carry with him, and what part of the winter equipment he must needs leave. They thought of any and every plea to prove that it must be dangerous to remain, and that the danger would be increased by the exhaustion of the troops in long watches. At dawn they marched forth from camp, as men persuaded that counsel had been given them not by an enemy, but by Ambiorix, a devoted friend; the column was very lengthy, and the baggage very heavy.

[32] When the enemy felt sure, by the noise and watchfulness of the night, that the Romans meant to march out, they posted a double ambush in the woods, in a convenient and covert spot about two miles away; and there they awaited the coming of the Romans. When the greater part of the column had descended into a big ravine, they showed themselves suddenly on either flank of the same, and sought to harass the rearguard, to prevent the vanguard from climbing the ascent, and to engage on ground the most unfavourable for our troops.

[33] Then indeed, as he had anticipated nothing, Titurius was alarmed: he ran hither and thither posting cohorts, yet even this he did in timid fashion and with all judgment evidently gone, as generally happens when men are forced to decide in the moment of action. Cotta, however, as he had thought this might happen on the march, and for that reason had opposed departure, neglected nothing for the safety of the force: in addressing and encouraging the troops he did his duty as a commander, in action his duty as a soldier. When by reason of the length of the column the generals found it too hard to control everything in their own person, and to provide for the action necessary at each point, they

ordered to pass the word along the line to abandon the baggage and form square. This plan, though not reprehensible in such an emergency, had an unfortunate result; for it diminished the hope of our own troops and made the enemy keener for the fight, since the movement could not but betray the greatest apprehension and despair. Moreover, it was an inevitable consequence that on all sides soldiers were deserting their standards, while each of them hastened to seek and to seize from the baggage-train all that he accounted dearest. So everything was a confusion of shouting and weeping.

[34] But the natives were not lacking in resource. Their leaders ordered the command to be given along the line that no one was to leave his rank, that the booty was theirs, and whatsoever the Romans abandoned was to be reserved for them; wherefore they must think that all depended on victory. The enemy were our equals in valour and in fighting zeal. Our troops, though deserted by their commander and by fortune, still set all hope of safety in valour; and as often as each cohort dashed forward a great number of the enemy would fall in that quarter. Noticing this, Ambiorix ordered the command to be given that his men should discharge their missiles at long range and not approach too near, and give way where the Romans made a charge, for that by reason of the lightness of their armament and their daily training no harm could be done to them, and when the enemy retired upon their standards they were to pursue in their turn.

[35] This instruction they most carefully observed. When any cohort left the square and made a charge the enemy would run back with great rapidity. Meanwhile that detachment was of necessity uncovered, and a discharge of missiles was received upon its exposed[17] flank. And when they sought to return back to the position from which they had started, they were like to be surrounded both by those who had given way and by those who had the nearest station. If, on the other hand, they were fain to hold their ground, there was no room left for valour, and in close array they could not avoid the missiles discharged by so great a host. Yet, handicapped by all these disadvantages, and with many men wounded, they stood firm; and though a great part of the day was so spent, for the battle lasted from dawn till the eighth hour, they did nothing unworthy of themselves. At this point Titus Balventius, a gallant man of great influence, who in the previous year had commanded the first century,[18] had both thighs pierced by a dart; Quintus Lucanius, of the same rank, was killed fighting most bravely to succour a son who had been

---

[17] *i.e.* the right.
[18] *i.e.* had been chief centurion of his legion.

surrounded; Lucius Cotta, the lieutenant-general, as he cheered on all the cohorts and centuries, was hit full in the face by a sling-bullet.

[36] Alarmed by these events, Quintus Titurius, who had remarked Ambiorix at a distance encouraging his men, sent his interpreter, Gnaeus Pompeius, to him to ask him to spare himself and his troops. Ambiorix replied to the appeal that, if Titurius wished to parley with him, he was at liberty so to do; he hoped that he could prevail on his host to save the soldiers alive; to Titurius himself certainly no harm would be done, and thereto he pledged his own word. Titurius communicated with the wounded Cotta to see if he agreed to withdraw with him from the fight and parley with Ambiorix, stating that he hoped he might prevail on him to save themselves and the troops. Cotta refused to go to an armed enemy, and persisted in the refusal.

[37] Sabinus ordered all the tribunes and the senior centurions he had about him at the time to follow him; and when he was come quite near to Ambiorix, and was ordered to cast away his arms, he obeyed the command and commanded his party to do the same. While they two were discussing terms together, and Ambiorix was purposely making a longer speech than necessary, Titurius was gradually surrounded and slain. Then at once they shouted victory after their own fashion, and, with a loud yell, charged our troops and threw the ranks into confusion. There Lucius Cotta was killed fighting, with the greatest part of the troops. The remainder retired to the camp from which they had marched out. One of them, the standard-bearer Lucius Petrosidius, hard pressed by a great host of the enemy, flung his eagle within the rampart, and was himself cut down, fighting most gallantly, before the camp. The others scarcely kept off the assault till nightfall; in the night, despairing of deliverance, they slew one another to a man. A few who had slipped away from the battle made their way by uncertain paths through the woods to the cantonments of Titus Labienus, the lieutenant-general, and informed him of what had happened.

[38] Elated by this victory, Ambiorix at once set out with his cavalry for the country of the Aduatuci, which lay next to his kingdom; he marched without a break, for a night and a day, ordering his infantry to follow after him. Having reported the battle and aroused the Aduatuci, he came the next day into the territory of the Nervii, and exhorted them not to let slip the chance of winning freedom for all time and of taking vengeance on the Romans for the outrages they had suffered. He made it clear that two lieutenant-generals had been slain and the great part of an army destroyed; that it was not a difficult business to fall suddenly upon the legion which was wintering with Cicero and cut it to pieces; and he offered his own assistance to that end. With this speech he easily persuaded the Nervii.

[39] Accordingly messengers were at once despatched to the Ceutrones, the Grudii, the Levaci, the Pleumoxii, the Geidumni, all of whom were under the sovereignty of the Nervii; they raised companies as large as they could, and of a sudden swooped upon the winter quarters of Cicero, who had not yet received report of the death of Titurius. In Cicero's case also it happened, as was inevitable, that some soldiers who had gone off into the woods to get timber for entrenching were cut off by the sudden arrival of the enemy's horsemen. They were surrounded; and then in a huge mass the Eburones, the Nervii, the Aduatuci, and the allies and dependents of them all, began the assault upon the legion. Our troops speedily ran to arms and mounted the rampart. Scarcely for that day could they hold out, because the enemy were putting all their hope in despatch, believing that if they won this victory they would be victorious right through.

[40] Despatches were at once sent by Cicero to Caesar, with promise of great rewards if the bearers carried them safe; but all the roads were blocked, and the messengers were cut off. During the night about one hundred and twenty towers were run up with incredible speed out of the timber which had been collected for the purpose of the entrenchment, and all apparent deficiencies in the earthworks were rectified. On the next day the enemy assaulted the camp with a far larger force which they had assembled, and filled in the trench. Our troops resisted in the same fashion as on the day before. And exactly the same was done on the other days following. For not a moment of the night season was there a break in the work; no chance of rest was given to sick or wounded. All that was needed against the next day's assault was made ready in the night: quantities of stakes fired at the end, a great number of pikes for wall-fighting were got ready; the towers were raised stage by stage,[19] battlements and breastworks of hurdles were attached to them. Cicero himself, though he was in very frail health, left himself not even the night season for rest, until at last he was actually forced to spare himself by the protests of the soldiers, who crowded about him.

[41] Then the leaders and chiefs of the Nervii who had some plea of friendship to give them access to conversation with Cicero said that they desired to parley. When the opportunity was given them they recounted the same arguments which Ambiorix had used with Titurius. All Gaul, they said, was in arms; the Germans had crossed the Rhine; the winter stations of Caesar and the rest were being assaulted. They told further of the death of Sabinus; they pointed to Ambiorix in order to inspire credit. "You are wrong," they said, "to hope for any security from others who

---

[19] Or "raised a stage"; or, according to others, "boarded over."

are themselves in desperate case; our own feeling, however, towards Cicero and Rome is to refuse nothing except winter quartering, for we are unwilling that this practice should become established. So far as we are concerned, you have liberty to depart safe from your winter quarters, and to march off without fear in whatsoever direction you please." To this Cicero made one remark only in reply: that it was not the practice of Rome to accept terms from an enemy in arms; if they would lay down their arms, they might use his good offices and send deputies to Caesar; he hoped that, having regard to the justice of Caesar, they would obtain their petition.

[42] Foiled of this hope, the Nervii encompassed the station with a rampart nine feet high and a trench fifteen feet wide. These expedients they had learnt from us in the intercourse of previous years, and they were further instructed by prisoners from the army whom they kept in secret; but, having no supply of the tools suitable for this purpose, they were striving to cut sods round with swords, and lifting out earth with hands and cloaks. And this circumstance made it possible to ascertain the number of their host; for in less than three hours they completed an entrenchment fifteen miles in circumference, and on the days that followed they set about their preparations, making towers to suit the height of the rampart, grappling-hooks,[20] and shelters, under the instruction of the prisoners aforesaid.

[43] On the seventh day of the siege-operations a very strong wind arose, and they began to sling red-hot bullets of softened clay and to hurl blazing darts on to the huts, which in Gallic fashion had been thatched with straw. These speedily caught fire, which the strength of the wind carried to every corner of the camp. With a huge shout, as though victory were already won and assured, the enemy began to move up their towers and shelters, and to mount the rampart with scaling-ladders. Yet so great was the valour of the troops, and such their presence of mind, that, although they were everywhere scorched by the flame and harassed by the vast multitude of missiles, and understood that all their own baggage and all their possessions were ablaze, not only did no man leave the rampart to withdraw from the fight, but scarcely a man even looked behind him, and all at that time fought with the greatest zeal and gallantry. This day was by far the most serious for our troops, with the result, however, that a greater number of the enemy were wounded and slain than on any other day, as they had pressed right up to the very rampart, the rear giving no chance of retirement to the van. When the flames had abated somewhat, in one place a tower was moved up to touch the

---

[20] See III. 14, and VII. 22.

rampart: whereupon the centurions of the third cohort withdrew from their station and moved back all their men, and then began to invite the enemy by signs and shouts, in case they should desire to come in; but not one of them durst advance. Then they were dislodged by volleys of stones from every side, and the tower was set on fire.

[44] In that legion there were two most gallant centurions, now not far from the first class of their rank,[21] Titus Pullo and Lucius Vorenus. They had continual quarrels together which was to stand first, and every year they struggled in fierce rivalry for the chief posts. One of them, Pullo, when the fight was fiercest by the entrenchments, said: "Why hesitate, Vorenus? Or what chance of proving your pluck do you wait for? This day shall decide our quarrels." So saying, he stepped outside the entrenchments, and dashed upon the section of the enemy which seemed to be in closest array. Neither did Vorenus keep within the rampart, but in fear of what all men would think he followed hard. Then, at short range, Pullo sent his pike at the enemy, and pierced one man as he ran forward from the host. When he was struck senseless the enemy sought to cover him with their shields, and discharged their spears in a volley at the foeman, giving him no chance of retirement. Pullo's shield was penetrated, and a dart was lodged in his belt. This accident threw his scabbard out of place, and delayed his right hand as he tried to draw his sword, and while he was in difficulty the enemy surrounded him. His enemy, Vorenus, ran up to him and helped him in his distress. Upon him at once all the host turned, and left Pullo, supposing him to be slain by the dart. Vorenus plied his sword at close quarters, and by slaying one man drove off the rest a little; while he pressed on too eagerly he fell down headlong into a dip in the ground. He was surrounded in his turn, but Pullo brought assistance; and both, unhurt, though they had slain several men, retired with the utmost glory within the entrenchments. In the eagerness of their rivalry fortune so handled the two that, for all their mutual hostility, the one helped and saved the other, and it was impossible to decide which should be considered the better man in valour.

[45] The more serious and burdensome the siege-operations each day became—and chiefly because, with a great part of the soldiers overcome by wounds, the burden had fallen on a small number of defenders—the more frequent were the despatches and messengers sent to Caesar. Part of these latter were captured and put to death with torture in sight of our own troops. There was a Nervian in the camp, named Vertico, born to an honourable estate, who at the very beginning of the blockade had fled to Cicero for refuge, and had since proved his loyalty to him. He per-

---

[21] There was a regular gradation of the centurions in a legion.

suaded a slave by the hope of freedom and by great rewards to deliver a
despatch to Caesar. The man carried forth the despatch bound on a
javelin,[22] and moving, all unsuspected, as a Gaul among Gauls, he made
his way to Caesar. It was he who brought the information about the dangers of Cicero and the legion.

[46] Caesar received the despatch about the eleventh hour of the day,
and at once sent a messenger into the country of the Bellovaci to Marcus
Crassus, the quartermaster-general, whose winter quarters were twenty-
five miles away from him; he bade the legion start at midnight and come
speedily to him. Crassus marched out on receipt of the message. Another
envoy was sent to Gaius Fabius, the lieutenant-general, bidding him bring
his legion into the borders of the Atrebates, through which Caesar knew
he himself would have to march. He wrote instructions to Labienus to
come with his legion as far as the borders of the Nervii, if he could so do
without damage to the public service. For the rest of the army he did not
think he ought to wait, because it was somewhat too far away; he assembled about four hundred horse from the nearest cantonments.

[47] About the third hour the advanced parties informed him of the
approach of Crassus, and he moved forward twenty miles that day. He put
Crassus in charge of Samarobriva, and assigned him a legion, because he
purposed to leave there the baggage of the army, the hostages of the
states, the public documents, and all the corn which he had brought in
thither to last through the winter. Fabius and his legion, as ordered, after
a brief delay met him on the march. Labienus learnt of the death of
Sabinus and the slaughter of the cohorts; but as all the forces of the
Treveri were come against him he feared that, if he started to march from
his cantonments with the appearance of flight, he would not be able to
withstand the onslaught of the enemy, especially as he knew them to be
elated by the recent victory. He accordingly sent back a despatch to
Caesar explaining the greatness of the danger if he were to bring the
legion out of cantonments. He wrote in detail of the operation in the
territory of the Eburones, and he informed him that all the horsemen
and footmen of the Treveri had stationed themselves three miles from his
own camp.

[48] Caesar approved his conclusion, although he was thereby disappointed in his expectation of obtaining three legions, and reduced to
two; none the less, he still regarded speed as the only means to the general safety, and proceeded by forced marches into the borders of the
Nervii. There he learnt from prisoners what was taking place at Cicero's

---

[22] The message was probably not tied to the javelin, but bound up inside the shaft, hol-
lowed for the purpose.

station, and how dangerous was his case. Then he persuaded one of the Gallic troopers with great rewards to deliver a letter to Cicero. The letter he sent written in Greek characters, lest by intercepting it the enemy might get to know of our designs. The messenger was instructed, if he could not approach, to hurl a spear, with the letter fastened to the thong, inside the entrenchment of the camp. In the despatch he wrote that he had started with the legions and would speedily be with him, and he exhorted Cicero to maintain his old courage. Fearing danger, the Gaul discharged the spear, as he had been instructed. By chance it stuck fast in the tower, and for two days was not noticed by our troops; on the third day it was sighted by a soldier, taken down, and delivered to Cicero. He read it through, and then recited it at a parade of the troops, bringing the greatest rejoicing to all. Soon the smoke of the fires[23] was to be seen in the distance, and this banished all doubts about the arrival of the legions.

[49] The Gauls were informed of it by their scouts, and, relinquishing the blockade, they pressed on to meet Caesar with all their forces. These amounted to some sixty thousand men under arms. When a chance offered, Cicero again asked Vertico, whom we mentioned above, for a Gaul to deliver a despatch to Caesar. He warned the man to make his way cautiously and carefully. He wrote explicitly in the despatch that the enemy had departed from him and that the whole host had turned round to meet Caesar. The despatch was brought in about midnight; Caesar informed his troops thereof, and encouraged them for the fight. At dawn next day he struck camp, and, having advanced about four miles, he caught sight of the enemy's host across a valley and a stream. It was a very dangerous thing for so slender a force to fight on unfavourable ground; further, as he knew that Cicero was freed from blockade, he was without anxiety, and thought that he should abate his speed. He halted, therefore, and proceeded to entrench his camp in the most favourable position to be found; and small as was the camp itself, as it was for scarce seven thousand men, and those, too, without baggage, he nevertheless compressed it by narrowing the streets[24] as much as possible, with the object of incurring the utmost contempt on the part of the enemy. Meanwhile, by scouts despatched in all directions, he sought to find the most convenient route by which to cross the valley.

[50] On that day petty encounters of cavalry took place by the water, but both armies kept to their own ground—the Gauls because they were waiting for larger forces which had not yet joined them; Caesar, to see if by pretending fear he could draw the enemy on to his own ground, and

---

[23] *i.e.* burning villages and the like.
[24] The roadways of a camp.

fight on this side of the valley, in front of the camp, or, if he might not do so, that, after reconnaissance of the routes, he might cross valley and stream with less danger. At break of day the enemy's horsemen came up to the camp and engaged our own cavalry. Caesar purposely ordered the cavalry to give way and to retire into camp; at the same time he ordered the camp to be fortified with a higher rampart on all sides, the gates to be barricaded, and as much confusion and pretence of fear as possible to be shown in the execution of these arrangements.

[51] All these proceedings tempted the enemy to lead their forces across and to form line on unfavourable ground; and then, as our troops had been withdrawn even from the rampart, they approached nearer and discharged their missiles from all sides into the entrenchment. Next they sent heralds round about, and ordered proclamation to be made that if anyone, Gaul or Roman, would go over to their side before the third hour, he was at liberty so to do without danger; after that time there would be no chance. And, indeed, they held our troops in such contempt that, thinking they could not break in by the gates, which had been barricaded for show with single rows of sods, some of them set to work to tear down the rampart with their hands, others to fill in the trenches. Then Caesar caused a sally to be made from all the gates, and sending out the cavalry put the enemy speedily to flight, so effectually that never a man stood to fight. He slew a great number of them and stripped all of their arms.

[52] He feared to pursue very far, because there were woods and marshes in the way, and, as he saw, there was no chance now of doing even slight damage to the enemy; therefore, with his whole force unhurt, he joined Cicero the same day. He marvelled at the towers erected, the shelters, the fortifications of the enemy. He paraded the legion and found that not one-tenth of the soldiers were left unwounded. From all these evidences he could judge with what danger and with what courage the operations had been carried out. He warmly praised Cicero according to his desert, and the legion likewise; he addressed severally the centurions and tribunes, whose valour, on the testimony of Cicero, he knew to have been exceptional. As touching the disaster of Sabinus and Cotta, he learnt more particularly from prisoners. The next day he held a parade and set forth all that had occurred, cheering and encouraging the troops, and admonishing them to bear with the greater equanimity the loss incurred through the fault and foolhardiness of a general, inasmuch as by the goodness of the immortal gods and by their own valour the misfortune had been made good, leaving to the enemy no lasting joy, to themselves no long-enduring grief.

[53] Meanwhile report of Caesar's victory was brought to Labienus with incredible speed through the agency of the Remi. In fact, though

Labienus was about sixty miles away from Cicero's cantonments, and Caesar had not reached the latter until after the ninth hour; before midnight a shout arose at the gates of Labienus' camp, to signify the victory and to express the congratulations of the Remi to Labienus. When the same report was brought to the Treveri, Indutiomarus, who had determined to attack Labienus' camp next day, fled away in the night and withdrew all his forces into the country of the Treveri. Caesar sent Fabius with his legion back into cantonments, and determined to winter himself with three legions in three separate stations around Samarobriva; and in view of the great disturbances which had arisen in Gaul, he decided to remain with the army in person throughout the winter. For when news was brought of Sabinus' great disaster almost all the states of Gaul began to think of war, despatching messengers and deputations in all directions to find out what the others purposed and where the war should start, and holding nightly councils in solitary places. And scarcely a moment the whole winter through passed without anxiety for Caesar, without the receipt of some message concerning the projected rising of the Gauls. Among other news he was informed by Lucius Roscius, whom he had put in command of the Thirteenth Legion, that a large force of Gauls, from the states called Armoric, had assembled to attack him and had stationed themselves not farther than eight miles from his cantonments; but that upon receiving report of Caesar's victory they had departed so hastily that their departure seemed like unto flight.

[54] Nevertheless, Caesar summoned to his quarters the chief men of each state; and by frightening some with the announcement that he knew what was afoot, and by encouraging others, he kept a great part of Gaul in submission. The Senones, however, a state of prominent power and great authority among the Gauls, took counsel together and attempted to slay Cavarinus, whom Caesar had appointed king among them, and whose brother Moritasgus had held the kingship at the time of Caesar's arrival in Gaul, and his ancestors before him. Cavarinus got wind of their design and escaped. They pursued him even to the boundaries and drove him out of kingship and home, and then sent deputies to Caesar to make excuse; but they did not obey his command that all their senate should come to him. Indeed, the fact that they had found men to take the lead in a war of offence had so much weight among the natives, and brought about such a universal change of feeling, that, save the Aedui and the Remi, whom Caesar always held in especial honour—the former for their old-established and unbroken loyalty towards Rome, the latter for their recent services in the Gallic war—scarcely a single state was free from suspicion on our part. And I am inclined to think that this is not so very remarkable, chiefly, among several other reasons, because this nation, which at one time surpassed all others in military

courage, was grievously indignant to have lost so much of that estimation as to submit to the sovereignty of the Roman people.

[55] So the Treveri and Indutiomarus, without intermission throughout the course of the winter, sent deputies across the Rhine, inviting the states, promising sums of money, and affirming that, as a great part of our army had been slain, a much smaller part was left. But still none of the German states could be persuaded to cross the Rhine: they had tried it twice, they said, in the war of Ariovistus and the passage of the Tencteri, and they would not tempt fortune further. Though disappointed in this hope, Indutiomarus none the less set to work to raise forces, to train them, to procure horses from his neighbours, and to attract to his standard by great rewards exiles and condemned persons throughout Gaul. And, indeed, by such means, he had already secured himself so great an authority in Gaul that deputations hastened to him from every direction, seeking favour and friendship for their states or for themselves.

[56] When he perceived that they were coming to him of their own motion, that on the one hand the Senones and Carnutes were spurred on by the sense of guilt, on the other the Nervii and the Aduatuci were preparing for war against the Romans, and that he would not lack forces of volunteers if he began to advance from out his own borders, he proclaimed an armed convention. This in the practice of the Gauls marks the beginning of a war; and by a general law all grown men are accustomed to assemble at it in arms, while the one who comes last to the assembly is put to death with every kind of torture in sight of the host. At the convention Indutiomarus declared Cingetorix an enemy and confiscated his goods. Cingetorix was his son-in-law, the chief man of the other party, who, as set forth above,[25] had sought the protection of Caesar and had not deserted him. This business despatched, Indutiomarus declared in the convention that he had been summoned by the Senones, the Carnutes, and several other Gallic states, and that he proposed to march to them through the borders of the Remi, laying waste their lands, and before so doing to attack the camp of Labienus. He gave instructions as to what he would have done.

[57] Labienus, secure as he was in a camp well fortified by natural position and by handiwork, had no apprehension of danger to himself and his legion; his purpose was to lose no chance of a successful operation. And so, having learnt from Cingetorix and his kinsfolk the speech which Indutiomarus had made in the convention, he sent messengers to the neighbouring states and called up cavalry from all quarters, appointing them a certain day for assembly. Meanwhile, almost every day, Indutiomarus,

[25] v. 3.

with all his horsemen, would range close to his camp, sometimes to reconnoitre the situation thereof, sometimes to parley or to intimidate; and generally all the horsemen would dislodge missiles within the rampart. Labienus kept his troops within the entrenchment, and sought by all means in his power to enhance the impression that he was afraid.

[58] Indutiomarus continued to come up to the camp with daily increasing contempt; but in one night Labienus brought inside the cavalry of all the neighbouring states, which he had caused to be summoned, and by means of guards he kept all his troops so carefully inside camp that the fact could by no means be disclosed or reported to the Treveri. Meanwhile, in accordance with his daily custom, Indutiomarus came up to the camp and spent there a great part of the day; his horsemen discharged missiles, and with great insolence of language called our troops out to fight. No reply was given by our men; and towards evening, when it seemed good, the Gauls began to depart, dispersing in disorder. Suddenly from two gates Labienus launched forth all his cavalry; he straitly charged them that when they had once frightened the enemy and sent them flying (foreseeing exactly what would, and did, happen), they should all make for Indutiomarus alone, and no one was to wound any until he saw the chieftain slain, as Labienus did not wish that delay over the rest might give him time to escape. He offered great rewards to those who should kill him, and sent up cohorts to support the horse. The event approved his plan, and as all the force were making for one man they caught Indutiomarus just in the ford of the river, slew him, and brought his head back to camp; during their return the cavalry chased and killed all they could. On learning of this all the forces of the Eburones and Nervii which had assembled departed, and thereafter Caesar found Gaul somewhat more tranquil.

# BOOK VI

[1] For many reasons Caesar anticipated a more serious rising in Gaul; and he decided to raise a levy through the agency of Marcus Silanus, Gaius Antistius Reginus, and Titus Sextius, lieutenant-generals. At the same time he made request of Gnaeus Pompeius, now[1] proconsul, that, as he was remaining near Rome for the service of the state while retaining his military authority,[2] he would order the recruits from Cisalpine Gaul sworn in by him as consul to join the colours and start for Caesar's headquarters. He conceived it to be of great importance, for the future as well as for the present, to create an impression in Gaul that the resources of Italy were extensive enough not only to repair in a short time any damage incurred in the war, but even to increase the establishment. Pompey made the concession to public service and private friendship, and as Caesar speedily completed the levy through his staff officers, before the winter was over three legions had been formed and brought to headquarters. Having thereby doubled the number of the cohorts lost with Quintus Titurius, he showed the Gauls, at once by his rapidity and by the strength of his reinforcements, what the system and resources of the Roman people could accomplish.

[2] After Indutiomarus was slain, as we have set forth, the Treveri tendered the chief command to his kindred, who were continuing to tempt the neighbouring Germans and to promise money. As they could not prevail on their immediate neighbours they made trial of the more distant; and, having found some states to their mind, they took an oath to confirm their engagement, and hostages to secure the money;[3] and they associated Ambiorix with themselves by a league and covenant. Caesar had report of this, and saw preparations for war on every hand: the

---

[1] 53 B.C.
[2] Pompeius, after his consulship in 55 B.C., had been appointed proconsul in Spain for five years, but had remained "near Rome" (which he could not enter, as being still *cum imperio*) to fulfil his duties as head of an extraordinary commission for the supply of corn.
[3] *i.e.* subsidies.

Nervii, Aduatuci, and Menapii, and all the Germans on this side of the Rhine with them, were in arms; the Senones came not at his command, as they were conspiring with the Carnutes and adjacent states; the Germans were being tempted by frequent deputations of the Treveri. He felt, therefore, that he must plan an earlier campaign than usual.

[3] Accordingly, before the winter was ended, he concentrated the four nearest legions; he made a sudden and rapid advance into the borders of the Nervii, and before they could assemble or escape he had captured a great number of cattle and human beings; and giving up such booty to the troops, and laying waste the fields, he compelled the natives to come in and surrender and to give him hostages. That business speedily despatched, he led the legions back into cantonments. At the beginning of spring a convention of Gaul was proclaimed, according to his practice. The arrival of all except the Senones, Carnutes, and Treveri made him think this exception the beginning of an armed rebellion; and to give the impression that he counted all else of secondary importance, he removed the convention to Lutetia, a town of the Parisii. (These were next neighbours to the Senones, and in the previous generation had formed one state with them; but it was believed that they had held aloof from the present design.) This decision having been proclaimed from the tribunal,[4] on the same day he set off with the legions against the Senones, and reached their territory by forced marches.

[4] Upon report of his coming, Acco, who had been the leader in the plot aforesaid, commanded the population to assemble in their strongholds. They tried so to do; but before it could be brought to pass news came that the Romans were at hand. Of necessity they abandoned the project, and sent deputies to Caesar to entreat his clemency, approaching him through the Aedui, the protectors of their state from ancient times. Caesar willingly granted pardon and accepted their plea at the instance of the Aedui; for he held that summer was the time for the coming war, not for judicial inquiry. He requisitioned one hundred hostages, and delivered the same to the Aedui for custody. The Carnutes also sent deputies and hostages to his camp, employing the Remi, whose vassals they were, to entreat for them, and received the same replies. Caesar closed the convention, and made requisition of cavalry upon the states.

[5] So this part of Gaul was brought to peace, and he applied himself with all his heart and soul to the war with the Treveri and Ambiorix. He commanded Cavarinus and the horsemen of the Senones to move with him, so as to prevent the occurrence of any commotion in the state as the result of his hot temper or of the enmity which he had earned.

---

[4] This was a mound or platform in the camp.

Then, having so arranged these matters, since he was convinced that Ambiorix would not fight a decisive action, he began to examine what other courses were left him. There were the Menapii, near the borders of the Eburones, defended by continuous marshes and forests; and they alone in Gaul had never sent deputies to Caesar to treat of peace. He knew that Ambiorix had a formal friendship with them; he had learnt also that through the Treveri they had made friends with the Germans. He considered that these supports should be withdrawn from Ambiorix before he provoked him to hostilities; otherwise, in despair of deliverance, he might hide among the Menapii, or be obliged to make common cause with the tribes beyond the Rhine. Adopting this plan, then, he despatched the baggage of the whole army to Labienus, in the territory of the Treveri, and commanded two legions to begin the march to him, while he himself with five legions in light order began to march against the Menapii. They had raised no force, but, relying only on the protection of the country, fled all into the forests and marshes, and gathered their stuff there also.

[6] Caesar divided his forces with Gaius Fabius, lieutenant-general, and Marcus Crassus, quartermaster-general; and after causeways had been speedily constructed he approached in three divisions, setting fire to farm-buildings and hamlets, and seizing a large number of cattle and human beings. This action obliged the Menapii to send deputies to him to seek for peace. He accepted their hostages, and assured them that he would regard them as enemies if they received either Ambiorix or his deputies within their borders. When these matters had been securely settled Caesar left Commius, of the Atrebates, with cavalry in the country of the Menapii by way of guard, and he himself set off against the Treveri.

[7] While Caesar was thus engaged, the Treveri collected a large force of infantry and cavalry, and prepared to attack Labienus and the one legion which had wintered within their borders. And by now they were no farther from him than two days' march, when they learnt that two legions were come, as despatched by Caesar. So they pitched their camp at a distance of fifteen miles, and determined to await their German auxiliaries. Labienus learnt the design of the enemy, and in the hope that their recklessness would afford some chance of engaging them, he left a guard of five cohorts for the baggage, and set off against the enemy with twenty-five cohorts and a large detachment of cavalry. He entrenched a camp at an interval of one mile. Between Labienus and the enemy was a steep-banked river,[5] difficult to cross. He had no intention of crossing this himself, nor did he suppose that the enemy would cross it. Their hope of auxiliaries was increasing daily. Labienus declared openly in a

---

[5] Perhaps the Moselle, or its tributary the Alzette.

council of war that, as the Germans were said to be approaching, he would not risk his own and his army's fortunes, and that he would strike camp at dawn next day. This information was speedily carried to the enemy, for of a large number of Gallic horsemen natural feeling would compel some, as Gauls, to favour the Gallic cause. At nightfall Labienus summoned the military tribunes and the senior centurions, and propounded his plan; and, the more easily to give the enemy a suspicion that he was afraid, he ordered the camp to be struck with greater noise and disorder than was customary among Romans. By this means he made his departure like a rout. The camps were so close that this, too, was reported to the enemy by scouts before daybreak.

[8] The rear of the column had scarcely moved clear of the entrenchment when the Gauls with mutual exhortations not to let slip from their grasp the booty for which they hoped—it would be tedious, they said, to wait for German assistance when the Romans were terror-stricken; and it was intolerable to their honour not to venture an attack with so large a force upon so puny a company, especially in the moment of its retreat and embarrassment—proceeded to cross the river without hesitation and to engage on unfavourable ground. Labienus had surmised that this would happen, and to entice them all to his side of the river he pretended to march as before, and calmly continued his advance. He sent the baggage a little forward and packed it on some rising ground. Then said he: "Soldiers, you have the chance you have sought; you hold the enemy on ground that hampers and handicaps them: display under our command the same valour that you have often displayed to the commander-in-chief, and think that he is present and beholds this action with his own eyes." At the same moment he commanded the troops to wheel towards the enemy and deploy into line, and, detaching a few troops of cavalry to act as baggage-guard, he disposed the rest of the cavalry on the flanks. Speedily our troops raised a shout and hurled their pikes at the enemy. When these unexpectedly saw men whom they believed to be in retreat advancing against them in attack formation, they could not even sustain the assault, and at the first charge they were put to rout and sought the nearest woods. Labienus chased them with the cavalry, slew a great number, took a good many prisoners, and a few days later received the allegiance of the state. Nor was this surprising, for the Germans who were coming to its assistance returned home when they heard of the rout of the Treveri; and the kinsfolk of Indutiomarus, who had initiated the revolt, followed them out of the state. The prerogative of chieftaincy was delivered to Cingetorix, who, as we have shown, had remained loyal from the beginning.

[9] After he had passed from the territory of the Menapii to that of the Treveri, Caesar decided for two reasons to cross the Rhine. One rea-

son was that the German tribes had sent auxiliaries to the Treveri against him; the other, to prevent Ambiorix from having a chance of retreating to them. This decision made, he set about to build a bridge a little above the place where he had crossed before with his army. The plan of it was known and definite; and, thanks to the great zeal of the troops, the work was accomplished in a few days. He left a strong guard at the bridge-head in the territory of the Treveri, to prevent the outbreak of any sudden commotion on their part, and led the rest of his forces across with the cavalry. The Ubii had given hostages before and made their surrender, and now, to clear themselves, they sent deputies to him to inform him that no auxiliaries had been despatched from their state to the territory of the Treveri, and that they had not broken faith. They begged and prayed him to spare them, so that in a general hatred of the Germans the innocent might not be punished for the guilty: if he wished for more hostages, they promised to give them. Caesar heard their case, and ascertained that the auxiliaries had been despatched by the Suebi: he accepted the plea of the Ubii, and began to inquire about lines of advance into the country of the Suebi.

[10] After a few days' interval he was informed by the Ubii that the Suebi were collecting all their forces into one place and proclaiming to the tribes under their dominion that they must send auxiliaries of foot and horse. Upon report of this, he made provision for the corn-supply and selected a suitable spot for the camp. He commanded the Ubii to bring in their cattle and to collect all their stuff from the fields into the strongholds, hoping that lack of provisions might act upon untrained natives and oblige them to fight at a disadvantage. He instructed them to send a number of scouting parties into the country of the Suebi and to ascertain their movements. The Ubii carried out his commands, and reported after a few days' interval. The Suebi, they said, after more definite accounts of the Roman army came to them, had all withdrawn, with all the forces of their own folk and of their allies which they had collected, to the uttermost parts of the territory. There was, they added, a forest there of immense size, called Bacenis: it extended a long way into the country and interposed as a natural wall to keep the Cherusci from raids and outrages on the part of the Suebi, and the Suebi likewise from the Cherusci. At the edge of the forest the Suebi had determined to await the coming of the Romans.

[11] Since I have arrived at this point, it would seem to be not inappropriate to set forth the customs of Gaul and of Germany, and the difference between these nations. In Gaul, not only in every state and every canton and district, but almost in each several household, there are parties; and the leaders of the parties are men who in the judgment of their fellows are deemed to have the highest authority, men to whose decision

and judgment the supreme issue of all cases and counsels may be referred. And this seems to have been an ordinance from ancient days, to the end that no man of the people should lack assistance against a more powerful neighbour; for each man refuses to allow his own folk to be oppressed and defrauded, since otherwise he has no authority among them. The same principle holds in regard to Gaul as a whole taken together; for the whole body of states is divided into two parties.

[12] When Caesar arrived in Gaul the leaders of one party were the Aedui, of the other the Sequani. The latter, being by themselves inferior in strength—since the highest authority from ancient times rested with the Aedui, and their dependencies were extensive—had made Ariovistus and the Germans their friends, and with great sacrifices and promises had brought them to their side. Then, by several successful engagements and the slaughter of all the Aeduan nobility, they had so far established their predominance as to transfer a great part of the dependents from the Aedui to themselves, receiving from them as hostages the children of their chief men, compelling them as a state to swear that they would entertain no design against the Sequani, occupying a part of the neighbouring territory which they had seized by force, and securing the chieftaincy of all Gaul. This was the necessity which had compelled Diviciacus to set forth on a journey to the Senate at Rome for the purpose of seeking aid; but he had returned without achieving his object. By the arrival of Caesar a change of affairs was brought about. Their hostages were restored to the Aedui, their old dependencies restored, and new ones secured through Caesar's efforts (as those who had joined in friendly relations with them found that they enjoyed a better condition and a fairer rule), and their influence and position were increased in all other respects: in result whereof the Sequani had lost the chieftaincy. To their place the Remi had succeeded; and as it was perceived that they had equal influence with Caesar, the tribes which, by reason of ancient animosities, could in no wise join the Aedui were delivering themselves as dependents to the Remi. These tribes the Remi carefully protected, and by this means they sought to maintain their new and suddenly acquired authority. The state of things then at the time in question was that the Aedui were regarded as by far the chief state, while the Remi held the second place in importance.

[13] Throughout Gaul there are two classes of persons of definite account and dignity. As for the common folk, they are treated almost as slaves, venturing naught of themselves, never taken into counsel. The more part of them, oppressed as they are either by debt, or by the heavy weight of tribute, or by the wrongdoing of the more powerful men, commit themselves in slavery to the nobles, who have, in fact, the same

rights over them as masters over slaves. Of the two classes above mentioned one consists of Druids, the other of knights. The former are concerned with divine worship, the due performance of sacrifices, public and private, and the interpretation of ritual questions: a great number of young men gather about them for the sake of instruction and hold them in great honour. In fact, it is they who decide in almost all disputes, public and private; and if any crime has been committed, or murder done, or there is any dispute about succession or boundaries, they also decide it, determining rewards and penalties: if any person or people does not abide by their decision, they ban such from sacrifice, which is their heaviest penalty. Those that are so banned are reckoned as impious and criminal; all men move out of their path and shun their approach and conversation, for fear they may get some harm from their contact, and no justice is done if they seek it, no distinction falls to their share. Of all these Druids one is chief, who has the highest authority among them. At his death, either any other that is pre-eminent in position succeeds, or, if there be several of equal standing, they strive for the primacy by the vote of the Druids, or sometimes even with armed force. These Druids, at a certain time of the year, meet within the borders of the Carnutes, whose territory is reckoned as the centre of all Gaul, and sit in conclave in a consecrated spot. Thither assemble from every side all that have disputes, and they obey the decisions and judgments of the Druids. It is believed that their rule of life was discovered in Britain and transferred thence to Gaul; and to-day those who would study the subject more accurately journey, as a rule, to Britain to learn it.

[14] The Druids usually hold aloof from war, and do not pay war-taxes with the rest; they are excused from military service and exempt from all liabilities. Tempted by these great rewards, many young men assemble of their own motion to receive their training; many are sent by parents and relatives. Report says that in the schools of the Druids they learn by heart a great number of verses, and therefore some persons remain twenty years under training. And they do not think it proper to commit these utterances to writing, although in almost all other matters, and in their public and private accounts, they make use of Greek letters. I believe that they have adopted the practice for two reasons—that they do not wish the rule to become common property, nor those who learn the rule to rely on writing and so neglect the cultivation of the memory; and, in fact, it does usually happen that the assistance of writing tends to relax the diligence of the student and the action of the memory. The cardinal doctrine which they seek to teach is that souls do not die, but after death pass from one to another; and this belief, as the fear of death is thereby cast aside, they hold to be the greatest incentive to

valour. Besides this, they have many discussions as touching the stars and their movement, the size of the universe and of the earth, the order of nature, the strength and the powers of the immortal gods, and hand down their lore to the young men.

[15] The other class are the knights. These, when there is occasion, upon the incidence of a war—and before Caesar's coming this would happen well-nigh every year, in the sense that they would either be making wanton attacks themselves or repelling such—are all engaged therein; and according to the importance of each of them in birth and resources, so is the number of liegemen and dependents that he has about him. This is the one form of influence and power known to them.

[16] The whole nation of the Gauls is greatly devoted to ritual observances, and for that reason those who are smitten with the more grievous maladies and who are engaged in the perils of battle either sacrifice human victims or vow so to do, employing the Druids as ministers for such sacrifices. They believe, in effect, that, unless for a man's life a man's life be paid, the majesty of the immortal gods may not be appeased; and in public, as in private, life they observe an ordinance of sacrifices of the same kind. Others use figures of immense size, whose limbs, woven out of twigs, they fill with living men and set on fire, and the men perish in a sheet of flame. They believe that the execution of those who have been caught in the act of theft or robbery or some crime is more pleasing to the immortal gods; but when the supply of such fails they resort to the execution even of the innocent.

[17] Among the gods, they most worship Mercury. There are numerous images of him; they declare him the inventor of all arts, the guide for every road and journey, and they deem him to have the greatest influence for all money-making and traffic. After him they set Apollo, Mars, Jupiter, and Minerva. Of these deities they have almost the same idea as all other nations: Apollo drives away diseases, Minerva supplied the first principles of arts and crafts, Jupiter holds the empire of heaven, Mars controls wars. To Mars, when they have determined on a decisive battle, they dedicate as a rule whatever spoil they may take. After a victory they sacrifice such living things as they have taken, and all the other effects they gather into one place. In many states heaps of such objects are to be seen piled up in hallowed spots, and it has not often happened that a man, in defiance of religious scruple, has dared to conceal such spoils in his house or to remove them from their place, and the most grievous punishment, with torture, is ordained for such an offence.

[18] The Gauls affirm that they are all descended from a common father, Dis, and say that this is the tradition of the Druids. For that reason they determine all periods of time by the number, not of days, but

of nights,[6] and in their observance of birthdays and the beginnings of months and years day follows night. In the other ordinances of life the main difference between them and the rest of mankind is that they do not allow their own sons to approach them openly until they have grown to an age when they can bear the burden of military service, and they count it a disgrace for a son who is still in his boyhood to take his place publicly in the presence of his father.[7]

[19] The men, after making due reckoning, take from their own goods a sum of money equal to the dowry they have received from their wives and place it with the dowry. Of each such sum account is kept between them and the profits saved; whichever of the two survives receives the portion of both together with the profits of past years. Men have the power of life and death over their wives, as over their children; and when the father of a house, who is of distinguished birth, has died, his relatives assemble, and if there be anything suspicious about his death they make inquisition of his wives as they would of slaves, and if discovery is made they put them to death with fire and all manner of excruciating tortures. Their funerals, considering the civilization of Gaul, are magnificent and expensive. They cast into the fire everything, even living creatures, which they believe to have been dear to the departed during life, and but a short time before the present age, only a generation since, slaves and dependents known to have been beloved by their lords used to be burnt with them at the conclusion of the funeral formalities.

[20] Those states which are supposed to conduct their public administration to greater advantage have it prescribed by law that anyone who has learnt anything of public concern from his neighbours by rumour or report must bring the information to a magistrate and not impart it to anyone else; for it is recognised that oftentimes hasty and inexperienced men are terrified by false rumours, and so are driven to crime or to decide supreme issues. Magistrates conceal what they choose, and make known what they think proper for the public. Speech on state questions, except by means of an assembly, is not allowed.

[21] The Germans differ much from this manner of living. They have no Druids to regulate divine worship, no zeal for sacrifices. They reckon among the gods those only whom they see and by whose offices they are openly assisted—to wit, the Sun, the Fire-god, and the Moon; of the rest they have learnt not even by report. Their whole life is composed of

---

[6] Because Dis is the god of the dark underworld; and *cf.* our "se'nnight," "fortnight."

[7] When the father appeared *in publico, i.e.,* as a warrior, he was disgraced (probably a survival of *taboo*) if a son, not yet a warrior also, appeared in his presence.

hunting expeditions and military pursuits; from early boyhood they are zealous for toil and hardship. Those who remain longest in chastity win greatest praise among their kindred; some think that stature, some that strength and sinew are fortified thereby. Further, they deem it a most disgraceful thing to have had knowledge of a woman before the twentieth year; and there is no secrecy in the matter, for both sexes bathe in the rivers and wear skins or small cloaks of reindeer hide, leaving great part of the body bare.

[22] For agriculture they have no zeal, and the greater part of their food consists of milk, cheese, and flesh. No man has a definite quantity of land or estate of his own: the magistrates and chiefs every year assign to tribes and clans that have assembled together as much land and in such place as seems good to them, and compel the tenants after a year to pass on elsewhere. They adduce many reasons for that practice—the fear that they may be tempted by continuous association[8] to substitute agriculture for their warrior zeal; that they may become zealous for the acquisition of broad territories, and so the more powerful may drive the lower sort from their holdings; that they may build with greater care to avoid the extremes of cold and heat; that some passion for money may arise to be the parent of parties and of quarrels. It is their aim to keep common people in contentment, when each man sees that his own wealth is equal to that of the most powerful.

[23] Their states account it the highest praise by devastating their borders to have areas of wilderness as wide as possible around them. They think it the true sign of valour when the neighbours are driven to retire from their lands and no man dares to settle near, and at the same time they believe they will be safer thereby, having removed all fear of a sudden inroad. When a state makes or resists aggressive war officers are chosen to direct the same, with the power of life and death. In time of peace there is no general officer of state, but the chiefs of districts and cantons do justice among their followers and settle disputes. Acts of brigandage committed outside the borders of each several state involve no disgrace; in fact, they affirm that such are committed in order to practise the young men and to diminish sloth. And when any of the chiefs has said in public assembly that he will be leader, "Let those who will follow declare it," then all who approve the cause and the man rise together to his service and promise their own assistance, and win the general praise of the people. Any of them who have not followed, after promise, are reckoned as deserters and traitors, and in all things afterwards trust is denied to them. They do not think it right to outrage a guest; men who

---

[8] *i.e.* with one spot which would become endeared to them.

have come to them for any cause they protect from mischief and regard as sacred; to them the houses of all are open, with them is food shared.

[24] Now there was a time in the past when the Gauls were superior in valour to the Germans and made aggressive war upon them, and because of the number of their people and the lack of land they sent colonies across the Rhine. And thus the most fertile places of Germany round the Hercynian forest (which I see was known by report to Eratosthenes and certain Greeks, who call it the Orcynian forest) were seized by the Volcae Tectosages, who settled there, and the nation maintains itself to this day in those settlements, and enjoys the highest reputation for justice and for success in war. At the present time, since they abide in the same condition of want, poverty, and hardship as the Germans, they adopt the same kind of food and bodily training. Upon the Gauls, however, the neighbourhood of our provinces and acquaintance with oversea commodities lavishes many articles of use or luxury; little by little they have grown accustomed to defeat, and after being conquered in many battles they do not even compare themselves in point of valour with the Germans.

[25] The breadth of this Hercynian forest, above mentioned, is as much as a nine days' journey for an unencumbered person; for in no other fashion can it be determined, nor have they means to measure journeys. It begins in the borders of the Helvetii, the Nemetes, and the Rauraci, and, following the direct line of the river Danube, it extends to the borders of the Daci and the Anartes; thence it turns leftwards, through districts apart from the river, and by reason of its size touches the borders of many nations. There is no man in the Germany we know who can say that he has reached the edge of that forest, though he may have gone forward a sixty days' journey, or who has learnt in what place it begins. It is known that many kinds of wild beasts not seen in any other places breed therein, of which the following are those that differ most from the rest of the animal world and appear worthy of record.

[26] There is an ox shaped like a stag,[9] from the middle of whose forehead between the ears stands forth a single horn, taller and straighter than the horns we know. From its top branches spread out just like open hands. The main features of female and of male are the same, the same the shape and the size of the horns.

[27] There are also elks so-called. Their shape and dappled skin are like unto goats, but they are somewhat larger in size and have blunted horns.[10] They have legs without nodes or joints, and they do not lie down to

---

[9] i.e. the reindeer, probably—but that has a pair of antlers.
[10] Or "stumps of horns."

sleep, nor, if any shock has caused them to fall, can they raise or uplift themselves. Trees serve them as couches; they bear against them, and thus, leaning but a little, take their rest. When hunters have marked by their tracks the spot to which they are wont to betake themselves, they either undermine all the trees in that spot at the roots or cut them so far through as to leave them just standing to outward appearance. When the elks lean against them after their fashion, their weight bears down the weakened trees and they themselves fall along with them.[11]

[28] A third species consists of the ure-oxen[12] so-called. In size these are somewhat smaller than elephants; in appearance, colour, and shape they are as bulls. Great is their strength and great their speed, and they spare neither man nor beast once sighted. These the Germans slay zealously, by taking them in pits; by such work the young men harden themselves and by this kind of hunting train themselves, and those who have slain most of them bring the horns with them to a public place for a testimony thereof, and win great renown. But even if they are caught very young, the animals cannot be tamed or accustomed to human beings. In bulk, shape, and appearance their horns are very different from the horns of our own oxen. The natives collect them zealously and encase the edges with silver, and then at their grandest banquets use them as drinking-cups.

[29] When Caesar had ascertained through scouts of the Ubii that the Seubi had retired into the forests, he decided to advance no farther, fearing scarcity of corn, because, as above mentioned, all the Germans care naught for agriculture. At the same time, in order not to remove altogether from the natives the fear of his return and to delay their reinforcements, after he had withdrawn his army he broke up to the extent of two hundred feet the farthest section of the bridge which touched the banks of the Ubii, and at the end of the bridge he set a tower of four stories, posting a garrison of twelve cohorts to protect the bridge and strengthening the station with considerable fortifications. He set young Gaius Volcatius Tullus in command of the station and garrison, and himself moved off, as soon as the corn-crops began to ripen, for the campaign against Ambiorix. His route ran through the forest of Ardennes, which is the largest in all Gaul and stretches from the banks of the Rhine and the borders of the Treveri to the country of the Nervii, extending lengthwise for more than five hundred miles, and he sent forward Lucius Minucius Basilus, with all the cavalry, to see if he could gain any advan-

---

[11] *Cf.* Shakespeare, *Julius Caesar*, II. i. 203:

> . . . for he [Caesar] loves to hear
> That unicorns may be betrayed with trees.

[12] The aurochs, *Bos primigenius,* was a prehistoric inhabitant of Britain.

tage by speed of march and chance of opportunity. He instructed him to prevent the. making of fires in camp in order to give no intimation from afar of his coming, and said that he himself would follow forthwith.

[30] Basilus did as he was commanded. He accomplished the march speedily, contrary, indeed, to the general expectation, and caught many persons in the fields off their guard. Their information led him to make for Ambiorix himself in the locality where he was reported to be with a few horsemen. In everything, and especially in warfare, great is the power of fortune. For just as it was by great good luck that he fell upon the chief himself actually off his guard and unprepared—in fact, his arrival was seen by everybody before any rumour or message thereof was brought—so likewise it was a great piece of fortune that, when all the military equipment he had about him had been captured, the carriages and horses seized, the chief himself should escape death. But this, too, came to pass because, the building being surrounded by forest, as the dwellings of the Gauls usually are—for to avoid the heat they generally seek the neighbourhood of woods and rivers—his companions and friends in so confined a place held off the attack of our cavalry for a short time. While they fought, one of his followers set him on a horse, and the woods covered his flight. Thus both in his exposure to danger and in his escape therefrom the influence of fortune was great.

[31] It is doubtful whether it was of set purpose that Ambiorix did not assemble his forces, thinking that he ought not to fight a decisive action, or whether he had no chance of so doing because he was prevented by the sudden arrival of the cavalry, believing that the rest of the army was following close behind. But certain it is that he despatched messengers in different directions through the fields with the order that each man should take thought for himself. Part of them escaped into the forest of Ardennes, part into the long stretches of morass;[13] those who were nearest the Ocean hid themselves in the islands which the tides are accustomed to form; many left their own borders and entrusted themselves and all their stuff to utter strangers. Catuvolcus, king of half the Eburones, who had shared the project of Ambiorix, was old and worn, and, finding that he could not endure the effort of war or flight, cursed Ambiorix by all his gods for suggesting such a project, and hanged himself to a yew-tree, of which there is great plenty in Gaul and Germany.

[32] The Segni and Condrusi, who are of the nation and number of the Germans and have their abode betwixt the Eburones and the Treveri, sent envoys to Caesar to beg him not to count them among his enemies, nor to consider that there was common cause among all the

---

[13] Or possibly "adjacent morasses."

Germans on the Roman side of the Rhine. They pleaded that they had had no idea of war, had sent no auxiliaries for Ambiorix. Caesar investigated the matter by examination of prisoners, and commanded that if any of the Eburones should have repaired to them in their flight they should be brought back to him; he said that if they did this he would not do violence to their territories. Then, dividing his forces into three parts, he concentrated the baggage of all the legions at Aduatuca. That is the name of a fort situated almost in the middle of the territory of the Eburones, where Titurius and Aurunculeius had stationed themselves to winter; and Caesar approved of the position on general grounds, and particularly because the fortifications of the previous year remained intact, in order thereby to lighten the labour of the troops. To guard the baggage he left the Fourteenth Legion, one of the three latest enrolled[14] which he had brought over from Italy. He put Quintus Tullius Cicero in command of the legion and the camp, and attached two hundred cavalry to his force.

[33] Having divided the army, he ordered Titus Labienus to proceed with three legions towards the districts which touch the Menapii; Gaius Trebonius with an equal number of legions to devastate the region which adjoins the Aduatuci; and he determined to march himself with the remaining three to the river Scheldt, which flows into the Meuse,[15] and to the uttermost parts of the Ardennes, whither he heard Ambiorix had started with a few horsemen. As he departed he guaranteed that he would return, after an interval of seven days, on the day by which he knew that the corn-ration was due for the legion left in garrison. He urged Labienus and Trebonius, if they could do so without danger to the commonwealth, to return by the same day, in order that they might again take counsel together, examine the tactics of the enemy, and so be able to start the campaign afresh.

[34] As above mentioned, there was nowhere any definite body of troops, any stronghold, any garrison to defend itself in arms; but the population was scattered in all directions. Each man had settled where a hidden valley or a wooded locality or an entangled morass offered some hope of defence or security. These localities were known to the dwellers round about, and thus the matter required great care, not for the protection of the army as a whole (for no danger could occur to united bodies from individuals scared and scattered), but for the preservation of single soldiers, although this latter consideration affected to some degree the safety of the army. For the passion for plunder was apt to draw many

---

[14] See ch. 1 *supra*.
[15] It no longer does so, if it ever did.

men too far afield, and at the same time the woods forbade the advance of any close-formed body along the hidden and uncertain tracks. If Caesar wished to finish off the business and to make away with a brood of malefactors, he must needs send several bands in different directions and move his troops at wide intervals; if he wished to keep the companies with the standards, as the established rule and custom of the Roman army required, the locality itself gave protection to the natives, and individuals among them lacked not the daring to lay secret ambush and surround scattered detachments. Considering these particular difficulties, all precaution that carefulness could take was taken; and Caesar preferred to forgo some chance of doing harm, although the spirit of every man was burning for vengeance, rather than to do harm with some damage to the troops. He sent messengers round to the neighbouring states and invited them all, in the hope of booty, to join him in pillaging the Eburones, so that he might hazard the lives of the Gauls among the woods rather than the soldiers of the legions, and at the same time, by surrounding it with a large host, destroy the stock and name of the tribe in requital for its horrid crime. A great number assembled speedily from every side.

[35] These operations were being carried out in all parts of the Eburones' country, and the seventh day drew nigh, by which Caesar had determined to return to the baggage and the legion. Herein it has been possible to note how great is the power of fortune in war, and how great the chances she brings in her train. The enemy were scared and scattered, as we have mentioned, and there was no body of troops that could suggest the slightest occasion for alarm. Across the Rhine the report reached the Germans that the Eburones were being pillaged; nay, more—that all were invited to come and plunder. Two thousand horsemen were collected by the Sugambri, who live nearest the Rhine, and, as we set forth above, had received the Tencteri and the Usipetes after their flight. On boats and rafts they crossed the Rhine thirty miles below the spot where the bridge had been built and a garrison left by Caesar; and, coming first to the borders of the Eburones, they caught many persons scattered in flight, and captured a great quantity of cattle, of which barbarians are very covetous. They were tempted by plunder to proceed further. No marsh, no woods check these children of war and brigandage. From prisoners they inquire in what district Caesar is; they find that he has gone on some distance, they learn that all his army is departed. And then one of their prisoners said: "Why do you pursue this miserable and slender booty, when you now have the chance of the utmost fortune? In three hours you may come to Aduatuca; in that spot the Roman army has concentrated all its stores; the garrison is so small that it cannot even man the wall, and no one dares to step outside the entrenchments." With this hope offered them, the Germans left in a secret place the plunder they

had got and made for Aduatuca, using as guide the very man by whose information they had learnt the news.

[36] For all the previous days Cicero, in obedience to Caesar's instructions, had most carefully confined his troops to camp, allowing not even a single camp-follower to pass beyond the entrenchment. On the seventh day he did not feel sure that Caesar would keep his word as touching the number of days, as he heard that he had advanced farther, and no report about his return was brought in. At the same time he was influenced by the remarks of those who called his patience almost a siege, since no leave to pass out of camp was given; and he did not anticipate any turn of fortune such as, with nine legions and a very large force of cavalry to confront a scattered and almost obliterated enemy, could cause disaster within the distance of three miles. He therefore sent five cohorts to get corn in the nearest fields, between which and the camp but a single hill interposed. Several men of the legions had been left behind sick, and those of them who had recovered during the intervening days, to the number of some three hundred, were sent together under a flag;[16] and, besides, a great host of camp-followers got leave to follow with a great number of pack-animals which had remained in the camp.

[37] Just at this moment, as it chanced, the German horsemen came on the scene, and immediately, at the same speed as had brought them thither, essayed to burst into camp at the main gate. There was a screen of woods on that side, so that they were not seen before they drew near the camp, so much so that the traders encamped close under the rampart had no chance of retreating. Our troops, not expecting them, were thrown into confusion by the surprise, and the cohort on guard scarcely stood the first attack. The enemy poured round the other faces of the camp, to see if they could find an entry. Our troops with difficulty defended the gates; all other chances of entrance were prevented by the nature of the place itself and by the entrenchment. There was confusion throughout the camp, and one sought from another the cause of the uproar; no one had a care to which point the companies[17] were to move or in what quarter each man was to assemble. One declared that the camp was already taken, another insisted that the barbarians were come victorious from the destruction of the army and the commander-in-chief, and the majority pictured to themselves new superstitions because of the place and set before their eyes the disaster of Cotta and Titurius, who (as they remembered) fell in the same fort. Owing to the universal

---

[16] *i.e.* they formed a single and separate detachment: *cf.* ch. 40.

[17] *i.e.* the companies which were assembling; the second clause indicates that individual soldiers did not know where to fall in.

panic caused by such fears, the barbarians were confirmed in the belief that, as they had heard from the prisoner, there was no garrison inside. They strove to break through, exhorting one another not to let so good a chance slip from their hands.

[38] With the garrison there had been left behind, sick, a certain Publius Sextius Baculus, who has been mentioned by us in previous battles.[18] He had now been five days without food, and, doubtful of his own and the general safety, he came forth from his tent unarmed. He saw that the enemy were threateningly close and that the issue was in the greatest danger; he took arms from the nearest men and stationed himself in the gate. He was followed by all the centurions of the cohort on guard, and together for a short space they bore the brunt of the battle. Sextius fainted after receiving severe wounds; with difficulty he was dragged from hand to hand into safety. In the respite thus given the rest took courage so far as to venture to their stations in the entrenchments and to afford a semblance of defence.

[39] Meanwhile, having finished corn-gathering, our troops heard the shouting; the cavalry sped forward, and learnt the great danger of the moment. But here was no entrenchment to receive the scared soldiers; lately enlisted, and unskilled in the practice of war, they turned their faces with one accord to the tribunes and centurions, waiting to see what these would direct. No one was so brave as not to be confused by so unexpected a situation. The natives, on the other hand, catching sight of the standards at a distance, desisted from the assault: at first they supposed that the legions had returned, which, according to the information given by the prisoners, had gone farther afield; afterwards, despising the small numbers, they made a charge on every side.

[40] The camp-followers dashed forward to the nearest rise. They were speedily hurled down from thence, and ran headlong into the company formations, scaring the soldiers into greater alarm. Some of these proposed to form a wedge and break through speedily, as the camp was so near at hand, feeling confident that if some part were surrounded and slain, yet the remainder could be saved. Others proposed to take post on the ridge and all face the same risk together. This course was not approved by the veterans, who, as we have shown, marched out together under a flag. So they encouraged one another, and, led by Gaius Trebonius, a Roman knight, who had been put in command of them, they broke through the midst of the enemy and came into camp all safe to a man. Close behind them in the same onrush came the camp-followers and the cavalry, who were saved by the valour of the soldiers.

[18] II. 25; III. 5.

But the party which had taken post on the ridge, still utterly untutored in the practice of war, had proved unable either to abide in the place they had approved and defend themselves on higher ground, or to imitate the vigour and the speed which they had seen to be of assistance to others; indeed, in the attempt to retire into camp they came down to unfavourable ground. Some of their centurions had been transferred, on account of valour, from the lower ranks of the other legions to the higher ranks of this; and these, that they might not lose the renown for military prowess won in the past, fell, fighting most gallantly. Part of the soldiers, when the enemy had been thrust aside by the valour of the centurions, arrived, though they did not expect it, safe in camp; part were surrounded by the natives and perished.

[41] The Germans despaired of storming the camp, for they could see that our men had now taken post in the entrenchments; they therefore retired across the Rhine with the booty which they had secreted in the woods. And even after their departure so great was the fear of the enemy that the same night, when Gaius Volusenus, who had been sent on with the cavalry, reached the camp, he could not make the troops believe that Caesar was close at hand with his army unhurt. Terror had so completely seized their minds that they were almost crazy, declaring that after the destruction of all the forces the cavalry had escaped from the rout, and insisting that if the army had been safe the Germans would not have attacked the camp. This terror was removed by the arrival of Caesar.

[42] When he returned, knowing well the accidents of war, he had but one complaint to make—that cohorts had been sent afield from outpost and garrison duty: he held that no room should have been left for even the slightest mischance, and that fortune had proved her power in the sudden arrival of the enemy—ay, and far more so, in that she had turned away the natives almost from the very rampart and gates of the camp. Of all these events the most remarkable seemed to be that the Germans, who had crossed the Rhine with the definite intention of devastating the territory of Ambiorix, by their descent on the Roman camp rendered Ambiorix the most acceptable service.

[43] Caesar marched forth again to harass the enemy, and, collecting a great host from the neighbouring states, he sent them off in every direction. Every hamlet, every homestead that anyone could see was set on fire; captured cattle were driven from every spot; the corn-crops were not only being consumed by the vast host of pack-animals and human beings, but were laid flat in addition because of the rainy season, so that, even if any persons succeeded in hiding themselves for the moment, it seemed that they must perish for want of everything when the army was withdrawn. And with so large a force of cavalry scattered in every direc-

tion, it often came to pass[19] that prisoners when taken were gazing about for Ambiorix, whom they had just seen in flight, and even insisting that he had not quite gone out of sight. The hope of catching the fugitive now offered to them inspired immense exertion, and the thought that they would win the highest favour with Caesar made their zeal almost more than human. Yet always it seemed that they had failed by a little to win supreme success, while Ambiorix stole away from covert or glade and, hidden by night, made for other districts or territories, with no more escort of horsemen than four troopers, to whom alone he durst entrust his life.

[44] When the districts had been devastated in such fashion, Caesar brought back the army with the loss of two cohorts to Durocortorum,[20] a city of the Remi; and, having summoned a convention of Gaul at that place, he determined to hold an inquisition touching the conspiracy of the Senones and Carnutes; and on Acco, the arch-conspirator, who had originated the plot, he pronounced a heavier sentence than usual, and executed punishment in our traditional fashion.[21] Some persons feared trial and fled, and these he outlawed. Then he stationed two legions in cantonments on the borders of the Treveri, two among the Lingones, and the remaining six at Agedincum, in the territory of the Senones; and, having provided a corn-supply for the army, set out for Italy, as he had determined, to hold the assizes.[22]

---

[19] Or, "it often came so nearly to pass," *i.e.* the capture of Ambiorix.
[20] Reims.
[21] By flogging him to death *(fustuarium)*.
[22] See note on I. 54.

# BOOK VII

[1] When Gaul was quiet Caesar set out for Italy, as he had determined, to hold the assizes. There he heard of the murder of Clodius;[1] and having been informed of the Senate's decree that all the younger men of military age[2] in Italy should be sworn in, he decided to hold a levy throughout his province.[3] These events were speedily reported to Transalpine Gaul. The Gauls added to the reports a circumstance of their own invention, which the occasion seemed to require, that Caesar was detained by the commotion at Rome and, in view of discords so serious, could not come to the army. Such an opportunity served as a stimulus to those who even before were chafing at their subjection to the sovereignty of Rome, and they began with greater freedom and audacity to make plans for a campaign. The chiefs of Gaul summoned conventions by mutual arrangement in remote forest spots and complained of the death of Acco. They pointed out that his fate might fall next upon themselves; they expressed pity for the common lot of Gaul; by all manner of promises and rewards they called for men to start the campaign and at the risk of their own life to champion the liberty of Gaul. First and foremost, they said, they must devise means, before ever their secret designs got abroad, to shut Caesar off from the army. It was an easy task, because the legions would not dare to march out of cantonments in the absence of the commander-in-chief, nor could the latter without a strong escort reach the legions. Finally, it was better, they urged, to be slain in battle than to fail of recovering their old renown in war and the liberty which they had received from their forefathers.

[2] When these subjects had been discussed, the Carnutes declared that there was no hazard they refused for the general welfare, and promised that they would be the first of all to make war; and, since in the present circumstances they could not give one another security by means

---

[1] By Milo, 52 B.C.
[2] *i.e.* from seventeen years upwards.
[3] *i.e.* Cisalpine Gaul.

of hostages, for fear the matter should get abroad, they asked for the sanction of an oath of honour before the assembled war-standards—the formality which represents their most solemn ritual—to make sure that after beginning the campaign they should not be abandoned by the rest. Thereupon all present praised the Carnutes with one accord and gave their oath, and after appointing a season for the enterprise departed.

[3] When the day came, the Carnutes, under the leadership of two desperate men, Cotuatus and Conconnetodumnus, rushed at a given signal on Cenabum, put to the sword the Roman citizens who had established themselves there for trading purposes—among them Gaius Fufius Cita, a Roman knight of distinction, who by Caesar's order was in charge of the corn-supply—and plundered their goods. Speedily the report thereof was carried to all the states of Gaul. As a matter of fact, whenever any event of greater note or importance occurs, the Gauls shout it abroad through fields and districts and then others take it up in turn and pass it on to their next neighbours; as happened on this occasion. For the deeds done at Cenabum at sunrise were heard of before the end of the first watch in the borders of the Arverni, a distance of about one hundred and sixty miles.

[4] There in like fashion Vercingetorix, son of Celtillus, an Arvernian youth of supreme influence (whose father had held the chieftainship of all Gaul and consequently, because he aimed at the kingship, had been put to death by his state),[4] summoned his own dependents and easily fired their spirit. Directly his design was known there was a general rush to arms. Gobannitio, his uncle, and the rest of the chiefs, who did not think this adventure should be hazarded, sought to prevent him; he was cast out of the town of Gergovia, but he did not give up for all that; and in the fields he held a levy of beggars and outcasts. Then, having got together a body of this sort, he brought over to his own way of thinking all the members of his state whom he approached, urging them to take up arms for the sake of the general liberty; and having collected large forces, he cast out of the state his opponents by whom he had been expelled a short time before. He was greeted as "King" by his followers. He sent out deputations in every direction, adjuring the tribesmen to remain loyal to him. He speedily added to his side the Senones, Parisii, Pictones, Cadurci, Turoni, Aulerci, Lemovices, Andi, and all the other maritime tribes; by consent of all, the command was bestowed upon him. In virtue of the power thus conferred he made requisition of hostages on all these states, and ordered a certain number of soldiers to be brought to him speedily; he determined what amount of arms, and by what date, each state should manufacture[5] at home, and he paid

---

[4] Celtillus evidently desired to advance from *principatus* to *regnum*.
[5] Or perhaps, in a less literal sense, "produce."

especial attention to the cavalry. To the utmost care he added the utmost strictness of command, compelling waverers by severity of punishment. Indeed for the commission of a greater offence he put to death with fire and all manner of tortures; for a lesser case he sent a man home with his ears cut off or one eye gouged out, to point the moral to the rest and terrify others by the severity of the penalty.

[5] By enforcing punishments of this sort he speedily raised an army, and he despatched Lucterius, a Cadurcan of the utmost intrepidity, with a part of the forces into the land of the Ruteni, while he himself started forth against the Bituriges. At his coming the Bituriges sent envoys to the Aedui, in whose allegiance they were, to ask for succour, so as to enable them the easier to withstand the enemy's forces. Acting on the advice of the deputies left by Caesar with the army, the Aedui sent a force of horse and foot to the support of the Bituriges. When they were come to the river Loire, which parts the Bituriges from the Aedui, they halted there for a few days; and, not venturing to cross the river, they returned home, and reported to the Roman deputies that their return was due to fear of treachery on the part of the Bituriges, who, they learnt, had planned that, if the Aedui crossed the river, they themselves should surround them on the one side, and the Arverni on the other. As we have no clear knowledge whether they acted as they did for the reason which they declared to the deputies, or from motives of treachery, it does not seem proper to state it as a certainty. Upon their departure the Bituriges at once joined the Arverni.

[6] When these matters were reported to Caesar in Italy, he had already received intelligence that affairs in Rome had been brought by the energy of Gnaeus Pompeius into a more satisfactory state, and he therefore set out for Transalpine Gaul. Upon arrival there he was confronted with a great difficulty, as to the means whereby he could reach the army. For if he should summon the legions to the Province, he realised that on the march they might have to fight an action without his presence; if, on the other hand, he himself pressed on to the army, he saw that it was a mistake to entrust his personal safety at that time even to the tribes which appeared to be at peace.

[7] Meanwhile Lucterius the Cadurcan, who had been sent into the country of the Ruteni, united that state with the Arverni. He then advanced into the land of the Nitiobriges and the Gabali, and received hostages from both tribes; and so, having collected a large force, he made an effort to overrun the Province in the direction of Narbo. On report of this Caesar thought that he should proceed to Narbo in preference to any other plan. When he was come thither he put new strength into timorous hearts by posting garrisons among the Ruteni of the Province, the Volci Arecomici, the Tolosates, and around Narbo—all localities adjacent to the enemy; and he ordered a part of the forces of the Province, and the sup-

plementary levy which he had brought with him from Italy, to assemble in the territory of the Helvii, which touches the borders of the Arverni.

[8] By these measures of security Lucterius was checked and set back, for he deemed it dangerous to penetrate the line of garrisons; and so Caesar was free to proceed into the district of the Helvii. Now the range of the Cevennes, which parts the Arverni from the Helvii, in this the severest season of the year was likely to hinder the march with great depth of snow; however, he cleared away snow six feet deep and, having thus opened up the roads by a supreme effort of the troops, reached the borders of the Arverni. They were caught off their guard, for they thought themselves fortified by the Cevennes as by a wall, and not even a solitary traveller[6] had ever found the paths open at that season of the year; and Caesar commanded the cavalry to extend on as broad a front and strike as much terror into the enemy as possible. Rumour and reports hereof were speedily brought to Vercingetorix, and all the Arverni gathered about him panic-stricken, beseeching him to have regard to their fortunes and not suffer them to be pillaged by the enemy, especially now that, as he saw, the whole war had been turned against them. He was prevailed upon by their prayers to move his camp from the country of the Bituriges towards that of the Arverni.

[9] Caesar, however, having anticipated that this would be the natural course of things for Vercingetorix, halted for two days in this locality; then he left the army on the pretext of assembling the supplementary levy and the cavalry. He put young Brutus in command of the force here, instructing him to let his cavalry range the district in every direction on as broad a front as possible, and saying that he would endeavour to be away from the camp no longer than three days. Having set these matters in order, he reached Vienna[7] by forced marches before his own army expected him.[8] There he found the cavalry which he had sent on thither many days beforehand fit for action, and without a break in his march by day or night he pressed on through the country of the Aedui into that of the Lingones, where two legions were wintering—so speedily as to forestall even the possibility of any design of the Aedui on his own safety. Upon arrival at the station he sent word to the rest of the legions and concentrated them all in one place, or ever report of his coming could reach the Arverni. When he was informed of this, Vercingetorix led his army back again to the country of the Bituriges, and starting thence determined to assault Gorgobina, a

---

[6] Much less a body of troops.

[7] Vienne.

[8] Or, "to the surprise of the army." The march to Vienne may have been expected, but not so soon, or it may have been quite unexpected.

stronghold of the Boii, whom, after their defeat in the battle against the Helvetii, Caesar had established there as dependents of the Aedui.

[10] This action of Vercingetorix caused Caesar great difficulty in forming his plan of campaign. If he were to keep the legions in one place for the rest of the winter, he was afraid that the reduction of the tributaries of the Aedui would be followed by a revolt of all Gaul, on the ground that Caesar was found to be no safeguard to his friends. If he were to bring the legions out of cantonments too soon, he was afraid that difficulties of transport would cause trouble with the corn-supply. However, it seemed preferable to endure any and every difficulty rather than to put up with so dire a disgrace[9] and thus to alienate the sympathies of all his own adherents. Therefore he urged the Aedui to see to the transport of supplies, and sent men forward to the Boii to apprise them of his own coming and urge them to remain loyal and courageously to withstand the attack of the enemy. Then, leaving two legions at Agedincum with the baggage-train of the whole army, he set off for the Boii.

[11] On the next day he came to Vellaunodunum, a stronghold of the Senones; and in order to leave no enemy in his rear, and so to expedite the corn-supply, he determined to assault the place, and in two days invested it. On the third day deputies were sent out of the town to treat for surrender, and Caesar ordered arms to be collected, pack-animals furnished, and six hundred hostages given. He left Gaius Trebonius, lieutenant-general, to carry out these orders. He himself, in order to end his march as soon as possible, started for Cenabum, a town of the Carnutes. The news of the siege of Vellaunodunum had been brought to them, and thinking that the business would be long drawn out, they were at this moment beginning to raise a garrison to be sent to Cenabum for the protection thereof. Caesar reached it in two days. He pitched his camp before the town, and as the hour of the day forbade further action he deferred the assault until the morrow. He commanded the troops to make ready the appliances required for the operation; and as the bridge over the river Loire was contiguous to the town of Cenabum, he ordered two legions to bivouac under arms, as he feared the inhabitants might escape from the town by night. A little before midnight the men of Cenabum moved out in silence from the town and began to cross the river. This was reported to Caesar by the scouts; and setting the gates on fire, he sent in the legions which he had ordered to be ready for action, and took possession of the town. Exceeding few of the enemy's total strength were lacking to make the capture complete, inasmuch as the narrowness of the bridge and the roads had prevented the escape of the general population. He plundered

---

[9] *i.e.* as proving unable to safeguard his friends.

and burnt the town, bestowed the booty on the troops, crossed the Loire with the army, and reached the borders of the Bituriges.

[12] As soon as he heard of Caesar's approach Vercingetorix abandoned the siege and started to meet him. Caesar, for his part, had determined to assault Noviodunum, a stronghold of the Bituriges stationed on his route. And as deputies came out to him from the place to entreat pardon for their faults and pity for their lives, he ordered arms to be collected, horses to be furnished, hostages to be given, with intent to complete the remainder of the business as speedily as he had accomplished the greater part thereof. Part of the hostages had already been handed over, and the other demands were in process of fulfilment, as some centurions and a few soldiers had been sent in to collect arms and animals, when the enemy's horsemen were sighted at a distance, the vanguard of the column of Vercingetorix. The moment the townsfolk caught sight of them and conceived a hope of assistance, they raised a shout and began to take up their arms, to shut the gates, and to man the wall. When the centurions in the town perceived by the demonstration on the part of the Gauls that some new design was afoot, they drew their swords, seized the gates, and withdrew all their parties in safety.

[13] Caesar ordered the cavalry to be brought out of camp, and engaged the cavalry of the enemy. When his own troops began to be distressed he sent in support some four hundred German horse, whom he had made a practice of keeping with him from the first. The Gauls could not resist their charge, and were put to flight, retiring to the main body with a loss of many men. At their discomfiture the townsfolk were once more panic-stricken, and seizing the persons by whose efforts they supposed the populace had been roused, they brought them to Caesar and surrendered themselves to him. When this business had been despatched, Caesar moved off to the town of Avaricum,[10] the largest and best fortified in the territory of the Bituriges, and situated in a most fertile district. He felt confident that by the recovery of that town he would bring the state of the Bituriges again into his power.

[14] Having experienced three continuous reverses—at Vellaunodunum, Cenabum, and Noviodunum—Vercingetorix summoned his followers to a convention. He pointed out that the campaign must be conducted in far different fashion from hitherto. By every possible means they must endeavour to prevent the Romans from obtaining forage and supplies. The task was easy, because the Gauls had an abundance of horsemen and were assisted by the season of the year. The forage could not be cut; the enemy must of necessity scatter to seek it from the homesteads; and all

---

[10] Bourges.

these detachments could be picked off[11] daily by the horsemen. Moreover, for the sake of the common weal, the interests of private property must be disregarded: hamlets and homesteads must be burnt in every direction for such a distance from the route as the enemy seemed likely to penetrate in quest of forage. The Gauls had a supply of such necessaries, because they were assisted by the resources of the tribes in whose territory the campaign was being carried on. The Romans would not endure scarcity, or else would advance farther from their camp at great risk; and it made no difference whether the Gauls killed them or stripped them of their baggage, the loss of which rendered the campaign impossible. Moreover, any towns which were not secure from all danger by fortification or natural position ought to be burnt, in order that they might not afford the Gauls a refuge for the avoidance of service, nor offer the Romans a chance to carry off plunder and store of supplies. If these measures seemed grievous or cruel, they ought to take into account that it was far more grievous that their children and their wives should be dragged off into slavery, that they themselves should be slaughtered—the inevitable fate of the conquered.

[15] This view was approved by general consent, and in a single day more than twenty cities of the Bituriges were set on fire. The same was done in the other states, and in every direction fires were to be seen. And although it was a bitter pain to all to endure this, yet they set before themselves thus much of comfort, that they were confident of recovering their losses by a well-nigh assured victory. They deliberated in a general convention whether Avaricum should be burnt or defended. The Bituriges flung themselves at the feet of all the Gauls, entreating that they might not be compelled with their own hands to set light to almost the fairest city in all Gaul, the safeguard and the ornament of their state. They declared that they would easily defend themselves by its natural strength, for it was surrounded by river and marsh on almost every side, and had a single and a very narrow approach. Leave was granted to their petition: Vercingetorix at first argued against it, but afterwards yielded to the prayers of the tribesmen and to compassion for the multitude. Suitable defenders for the town were chosen.

[16] Vercingetorix followed after Caesar by shorter stages, and chose for his camp a place fenced by marshes and woods, about sixteen miles from Avaricum. There, by means of scouting parties appointed for each section of the day, he could keep himself informed of the operations about Avaricum, and give such orders as he desired. He kept all our foraging and corn-collecting parties under observation, and when they were scattered, since they had of necessity to advance farther afield, he would

---

[11] Or perhaps "destroyed."

attack them and inflict serious loss; at the same time our men took every precaution they could think of to counteract this, by moving at uncertain times and by different routes.

[17] Caesar pitched his camp on that side of the town which was unenclosed by the river and the marshes, and had, as above mentioned, a narrow approach. He began to prepare a ramp, to move up mantlets, to build two towers; for the nature of the locality precluded an investment. He did not cease to importune the Boii and the Aedui in the matter of the corn-supply; but the latter, with no zeal for the task, did not help much, and the former, having no great resources, because their state was small and feeble, speedily consumed what they had. So the army suffered from the utmost difficulty in its corn-supply, because of the indigence of the Boii, the apathy of the Aedui, and the burning of the homesteads— so much so that for several days the troops were without corn, and staved off the extremity of famine by driving in cattle from the more distant hamlets. Yet never a word was heard from their lips unworthy of the dignity of Rome and of their previous victories. Nay more, when Caesar addressed single legions at work, and declared that if the burden of scarcity were too bitter for them to bear he would raise the siege, one and all would beseech him not to do so. They had served, they said, for many years under his command without once incurring disgrace, without anywhere leaving a task unaccomplished; they would regard it in the nature of a disgrace if they relinquished the siege they had begun; it were better to endure any and every bitterness than to fail of avenging the Roman citizens who had perished at Cenabum by the treachery of the Gauls. They entrusted messages in the same spirit to the centurions and tribunes, to be tendered to Caesar through them.

[18] By the time that the towers had come near to the wall, Caesar learnt from prisoners that Vercingetorix had exhausted his forage and moved his camp nearer to Avaricum, and was gone forward in person, with horsemen and the light troops that were accustomed to do battle among the horse, to set an ambush in the place whither he believed our troops would come next day to get forage. Having learnt this, Caesar marched in silence at midnight, and reached the enemy's camp in the morning. They had speedily learnt through their scouts of Caesar's coming, and having hidden away their wagons and baggage in the denser part of the woods, they drew up all their force on high, open ground. On report of this Caesar ordered packs to be speedily piled and arms got ready.

[19] There was a hill sloping gently from the base, and surrounded on almost every side by a difficult and troublesome marsh, not more than fifty feet across. On this hill, having broken up the causeways, the Gauls were established, with all confidence in the position; distributed according to their several nationalities, they held every ford and thicket by the

marsh. They were resolved, if the Romans tried to burst through the marsh, to overwhelm them from the higher ground as they stuck fast. So anyone who remarked how near they were thought them prepared to fight to a finish in almost equal battle; but anyone who observed the inequality of the conditions recognised that they were displaying themselves in empty bravado. The troops were furious that the enemy were able to endure the sight of themselves at so brief an interval, and demanded the signal for action. But Caesar pointed out what great loss, in the death of so many gallant men, a victory must necessarily cost, and said that, when he saw them resolved to refuse no risk that might win him renown, he deserved to be condemned for the uttermost injustice if he did not count their life dearer than his own welfare. Having thus pacified the troops, he led them back to camp the same day, and began to set in order everything else required for the siege of the town.

[20] When Vercingetorix returned to his followers, he was accused of treachery because he had moved the camp nearer to the Romans, because he had gone off with all the horse and had left so large a force without a commander, and because on his departure the Romans had come with such speed upon their opportunity. All these circumstances, they said, could not have happened by chance or without design; he preferred to possess the kingship of Gaul by the leave of Caesar rather than by favour of themselves. Accused in such sort, he replied to the charges. As for having moved the camp, it had been done, he said, actually at their own instance, through lack of forage; as for having gone nearer the Romans, he had been influenced by the advantage of a position which could protect itself by its own defences; further, the service of the horse should not have been needed on marshy ground, and it had been useful in the place to which they had marched. It was of purpose that he had committed the chief command to no one at his departure, for fear that his deputy might be driven by the zeal of the host to an engagement—an object for which he saw that all were zealous through weakness of spirit, because they could not longer endure hardship. If the appearance of the Romans on the scene had been due to chance, the Gauls had fortune to thank; if they had been summoned thither by some informer, the Gauls had that man to thank for the satisfaction of having been able to learn from their higher station the scantiness of their numbers, and to despise a courage which had not ventured to fight but had retired disgracefully to camp. He had no need to obtain from Caesar by treachery a title of command which he could enjoy by a victory already assured to himself and all the Gauls. Nay more, he gave the title back to them if they thought that they were bestowing honour on him rather than deriving security from him. "That you may perceive," he continued, "the sincerity of this statement on my part, listen to Roman soldiers." He brought forward slaves whom he had caught foraging a few days before and

## THE ROMAN *AGGER* AT AVARICUM (VII. 17, 24.) (*After Colonel Stoffel*)

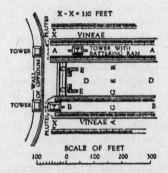

At A . . . A, B . . . B, the *agger* is built up in inclined planes, on which towers (T, T) with battering-rams are pushed up to the wall. C . . . C is a terrace, level or nearly level with the top of the wall: from the *vineae* here a covering fire is kept up to assist the operations. The area D . . . D is not built up, but left at the natural level; from it the troops move by steps, as at E, E to the level C, C.

## GALLIC WALL (VII. 23.)

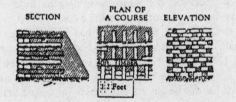

had tortured with hunger and chains. These had been previously instructed what to state when questioned, and said that they were soldiers of the line; they had been induced by hunger and want to go secretly out of the camp, to see if they could find any corn or cattle in the fields; the whole army was suffering from similar want, no man had any strength left, none could endure the strain of work, and therefore the commander-in-chief had decided, if they made no progress in the siege of the town, in three days to withdraw the army. "These," said Vercingetorix, "are the benefits you have from me, whom you accuse of treachery, by whose effort, without shedding of your own blood, you behold this great victorious army wasted with hunger; while it is I who have seen to it that, when it takes shelter in disgraceful flight, no state shall admit it within its borders."

[21] The whole host shouted with one accord, and clashed their arms together in their peculiar fashion, as they always do for a man whose speech they approve. They declared that Vercingetorix was a consummate leader, that there could be no doubt of his loyalty, and that the campaign could not be conducted with greater intelligence. They decided that ten thousand men picked from the whole force should be sent into the town, and resolved that the common safety of all must not be entrusted to the Bituriges alone, for they perceived that in keeping possession of the town rested almost the whole issue of victory.

[22] The matchless courage of our troops was met by all manner of contrivances on the part of the Gauls; for they are a nation possessed of remarkable ingenuity, and extremely apt to copy and carry out anything suggested to them. So now they sought to drag aside the grappling-hooks with nooses, and, when they had caught them, to pull them back inwards with windlasses; and they tried to under-cut the ramp by mines, the more scientifically because they have large iron-workings in their country, and every kind of mine is known and employed. Further, they had furnished the whole wall on every side with a superstructure of wooden turrets, and covered these over with hides. Then in frequent sallies by day and night they tried to set fire to the ramp or to attack the troops engaged in the works; and whatever increase was made in the height of our turrets by daily additions to the ramp,[12] they equalised by joining fresh scaffolding[13] to their own turrets, and tried to check the progress of our own mines where they opened up,[14] and to prevent their approach to the walls by means of timbers[15] hardened in the fire and sharpened, boiling pitch, and stones of very great weight.

[12] As the Roman ramp rose day by day, the turrets on it were, not actually, but relatively higher.
[13] Or, "by joining poles together on their own turrets," and so building up a fresh story.
[14] Or, "opened up our mines, and tried to check their progress."
[15] Presumably these were long stout poles thrust into the end of the mine, when it had been pushed close up to the wall, from a counter-mine.

[23] All Gallic walls are, as a rule, of the following pattern. Balks are laid on the ground at equal intervals of two feet throughout the length of the wall and at right angles thereto. These are made fast on the inside and banked up with a quantity of earth, while the intervals above mentioned are stopped up on the front side with big stones. When these balks have been laid and clamped together a second course[16] is added above, in such fashion that the same interval as before is kept, and the balks[17] do not touch one another, but each is tightly held at a like space apart by the interposition of single stones. So the whole structure is knit together stage by stage until the proper height of wall is completed. This work is not unsightly in appearance and variety, with alternate balks and stones which keep their proper courses in straight lines; and it is eminently suitable for the practical defence of cities, since the stone protects from fire and the timber from battery,[18] for with continuous balks, generally forty feet long, made fast on the inside it can neither be breached nor pulled to pieces.

[24] All these circumstances impeded the siege; but though the troops were delayed throughout by cold and constant showers, still by continuous effort they overcame all these obstacles, and in twenty-five days they built a ramp three hundred and thirty feet broad and eighty feet high. This was almost touching the enemy's wall, and Caesar, according to his custom, bivouacked by the work, urging the troops not to leave off working even for a moment: when shortly before the third watch[19] the ramp was observed to be smoking, for the enemy had set fire to it from a counter-mine. At the same moment a shout was raised all along the wall, and a sortie was made from two gates on either side of the Roman turrets. Others began at long range to hurl torches and dry wood from the wall on to the ramp, and to pour down pitch and everything else that can kindle a fire, so that it was scarcely possible to form an idea in which direction the troops should hasten first or to what point bring assistance. However, as by Caesar's standing order two legions were always in bivouac before the camp, and more, by a succession of reliefs, were engaged on the earthwork, it was speedily arranged that some troops should resist the sorties, while others dragged back the turrets and cut a gap in the ramp, and the whole host from the camp rushed up to extinguish the fire.

[25] Even when the rest of the night was spent, there was fighting at every point, and ever the enemy's hope of victory was renewed—the more so because they saw that the breastworks of the turrets[20] were burnt up,

---

[16] Of balks and stones.

[17] The balks of the second course are laid on the stones of the first.

[18] *i.e.* the battering-ram.

[19] The Roman night, from sunset to sunrise, was divided into four equal "watches."

[20] Or "the screens round the turrets," which gave cover to the forward working-parties.

and observed that without cover it was not easy for the troops to advance in support; and ever, on their side, fresh men replaced the weary, and they believed that the deliverance of Gaul depended on that moment of time. Then there occurred before our eyes a thing which, as it seemed worthy of record, we have not thought it right to omit. A certain Gaul before the gate of the town was hurling into the fire over against a turret lumps of grease and pitch that were handed to him. He was pierced by a dart from a "scorpion"[21] in the right side and fell dead. One of the party next him stepped over his prostrate body and went on with the same work; and when this second man had been killed in the same fashion by a scorpion-shot, a third succeeded, and to the third a fourth; and that spot was not left bare of defenders until the ramp had been extinguished, the enemy cleared away on every side, and a stop put to the fighting.

[26] The Gauls had tried every expedient, and as nothing had succeeded they resolved next day to escape from the town, as Vercingetorix urged and ordered. They hoped that by attempting it in the silence of night they would accomplish it with no great loss of their men, because the camp of Vercingetorix was not far from the town, and the marsh, which filled without break all the space between, must hinder the Romans in pursuit. And it was now night and they were already preparing to do this, when the matrons suddeny rushed out of doors, and, flinging themselves with tears at the feet of their men, with prayers and supplications besought them not to surrender, to the tender mercies of the enemy, themelves and their common children, whom natural weakness hampered from taking flight. When they saw that the men were firm in their purpose, for as a rule in extreme peril fear admits no sense of pity, they began to cry out in a body and to make signs to the Romans as touching the flight. So the Gauls were terror-struck by the fear that the Roman cavalry might seize the roads before them, and they abandoned their design.

[27] On the morrow, when a turret had been advanced and the works which Caesar had begun to construct were finished, a heavy shower of rain came on. He thought the moment suitable for the execution of his plan, as he observed that the guards on the wall were less carefully posted than usual; so he ordered his men to move more leisurely about the work, and showed them what he wanted to be done. The legions made ready for action secretly under the cover of the mantlets; and having urged them to reap at length the fruit of victory in return for their great labours, he offered prizes to those who should first mount the wall, and gave the signal to the troops. They dashed out suddenly from all sides and speedily lined the wall.

---

[21] A kind of small catapult, the Roman machine-gun.

[28] The enemy were panic-stricken by the surprise, and when they were hurled down from the wall and the turrets they stood fast in wedge-formations in the market-place and the more open places, with intent, if a movement were made from any side upon them, to deploy into line and fight to a finish. When they saw no one coming down on to the level ground, but that the troops were pouring round everywhere all along the wall, they feared that the hope of escape might be cut off altogether, and, casting away their arms, they made in a continuous rush for the farthest parts of the town; and part, as they crowded one another at the narrow passage of the gates, were slain there by the troops, part after they had got out of the gates by the cavalry, and no one had any thought for plunder. In such fashion the troops, maddened by the massacre at Cenabum and the toil of the siege-work, spared not aged men, nor women, nor children. Eventually of all the number, which was about forty thousand, scarcely eight hundred, who had flung themselves out of the town when they heard the first shout, reached Vercingetorix in safety. He intercepted the refugees late at night in silence, fearing that a mutiny might arise if they were met and pitied by the common sort: therefore, by stationing his own friends and the chiefs of states at some distance along the roads, he took steps to separate them and conduct them to their friends in the part of the camp allotted to each state from the beginning.

[29] On the next day, summoning a conference, he comforted them, and exhorted them not greatly to lose heart, nor to be disturbed by the disaster. The Romans had not conquered by courage nor in pitched battle, but by stratagem and by knowledge of siege operations, in which the Gauls had had no experience. It was a mistake to expect in war that all events would have a favourable issue. He himself had never agreed with the defence of Avaricum, and of that he had themselves as witnesses; but this experience of disaster had been brought about by the unwisdom of the Bituriges and the undue complaisance of the rest. However, he would speedily remedy it by greater advantages. He would by his own efforts bring to their side the states which disagreed with the rest of Gaul, and establish one policy for the whole of Gaul, whose unanimity not even the world could resist; and already he had almost brought that to pass. Meanwhile it was reasonable that for the sake of the common weal they should do as he asked and set to work to fortify the camp, in order more easily to resist sudden attacks of the enemy.

[30] This speech was not unpleasing to the Gauls, chiefly because the commander himself had not failed them after the great disaster they had suffered, nor hidden out of their sight and avoided the gaze of the host; and they considered his foresight and forethought the greater because, while the matter was still open, he had first advocated the burning, and afterwards the abandonment, of Avaricum. And thus, whereas the

authority of commanders in general is diminished by reverses, so his position, on the contrary, was daily enhanced by the disaster they had suffered. At the same time they were inclined to be hopeful, by reason of his assurance, about bringing in the remaining states; and on this occasion for the first time the Gauls set to work to fortify the camp, and they were so strengthened in spirit that, although unaccustomed to toil, they thought that they must submit to any commands.

[31] As good as his promise, Vercingetorix worked with a will to bring in the remaining states, and tried to attract them by presents and promises. He selected for the purpose suitable persons, each of whom, by guileful speech or by friendly demeanour, should be able most easily to captivate. The men who had escaped at the storming of Avaricum he caused to be armed and clothed; at the same time, to recruit his diminished force, he made requisition of a certain number of soldiers from the states, saying what number he wished for and by what day they should be brought into camp; and he ordered all archers, of whom there was a very great number in Gaul, to be sought out and sent to him. By this means the loss at Avaricum was speedily made up. Meanwhile Teutomatus, the son of Ollovico and king of the Nitiobriges, whose father had been saluted as Friend by the Roman Senate, came to him with a large number of horsemen: some were his own, and others he had hired from Aquitania.

[32] Caesar halted at Avaricum for several days, and by the immense quantity of corn and all other supplies which he found there recuperated the army after toil and want. The winter was now almost spent; the very season was inviting him to continue the war, and he had decided to march against the enemy to see whether he could entice them out of the marshes and woods or reduce them by blockade, when at this juncture chiefs of the Aedui came on a mission to him to beseech his succour for the state in a crisis of absolute urgency. The administration, they said, was in the utmost peril, because, in spite of their ancient custom of electing single magistrates to hold kingly power for a year, two persons were exercising office, and each of them declared himself legally elected. One of the two was Convictolitavis, a successful and distinguished young man; the other Cotus, the scion of a most ancient house, and himself a man of dominant power and noble connection, whose brother Valetiacus had exercised the same office in the previous year. The whole state was in arms, the senate was divided, and each claimant had his own following. If the quarrel were any longer fomented, one part of the state must inevitably come to blows with the other. The prevention of that depended upon Caesar's energy and authority.

[33] Caesar thought it disastrous to move away from the war and the enemy, but at the same time he knew full well what great troubles generally arose from such dissensions; and therefore, to prevent this large state, so closely connected with Rome—a state which he himself had

always cherished and by every means distinguished—from resorting to armed violence, wherein the party which had less confidence in itself would seek succours from Vercingetorix, he thought the matter should receive his first attention. And, inasmuch as the laws of the Aedui did not suffer those who exercised the highest office to leave the country, he determined, in order that he might not appear in any way to disparage their rights or laws, to proceed in person into the territory of the Aedui, and summoned all their senate, together with the parties to the quarrel, to join him at Decetia. Almost the whole state assembled there, and he was informed that in a small and secret assembly, held in a place and at a time which were irregular, one brother had declared the other elected, although the law not only forbade two of one house, in the lifetime of both, to be elected as officers of state, but even precluded them from membership of the senate. He therefore compelled Cotus to lay down the supreme authority, and ordered Convictolitavis, who had been elected by the priests, according to the tradition of the state when the succession of civil officers had been interrupted, to hold the power.

[34] Having made this decision between them, he urged the Aedui to forget disputes and discord and, leaving all such matters alone, to devote themselves to the present campaign, in anticipation of the rewards they deserved from himself so soon as the conquest of Gaul was complete. He bade them send him speedily all their horsemen and ten thousand infantry, that he might put them in various garrisons to protect the corn-supply. He then divided the army into two parts. Four legions he gave to Labienus to be led against the Senones and Parisii, six he led in person along the river Allier towards the town of Gergovia, in the country of the Arverni; he assigned part of the cavalry to Labienus, part he left for himself. As soon as Vercingetorix heard of it he broke up all the bridges over that river and began to march along the other side thereof.

[35] When the two armies had drawn apart, they proceeded to pitch camp in sight of each other and almost opposite, with the enemy's scouts posted about to prevent the Romans from constructing a bridge and effecting a passage. Caesar's position was thus beset by great difficulties; for there was danger that the river would block him for the greater part of the summer, as the Allier is not usually fordable before the autumn. To prevent this, therefore, he pitched camp in a wooded spot opposite one of the bridges which Vercingetorix had caused to be cut away, and on the morrow he kept two legions hidden, sending on the rest of the force with all the baggage, according to his custom, and opening out some of the cohorts to make the number of the legions appear the same as usual. This force was ordered to march out as far as possible, and when by the time of day he conjectured that they were safe in camp, he began to rebuild the bridge on the same piles as before, the lower part of which was still intact. The

PLAN OF GERGOVIA
(after Colonel Stoffel)

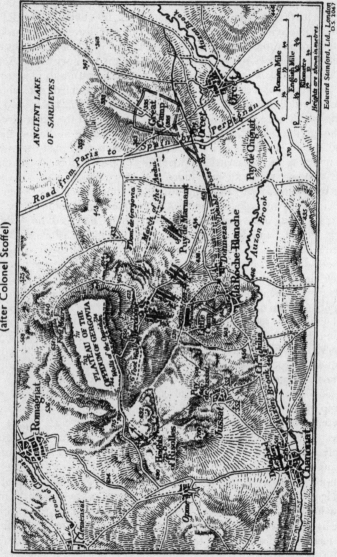

Edward Stanford, Ltd., London
D.S 3047

work was speedily completed and the legions put across; and when a suitable camping-ground had been chosen, he recalled the rest of the force.
On report of this, Vercingetorix moved ahead by forced marches, in order
that he might not be forced to fight against his own wish.

[36] From that position Caesar reached Gergovia[22] in five days' march.
On the fifth day a slight cavalry skirmish took place; and having reconnoitred the position of the city, which was set upon a very lofty height,
with difficult approaches on every side, he despaired of taking it by
storm, and he determined not to attempt a blockade until he had secured
his corn-supply. Vercingetorix, for his part, had pitched camp near the
town, and posted the contingent of each state separately at short intervals around himself. Every eminence on the ridge from which a bird's-
eye view was possible had been seized, and the appearance was formida-
ble. He would order the chiefs of the states, whom he had chosen to assist
him in council, to assemble at dawn daily at his quarters in case there
should seem to be anything to communicate or to arrange. And scarcely
a day passed that he did not put to the test, by an encounter of horsemen with archers placed among them, the spirit and the courage of each
of his followers. Opposite the town there was a hill at the very foot of
the mountain, an exceedingly strong position, precipitous on every side.
If our troops secured this they thought they could cut off the enemy at
once from great part of their water-supply and from freedom of foraging. The post was held, however, by the enemy with a garrison, albeit not
a very strong one. None the less, Caesar marched out of camp in the
silence of the night, dislodged the garrison before it could be reinforced
from the town, and made himself master of the position. He posted two
legions there, and ran a double ditch, twelve feet broad in each case, from
the greater to the lesser camp, so that even single soldiers could pass to
and fro safe from a sudden onset of the enemy.

[37] During these operations about Gergovia Convictolitavis the
Aeduan, to whom, as above mentioned, the magistracy had been
adjudged by Caesar, was tempted by a bribe on the part of the Arverni,
and held converse with certain young men, among whom the leaders
were Litaviccus and his brethren, young scions of a most distinguished
house. The Aeduan shared his bribe with them, and urged them to
remember that they were born to freedom and command. The state of
the Aedui was the only bar to the absolutely certain victory of Gaul; by
its influence the rest were held in check; if it were brought over, the
Romans would have no foothold in Gaul. It was true that he himself had
received some benefit at Caesar's hands, but simply in the sense that he

---

[22] For all the operations round Gergovia the plan should be consulted, page 132.

had won an entirely just cause before him, and he had a greater duty to the general liberty. Why should the Aedui come to Caesar to decide a question of their own right and law, rather than the Romans to the Aedui? The young men were speedily won over by the speech of the magistrate and by the bribe, and avowed that they would be the very first to support his design. Then they began to seek a means of executing it, because they were not sure that the state could be induced off-hand to undertake a war. It was resolved that Litaviccus should be put in command of the ten thousand soldiers who were to be sent to Caesar for the war, and should be responsible for their leading, while his brethren hastened forward to Caesar. They determined the plan to be adopted for carrying out the rest of the scheme.

[38] Litaviccus took over the army, and when he was about thirty miles from Gergovia he suddenly called together the troops, and with tears addressed them: "Whither, soldiers, are we proceeding? All our horsemen, all our chivalry is perished; Eporedorix and Viridomarus, chief men of our state, have been accused of treachery by the Romans, and put to death with their cause unheard. This you shall learn from men who actually escaped from that same massacre; for all my own brethren and all my kindred have been put to death, and grief prevents me from declaring what was brought to pass." The persons whom he had instructed what they were to say were brought forward, and set forth to the host the same tale which Litaviccus had declared—that many horsemen of the Aedui had been put to death because it was alleged that they had held converse with the Arverni; that they themselves had hidden in the general throng of soldiers, and so had escaped from the midst of the massacre. The Aedui shouted with one accord and entreated Litaviccus to take counsel for their safety. "As if," quoth he, "this were a matter of counsel, and it were not necessary for us to make speed to Gergovia and join ourselves to the Arverni! Or can we doubt that after committing an abominable crime the Romans are already hastening hither to slay us? Wherefore, if we have any spirit in us, let us avenge the death of those who have perished most shamefully, and let us slay these brigands." He pointed to Roman citizens, who were accompanying his force in reliance on his safeguard; he plundered a large quantity of corn and supplies, and put the Romans to death with cruel tortures. He sent messages throughout the state of the Aedui and sought to arouse them by the same falsehood concerning the massacre of horsemen and chiefs, urging them to avenge their own wrongs in the same fashion as he himself had done.

[39] Eporedorix the Aeduan, a young man of the highest rank and of supreme influence in his own country, and with him Viridomarus, his peer in age and popularity, but not in birth—he had been commended by Diviciacus to Caesar, who had advanced him from a humble station

to a pre-eminent position—had come along with the horsemen in response to a personal summons from Caesar. These two had a struggle between them for chieftancy, and in the late dispute[23] between the magistrates the one had fought with might and main for Convictolitavis, the other for Cotus. Of these two, Eporedorix, when he learnt the design of Litaviccus, reported the matter about midnight to Caesar. He besought him not to allow the state to fall away from the friendship of Rome through the mischievous designs of the young men; yet this, as he foresaw, would happen if those thousands of troops joined forces with the enemy, for their kindred could not ignore their safety, nor could the state account it of slight importance.

[40] This report caused Caesar great anxiety, because he had always shown especial indulgence to the state of the Aedui; and without a moment's hesitation he marched four legions in light order, and all the cavalry, out of camp. There was no time at such a crisis to reduce the camp-area,[24] as the issue seemed to depend on speed; he left Gaius Fabius, lieutenant-general, with two legions as camp-garrison. He ordered the brethren of Litaviccus to be arrested, but found that they had fled to the enemy shortly before. He urged the troops not to be disturbed by the fatigue of a march which the emergency rendered necessary, and then, amid the greatest eagerness of all ranks, he advanced for five-and-twenty miles, when he caught sight of the column of the Aedui. By sending on the cavalry he checked and hampered the enemy's march, and he forbade all to put any man to the sword. Eporedorix and Viridomarus, whom the other side supposed to be slain, he ordered to move among the horsemen and address their own people. When they were recognized, and the deceit of Litaviccus was discovered, the Aedui began to stretch out their hands in token of surrender and, casting away their arms, to beg for mercy. Litaviccus escaped to Gergovia with his dependents; for, according to the custom of Gaul, it is a crime in dependents to desert their patrons, even in desperate case.

[41] Caesar sent messengers to the state of the Aedui to report that the men, whom by right of war he might have put to death, had by his own favour been saved; and then, having given the army three hours of the night for rest, struck camp for Gergovia. About half-way thither some troopers sent by Fabius related how perilous had been their case. They reported that the camp had been attacked in full force, fresh men frequently taking the place of the fatigued and wearing down our troops by incessant toil, inasmuch as the size of the camp obliged the same men to continue throughout on the rampart. Many men, they said, had been

---

[23] See ch. 33.

[24] The fortified camp of the six legions was obviously far too large for the two left behind, which were likely to have difficulty in defending it.

wounded by the swarms of arrows and of every kind of missile; the artillery, however, had proved of great use in resisting these assaults; and, on the withdrawal of the enemy, Fabius was barricading all the gates except two, setting screens to the rampart, and preparing for a like event on the morrow. On report of this, Caesar reached the camp before sunrise, by a supreme effort of the troops.

[42] During these operations about Gergovia the Aedui received the first messages sent by Litaviccus. They left themselves no time to investigate: some were influenced by avarice, others by anger and the recklessness which is specially characteristic of their race,[25] treating frivolous hearsay as assured fact. They plundered the goods of Roman citizens, massacred some, dragged off others into slavery. Convictolitavis encouraged the general tendency, and urged the common folk to fury, that by committing crime they might be ashamed to return to a right mind. By giving him a pledge of safety they then induced Marcus Aristius, a military tribune, who was travelling to his legion, to quit the town of Cabillonum; those who had settled there for the sake of trade they compelled to do the same. Then they attacked them the moment they started on their journey, stripped them of all their baggage, and, when they defended themselves, blockaded them for a day and a night. After many persons had been slain on both sides, they brought up a still greater multitude of armed men.

[43] In the midst of this a message was brought that all their soldiers were prisoners in the power of Caesar. At once they ran with one consent to Aristius, declaring that the state had had no share in their design or deed. They ordered an inquiry as touching the plundered goods, they confiscated the goods of Litaviccus and his brethren, and sent deputies to Caesar to clear themselves. This they did to recover their kith and kin; but they were stained with crime, they were tempted by the profit to be made of plundered goods, as the business concerned a large number of persons; so, as they were alarmed by the fear of penalty, they began to entertain secret designs of war and to sound the other states by means of deputations. Caesar was fully aware of this; nevertheless he accosted their deputies as gently as possible, assuring them that the ignorance and inconsequence of the common people did not make him judge more severely of the state, nor diminish aught of his personal goodwill towards the Aedui. He himself was anticipating a greater rising in Gaul; and that he might not be surrounded by all the states, he began to plan how he might withdraw from Gergovia and once more concentrate the whole army without allowing a departure occasioned by fear of the revolt to resemble flight.

[44] While he reflected on these matters, a chance of successful action

---

[25] *i.e.* the Gallic race generally.

seemed to offer itself. He had come to the lesser camp to inspect the works, when he noticed that a hill held by the enemy, and on the previous days scarcely visible for the crowd upon it, was undefended. Surprised thereat, he asked deserters, a large number of whom were flocking to him daily, for the reason. All agreed in stating, what Caesar himself had already learnt through scouts, that the crest of the ridge there[26] was almost level, but that this hill was wooded and narrow where it gave access to the other[27] side of the town. For this spot the Gauls, they said, were grievously alarmed, and had now no alternative but to believe that if, after the seizure of one hill by the Romans, they lost the other, they would find themselves to be almost invested, and cut off from all egress and from foraging. Vercingetorix had accordingly called out every man to fortify this hill.

[45] On this information Caesar sent several troops of cavalry thither just after midnight, with orders to range in every direction in rather more noisy fashion than usual. At daybreak he commanded a large quantity of baggage-mules to be brought forth from camp, and the muleteers to take off the packs, and with helmets on their heads to ride round the hills, like cavalry to all seeming. With them he put a few cavalry, to range more widely by way of demonstration, and ordered them all to make for the same general destination by a long circuit. The proceeding was noticed afar from the town, as there was a bird's-eye view from Gergovia into the camp; but at so great a distance the real meaning thereof could not be discovered. He despatched one legion in the same direction, and when it had advanced a little way he halted it on the lower ground and concealed it in the woods. The suspicion of the Gauls was increased, and all their force was brought across to that spot to fortify it. When Caesar saw that the enemy's camp was empty, covering the badges of his men and concealing the war-standards, he moved soldiers from the greater to the lesser camp in small parties so as not to attract attention from the town. He showed the lieutenant-generals whom he had put in command of each legion what he wished to be done: first and foremost he instructed them to keep the troops in hand, lest in the zeal for battle or the hope of booty they might advance too far. He explained the disadvantage caused by the inequality of the ground, and said that this could be remedied by speed alone: it was a question of surprise, not of battle. After these explanations he gave the signal, and started the Aedui at the same moment by another ascent, on the right side.

[46] From the level where the ascent began the wall of the town was

---

[26] i.e. the ridge S.W. of Gergovia, of which the hill in question formed part.
[27] i.e. the side not directly attacked by the Romans.

twelve hundred paces distant in a straight line, if there were no curve to consider. Any deviation added to ease the slope of necessity increased the distance to be marched. About half-way up the hill, the Gauls had put up a six-foot covering-wall of large stones, running lengthways so as to follow the contour of the height, to check our attack; and leaving all the lower area unoccupied, they had filled all the upper part of the hill, right up to the wall of the town, with their camps, closely crowded together. When the signal was given, the troops speedily reached the fortification, crossed it, and took possession of three camps, and so great was their speed in capturing the camps that Teutomatus, king of the Nitiobriges, caught suddenly in his tent in a noonday sleep, barely escaped from the hands of the plundering troops, with the upper part of his body bare, and his horse wounded.

[47] Having thus secured his particular purpose, Caesar ordered the retreat to be sounded, and at once halted the Tenth Legion, which he had accompanied. But the rank and file of the other legions did not hear the trumpet-call, as a considerable valley lay in between; none the less, efforts were made by the tribunes and lieutenant-generals to hold them back, according to Caesar's instructions. Elated, however, by the hope of a speedy victory, by the flight of the enemy, and their successful engagements on previous occasions, they thought that nothing was so difficult as to be unattainable by their valour, and they did not make an end of pursuing until they neared the wall and the gates of the town. Then, indeed, shouting arose from all parts of the city, and those who were farther away were terror-struck at the sudden uproar, and, believing that the enemy was within the gates, flung out of the town. Matrons cast clothing and silver from the wall, and with bare breast and outstretched hands implored the Romans to spare them, and not to do as they had done at Avaricum, holding their hand not even from women and children. Some of the women were lowered by hand from the wall, and were fain to deliver themselves to the troops. Lucius Fabius, a centurion of the Eighth Legion, who was known to have said that day among his company that he was spurred on by the rewards at Avaricum, and would allow no one to mount the wall before him, got three men of his company, was lifted up by them, and mounted the wall. Then he in turn took hold of them one by one and pulled them up on to the wall.

[48] Meanwhile the Gauls who had assembled, as above mentioned, at the other side of the town to make a fortification first of all heard the shouting, and then came frequent messages that the town was held by the Romans to arouse them further; so they sent the horsemen in advance and hastened thither in a mighty stream. Each as he arrived took his stand under the wall and swelled the number of their fighting men. When a great host of them had assembled, the matrons who a moment before were stretching out their hands to the Romans from the wall began to adjure their own

men and, in Gallic fashion, to show dishevelled hair and to bring their children forward into view. The Romans had no fair contest in ground or numbers; they were tired out by the speedy march and the duration of the battle, and could not easily resist men that were fresh and unhurt.

[49] Caesar saw that the battle was being fought on unfavourable ground and that the strength of the enemy was increasing. Anxious, therefore, for his troops, he sent a message to Titus Sextius, the lieutenant-general, whom he had left to guard the lesser camp, bidding him bring the cohorts speedily out of the camp and post them at the foot of the hill on the right flank of the enemy, so that, if he saw our troops driven down from the position, he might deter the enemy from an indiscriminate pursuit. He himself advanced a little with the legion from the place where he had halted, and awaited the issue of the battle.

[50] The battle was continued most fiercely at close quarters: the enemy trusted to position and numbers, our troops to courage. Suddenly the Aedui, whom Caesar had sent on the right by another line of ascent to divert the enemy's forces, were seen on the exposed flank of our troops. The similarity of their armament to that of the Gauls grievously alarmed the Romans; and although it was noticed that they had their right shoulders uncovered—the distinction agreed upon by custom[28]—still the troops were disposed to think that even this had been done by the enemy to deceive them. At the same moment the centurion Lucius Fabius and those who had mounted the wall along with him were surrounded, slain, and hurled from the wall. Marcus Petronius, a centurion of the same legion, had tried to cut down a gate, but was overpowered by superior numbers and in desperate case. Already he had received many wounds, and he cried to the men of his company who had followed him: "As I cannot save myself with you, I will at any rate provide for *your* life, whom in the eager desire for glory I have brought into danger. When the chance is given do you look after yourselves." With this he burst into the midst of the enemy, and by slaying two shifted the rest a little from the gate. When his men tried to assist him he said: "In vain do you try to rescue *my* life, for blood and strength are already failing me. Wherefore depart while you have a chance and get you back to the legion." So, a moment later, he fell fighting and saved his men.

[51] Our troops were hard pressed on every side, and were dislodged from the position with a loss of six-and-forty centurions. But any immoderate pursuit on the part of the Gauls was checked by the Tenth Legion, which had taken post in support on rather more even ground. This legion

---

[28] It is probable that the Gauls who fought on the Roman side left their right shoulders bare in action as a distinguishing mark.

was covered in turn by cohorts of the Thirteenth, which had marched out
of the lesser camp with Titus Sextius, the lieutenant-general, and had occupied higher ground. As soon as the legions touched the plain they turned
the standards against the enemy and halted. Vercingetorix led his men back
from the base of the hill within the fortifications. On that day little less than
seven hundred soldiers were missing.

[52] On the morrow Caesar called a parade and reprimanded the
troops for their recklessness and headstrong passion: they had decided for
themselves whither they should advance or what they should do, they
had not halted when the signal for retirement was given, and had not
been amenable to the restraint of tribunes and lieutenant-generals. He
showed what might be the effect of unfavourable ground, what he himself had borne in mind at Avaricum, when, though he had caught the
enemy without general and without cavalry, he had given up an assured
victory in order that even slight loss in action might not be caused by
unfavourable ground. Greatly as he admired the high courage of men
whom no camp fortifications, no mountain-height, no town-wall had
been able to check, he blamed as greatly their indiscipline and presumption in supposing that they had a truer instinct than the commander-in-
chief for victory and the final result. He required from his soldiers, he
said, discipline and self-restraint no less than valour and high courage.

[53] After delivering this harangue, and at the end thereof encouraging the troops not to be cast down on this account, nor to attribute to
the courage of the enemy a result caused by unfavourable ground,
though he was still minded, as he had been before, to march off, he led
the legions out of camp and formed line-of-battle on suitable ground.
When Vercingetorix, notwithstanding, refused to come down to level
ground, a cavalry skirmish ensued, favourable to the Romans, after which
Caesar led the army back to camp. After a repetition of the same action
on the morrow he thought enough had been done to reduce the bravado
of the Gauls and to establish the spirit of the troops, and he moved camp
accordingly into the territory of the Aedui. Even then the enemy did
not pursue; and on the third day he reached the river Allier, rebuilt the
bridge, and brought the army across to the other side.

[54] There he was greeted by Viridomarus and Eporedorix, the
Aeduans, from whom he learnt that Litaviccus with all his horse was
gone to rouse the Aedui, and that they themselves must be before him
in order to keep the state loyal. Caesar already had abundant evidence to
prove the treachery of the Aedui, and he believed that the departure of
these two served but to hasten a revolt of the state; however, he determined not to detain them, lest he might seem to be inflicting an injury
or affording some suspicion of fear. As they departed he set forth briefly
his own services to the Aedui: their position, their humiliations at the

time when he had received them—crowded into towns, deprived of fields, all their resources plundered, a tribute imposed, hostages wrung from them with the utmost insolence—the success and the distinction to which he had brought them, with the result that they had not only returned to their ancient position, but, to all appearance, had surpassed the dignity and influence of all previous ages. With these monitions he dismissed them from his presence.

[55] Noviodunum was a town of the Aedui situated in an advantageous position by the banks of the Loire. Here Caesar had concentrated all the hostages of Gaul, the corn, the state chest, and great part of his own and the army's baggage; hither he had sent a great number of horses purchased for this war in Italy and Spain. When Eporedorix and Viridomarus were come to the town they learnt how it was with the state. Litaviccus had been received by the Aedui at Bibracte, the town of supreme influence among them; the magistrate, Convictolitavis, and a great part of the senate had gone to join him; deputies had been despatched officially to Vercingetorix to secure peace and friendship. So signal an advantage should not, the two men thought, be forgone. So they put to the sword the troops on guard at Noviodunum and the traders who had gathered there, and divided the money and the horses between them; they caused the hostages of the states to be conducted to the magistrate at Bibracte. As they judged that they could not hold the town they set it on fire, that it might be of no service to the Romans; all the corn that they could handle at once they removed in boats, the rest they spoilt with fire and river-water. They began themselves to collect forces from the neighbouring districts, to post garrisons and piquets on the banks of the Loire, and to display horsemen everywhere in order to strike terror, in the hope that they might be able to cut the Romans off from their corn-supply, or to reduce them by scarcity and drive them out into the Province. In this hope they were much assisted by the fact that the Loire was so swollen after the snows that it appeared to be altogether unfordable.

[56] On learning this Caesar decided that he must make speed, if the completion of the bridges was to be adventured, in order to fight a decisive battle before larger forces had been collected at the river. As for changing his plan and turning his march into the Province, even apprehension did not seem to necessitate it: there was the shame and disgrace of the thing, as well as the barrier of the Cevennes and the difficulty of the roads, to prevent it, and more especially there was his pressing anxiety for Labienus and the legions which he had sent with him on a separate mission. Therefore he executed very long marches by day and night, and came, altogether unexpected, to the Loire; found by means of the cavalry a ford to suit the need of the case, where the troops could just keep arms and shoulders clear of the water, to hold up their weapons;

posted the cavalry at intervals to break the force of the stream, and brought the army safe across, as the enemy were put to confusion by the first sight of him. In the country he found corn and store of cattle, and as soon as these requirements of the army had been duly supplied he decided to march into the country of the Senones.

[57] While this was happening with Caesar, Labienus had left the draft of recruits newly arrived from Italy and Agedincum to guard the baggage, and with four legions started for Lutetia (Paris), a town of the Parisii, situated on an island in the river Seine. When the enemy had news of his coming a large force assembled from the neighbouring states. The chief command was entrusted to Camulogenus the Aulercan, who, though old and well-nigh worn out, was nevertheless singled out for the distinction because of his exceptional knowledge of warfare. He, noticing a continuous marsh which flowed into the Seine and greatly increased the difficulties of the whole locality, halted there and decided to prevent our troops from crossing.

[58] Labienus at first tried to move up mantlets, fill in the marsh with hurdles and earth, and build a roadway. When he found that task too difficult he silently marched out of camp in the third watch, and reached Metiosedum by the same route by which he had come. This is a town of the Senones, situated, as was said just now of Lutetia, on an island in the Seine. Seizing some fifty vessels and fastening them speedily together, he hurried his troops on board, and by the suddenness of the operation struck such terror into the townsfolk, of whom a great proportion had been called out for the war, that he gained possession of the town without a struggle. Repairing the bridge, which the enemy had cut down in the days preceding, he led the army across, and began to march down stream towards Lutetia. The enemy were told of it by refugees from Metiosedum. They ordered Lutetia to be set on fire and the bridges belonging to the town to be cut down, and advancing from the marsh to the banks of the Seine, they halted opposite Lutetia over against the camp of Labienus.

[59] By this time it came to be known that Caesar had withdrawn from Gergovia, and rumours began to be brought in touching the revolt of the Aedui and the successful rising in Gaul; and in conversation[29] the Gauls affirmed that Caesar's march and passage of the Loire had been blocked, and that scarcity of corn had compelled him to make for the Province with speed. The Bellovaci were disloyal in themselves before the revolt of the Aedui, and when they heard thereof they began to collect companies and openly to prepare for war. With the case so completely altered, Labienus perceived that he must adopt a course quite

---

[29] i.e. probably between Gallic cavalry, serving with the Romans, and their own countrymen.

different from his previous design, and he began now to consider the means, not of further acquisition or of provoking the enemy to fight, but of bringing the army safely back to Agedincum. For the Bellovaci, the state which has the greatest reputation for courage in Gaul, were pressing upon him from one side,[30] while the ground on the other was held by Camulogenus with an army regularly equipped and organized; and further, the legions were cut off from their baggage and its guard with a mighty river between. Confronted suddenly with these supreme difficulties, he saw that he must have recourse to personal courage.

[60] Towards evening he called together a council of war. Urging them to carry out his commands with care and energy, he assigned each of the vessels which he had brought down from Metiosedum to a Roman knight, and ordered them at the end of the first watch to proceed silently four miles down stream and there to await him. He left as garrison for the camp the five cohorts which he regarded as least steady for action; he commanded the remaining five of the same legion to start up stream at midnight with all the baggage, with great uproar. He got together small boats also, and despatched these in the same direction with great noise of oars in the rowing. A short time afterwards he himself marched out silently with three legions, and made for the spot where he had ordered the vessels to put in.

[61] Upon his arrival there the enemy's scouts, posted all along the river, were caught unawares by our men and overcome, owing to a great storm which had suddenly got up. The legions and the cavalry were speedily sent across under the direction of the Roman knights in charge of the business. At almost the same moment, just before daylight, it was reported to the enemy that in the Roman camp there was unusual uproar, that a large column was moving up stream, that the sound of oars was audible in the same quarter, and that a little way down stream troops were being carried across in boats. When they heard this they supposed that the legions were crossing at three places and that all were preparing for flight in the disorder caused by the revolt of the Aedui; so they, too, distributed their force in three divisions. A guard was left opposite the camp; a small company was sent towards Metiosedum, to advance as far as the vessels should have proceeded; the rest of the force they led against Labienus.

[62] By daybreak our own troops had all been carried across, and the enemy's line began to be seen. Labienus urged the troops to remember well their own courage in the past and the brilliant success of their battles, and to think that Caesar himself, under whose leadership they had often overcome the enemy, was present to see them; then he gave the

---

[30] i.e. on his rear from the north.

signal for action. At the first encounter on the right wing, where the Seventh Legion was posted, the enemy were driven back and put to rout; on the left, which was held by the Twelfth Legion, although the first ranks of the enemy had fallen pierced by the missiles, the remainder nevertheless resisted most stoutly, and not a man gave an inkling of flight. The leader of the enemy, Camulogenus, was present in person to urge on his men. The ultimate victory, however, was still uncertain; but when the tribunes of the Seventh Legion were told what was afoot on the left wing, they brought out their legion in rear of the enemy and attacked. Not even then did any man yield his ground, but all were surrounded and slain. Camulogenus met with the same fate. As for the detachment which had been left on guard over against the camp of Labienus, when they heard that the fight had begun they marched to the support of their comrades, and occupied a hill. But they could not withstand the attack of our victorious troops; and thus, as they became intermingled with their fugitive comrades, all who did not win the shelter of woods or heights were slain by the cavalry. Having finished this business, Labienus returned to Agedincum, where the baggage of the whole army had been left. Marching thence with all his force, he reached Caesar on the third day.

[63] When the revolt of the Aedui became known the war increased in extent. Deputations were sent round in all directions: with all the power of influence, authority, money, they strove to stir up the states, and having got possession of the hostages whom Caesar had lodged among them, they sought by the execution of these to terrify waverers. The Aedui requested Vercingetorix to come to them and concert plans for the conduct of the war. When their request was granted, they insisted that the supreme command should be assigned to them. The matter was disputed, and a convention of all Gaul was summoned at Bibracte. Thither assembled many persons from all quarters. The question was put to the vote of the host, and all to a man approved Vercingetorix as commander-in-chief. From this convention the Remi, Lingones, and Treveri were absent: the former two out of consideration for the friendship of Rome, the Treveri because they were too far distant and were hard pressed by the Germans, which was the reason why they took no part throughout the war and sent no succours to either side. The Aedui were greatly distressed at their rejection from the leadership, complaining of the change in their fortune and feeling the loss of Caesar's kindness towards them; but nevertheless, having undertaken the campaign, they durst not part counsel from the rest. Unwillingly, for they were young and very ambitious, Eporedorix and Viridomarus obeyed Vercingetorix.

[64] He for his part made requisition of hostages from the other states, and appointed a day for the same, ordering all the horsemen, to the number of fifteen thousand, to assemble with speed. He said that he would

be content with the footmen that he had beforehand, as he did not purpose to try his fortune or fight a pitched battle; but, as he had abundance
of horsemen, it was easy enough to prevent the Romans from getting
corn and forage. Only, the Gauls must consent to destroy with their own
hands their corn-supplies and burn their buildings, seeing that by such
loss of property they were acquiring dominion and liberty for all time.
When he had made these arrangements he required of the Aedui and
the Segusiavi, who are neighbours of the Province, ten thousand foot-
soldiers; to this total he added eight hundred horsemen. He set the brother
of Eporedorix in command of them, and ordered them to make war on
the Allobroges. On the other side he sent the Gabali and the cantons of
the Arverni next them against the Helvii, and likewise the Ruteni and
Cadurci to devastate the borders of the Volcae Arecomici. At the same
time, by secret messages and deputations, he sought to rouse the Allobroges,
hoping that their temper had not yet settled down after the late war.[31]
To their chiefs he promised sums of money, to their state the dominion
over the whole Province.

[65] To meet all these emergencies there had been provided contingents to the number of two-and-twenty cohorts, drafted from the whole
Province by Lucius Caesar, lieutenant-general, and now set to oppose the
enemy at all points. The Helvii of their own motion joined battle with
their neighbours, and were repulsed; the chief of their state, Gaius
Valerius Donnotaurus, son of Caburus, and several others were slain, and
they were shut up within the walls of their towns. The Allobroges posted
numerous detachments at intervals along the Rhone and protected their
borders with great care and efficiency. Caesar was aware that the enemy
were superior in mounted troops and that, as all the lines of communi-
cation were interrupted, he could in no wise be assisted from the
Province and from Italy; accordingly, he sent across the Rhine into
Germany to the states which he had reduced to peace in previous years,
and fetched horsemen from them and light-armed infantry trained to
fight along with the horsemen. On their arrival he found that the horses
they were using were unsuitable, and therefore he took the horses from
the military tribunes and the rest of the Roman knights and the re-
enlisted veterans, and distributed them among the Germans.

[66] In the meanwhile the enemy's contingent from the Arverni and the
horsemen requisitioned from the whole of Gaul were assembling. While
Caesar was marching to the country of the Sequani across the outermost
borders of the Lingones, so as to be able to lend support more easily to the
Province, Vercingetorix got together a great number of these contingents

---

[31] 61 B.C.

and established himself in three camps about ten miles from the Romans. He called the cavalry commanders together to a council of war, and stated that the hour of victory was come. The Romans were fleeing to the Province and leaving Gaul. In his opinion that was enough to secure a temporary liberty, but it was too small a gain to give peace and quiet for the future; for they would return when they had collected a large force and would make no end of the war. Therefore, the Gauls must attack them while encumbered with baggage in column of route; then, if the legionaries hung back to give support to their comrades, they could not pursue the march; if, as he felt sure was more likely to happen, they left the baggage and looked to their own safety, they would be stripped at once of necessaries and of reputation. For, as touching the enemy's cavalry, they themselves,[32] at any rate, ought to have no doubt that not a man of them would dare even to advance beyond the column; and further, to make the commanders act with more spirit, he would have all his force paraded in front of the camp and strike terror into the enemy. The horsemen shouted with one accord that they should be bound by a most solemn oath—that no man should be received beneath a roof, nor have access to children, or to parents, or to wife, who had not twice ridden through the enemy's column.

[67] This was approved, and all were sworn, and on the morrow the horsemen were divided into three detachments. Two, in battle array, made a demonstration on the two flanks, and one began to hinder the march at the head of the column. On report of this Caesar divided his own cavalry likewise into three, and ordered it to advance against the enemy. The battle began simultaneously in every quarter. The column halted, and the baggage was drawn back inside the legions. At any point where our troops seemed to be distressed or too hard pressed Caesar would order the standards to advance and line of battle to be formed. This served to check the enemy in pursuit and to encourage our troops by hope of succour. At length the Germans on the right flank gained the top of a ridge and dislodged the enemy, drove them headlong as far as the river, where Vercingetorix had halted with the footmen of his force, and slew not a few. The rest remarked this and, fearing they might be surrounded, betook themselves to flight. Everywhere slaughter ensued. Three Aeduans of distinguished rank were captured and brought to Caesar. They were Cotus, a commander of horse, who had had the quarrel with Convictolitavis at the last election; Cavarillus, who after the revolt of Litaviccus had commanded the footmen of the force; and

---

[32] The Gallic cavalry commanders. Vercingetorix tells them that *they* have no right or reason to doubt; and that *he* will make assurance doubly sure by parading the forces.

Eporedorix, under whose leadership before the coming of Caesar the
Aedui had fought a campaign with the Sequani.

[68] When all the horsemen had been put to flight Vercingetorix
drew his forces back from their position in front of the camps and at once
began the march to Alesia, a town of the Mandubii, ordering the baggage to be brought speedily out of camp and to follow close after him.
Caesar withdrew his baggage to the nearest hill and, leaving two legions
to guard it, pursued as long as daylight allowed. Some three thousand of
the enemy's rearguard were slain, and on the next day he pitched camp
near Alesia. He reconnoitred the situation of the city, and as the enemy
were terror-struck by the rout of their horsemen, the branch of their
army on which they most relied, he urged his soldiers to the task and
began the investment.

[69] The actual stronghold of Alesia[33] was set atop of a hill, in a very
lofty situation, apparently impregnable save by blockade. The bases of the
hill were washed on two separate sides by rivers. Before the town a plain
extended for a length of about three miles; on all the other sides there
were hills surrounding the town at a short distance, and equal to it in
height. Under the wall, on the side which looked eastward, the forces of
the Gauls had entirely occupied all this intervening space, and had made
in front a ditch and a rough wall six feet high. The perimeter of the
siege-works which the Romans were beginning had a length of eleven
miles. Camps had been pitched at convenient spots, and three-and-
twenty forts had been constructed on the line. In these piquets would be
posted by day to prevent any sudden sortie; by night the same stations
were held by sentries and strong garrisons.

[70] When the siege-work had been started, a cavalry encounter took
place in the plain which we have described above as set between hills and
extending to a length of three miles. Both sides strove with the utmost
vigour. When our men were distressed Caesar sent up the Germans, and
posted the legions in front of the camp to prevent any sudden inrush on
the part of the enemy's footmen. With the reinforcement of the legions
behind them our men's spirit was increased; the enemy were put to flight,
and, hampering one another by sheer numbers, as the gates were left too
narrow, were crowded together in a press. The Germans pursued most
vigorously right up to the fortifications.[34] A great slaughter ensued; some
of the enemy abandoned their horses, and tried to cross the ditch and
scale the wall. Caesar ordered the legions posted in front of the rampart
to advance a short distance. The Gauls inside the fortifications were in

---

[33] For the operations at Alesia see the plan, page 148.
[34] i.e. the ditch and wall mentioned in ch. 69.

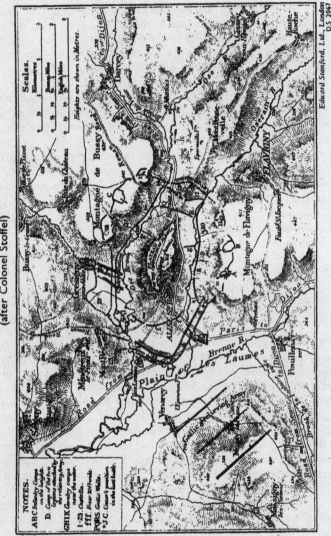

PLAN OF ALESIA
(after Colonel Stoffel)

NOTES.
ABC Infantry Camps on the Heights.
D. Camp of Our two Legions attacked by the relieving Army.
GHIK Cavalry camps near the same.
1-23. Castella.
fff. Four 20 ft. walls.
PQRS Great Walls.
•J.C. Caesar's position in the last battle.

Scales.
Heights are shown in Metres.

Edward Stanford, Ltd., London.
D.S. 2067

just as great a confusion as the rest; believing that the enemy were coming on them at once, they shouted the call to arms, and some in panic burst into the town. Vercingetorix ordered the gates to be shut, lest the camp should be deserted. After much slaughter and the capture of many horses the Germans retired.

[71] Vercingetorix now made up his mind to send away all his horsemen by night, before the Romans could complete their entrenchments. His parting instructions were that each of them should proceed to his own state and impress for the campaign all men whose age allowed them to bear arms. He set forth his own claims upon them, and adjured them to have regard for his personal safety, and not to surrender to the torture of the enemy one who had done sterling service for the general liberty. He showed them that if they proved indifferent eighty thousand chosen men were doomed to perish with him. He had calculated that he had corn in short rations for thirty days, but that by economy he could hold out just a little longer. After giving these instructions he sent the horsemen silently away in the second watch, at a point where a gap was left in our works. He ordered all the corn to be brought in to his headquarters; he appointed death as the penalty for any disobedience of the order; the cattle, of which great store had been driven together by the Mandubii, he distributed man by man; he arranged that the corn should be measured out sparingly and gradually; he withdrew into the town all the force which he had posted in front of it. By such measures did he prepare for the conduct of the campaign, in anticipation of the succours from Gaul.

[72] Caesar had report of this from deserters and prisoners, and determined on the following types of entrenchments.[35] He dug a trench twenty feet wide with perpendicular sides, in such fashion that the bottom thereof was just as broad as the distance from edge to edge at the surface. He set back the rest of the siege-works four hundred paces from the trench; for as he had of necessity included so large an area, and the whole of the works could not easily be manned by a ring-fence of troops, his intention was to provide against any sudden rush of the enemy's host by night upon the entrenchments, or any chance of directing their missiles by day upon our troops engaged on the works. Behind this interval he dug all round two trenches, fifteen feet broad and of equal depth; and the inner one, where the ground was level with the plain or sank below it, he filled with water diverted from the river. Behind the trenches he constructed a ramp and palisade[36] twelve feet high; to this he

---

[35] See diagrams on page 151.
[36] Probably the two words form one idea, a ramp revetted with palisades.

added a breastwork and battlements, with large fraises[37] projecting at the junctions of screens[38] and ramp, to check the upward advance of the enemy; and all round the works he set turrets at intervals of eighty feet.

[73] As it was necessary that at one and the same time timber and corn should be procured, and lines of such extent constructed, our forces, having to proceed to a considerable distance from camp, were reduced in number; and sometimes the Gauls would try to make an attempt upon our works by a sortie in force from several gates of the town. Caesar, therefore, thought proper to make a further addition to these works, in order that the lines might be defensible by a smaller number of troops. Accordingly, trunks or very stout branches of trees were cut, and the tops thereof barked and sharpened, and continuous trenches five feet deep were dug. Into these the stumps were sunk and fastened at the bottom so that they could not be torn up, while the bough-ends were left projecting. They were in rows of five fastened and entangled together, and anyone who pushed into them must impale himself on the sharpest of stakes. These they called "markers."[39] In front of these, in diagonal rows arranged like a figure of five,[40] pits three feet deep were dug, sloping inwards slightly to the bottom. In these, tapering stakes as thick as a man's thigh, sharpened at the top and fire-hardened, were sunk so as to project no more than four fingers' breadth from the ground; at the same time, to make all strong and firm, the earth was trodden down hard for one foot from the bottom, and the remainder of the pit was covered over with twigs and brushwood to conceal the trap. Eight rows of this kind were dug, three feet apart. From its resemblance to the flower the device was called a "lily." In front of all these, logs a foot long, with iron hooks firmly attached, were buried altogether in the ground and scattered at brief intervals all over the field, and these they called "spurs."

[74] When all these arrangements had been completed Caesar constructed parallel entrenchments of the same kind facing the other way, against the enemy outside, following the most favourable ground that the locality afforded, with a circuit of fourteen miles. This he did to secure the garrisons of the entrenchments from being surrounded by a host, however large it might chance to be. And in order that he might not be constrained to dangerous excursions from camp, he ordered all his men to have thirty days' corn and forage collected.

[75] While this was proceeding about Alesia, the Gauls summoned a

---

[37] i.e. pointed stakes projecting horizontally—a sort of *chevaux-de-frise*.

[38] The wooden hoarding which formed the breastwork on the top of the ramp.

[39] The word *cippus* means both a boundary-stone and a tombstone, and its use here probably represents a rough jest of the Roman soldiers.

[40] A *quincunx*, ∶·∶

# ROMAN SIEGE APPLIANCES

VINEA, mantlet: the sides were covered with
skins or wickerwork when required.

The TESTUDO was similar to the VINEA, but
squarer and more stoutly built, with a sloping
roof or shutter on the side next the enemy's
walls: it was covered over with hides or other
non-inflammable substances.

The MUSCULUS was longer, lower, and narrower
than the VINEA, forming a covered gallery,
pushed up at right angles to the enemy's wall.

PLUTEUS, a screen of wickerwork on wheels,
generally semicylindrical in form.

## ROMAN WORKS AT ALESIA (VII. 72, 73.) (*After Colonel Stoffel*)

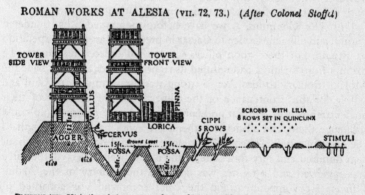

PLUTEUS (VII. 73) is the whole screen made up of LORICA with PINNAE, with VALLUS behind.

council of chiefs and determined not to call up (according to the proposal of Vercingetorix) all who could bear arms, but to require of each
chief a certain quota from his state; for they feared that with so large a
host herded together they might not be able to preserve discipline, to dis-
tinguish their several contingents, or to secure a supply of corn. Of the
Aedui and their dependents, Segusiavi, Ambivareti, Aulerci Brannovices,
and Blannovii, they required five-and-thirty thousand; an equal number
from the Arverni, together with the Eleuteti, Cadurci, Gabali, and
Vellavii, who are regularly under the sovereignty of the Arverni; from the
Sequani, Senones, Bituriges, Santoni, Ruteni, and Carnutes, twelve thousand each; from the Bellovaci ten thousand, and as many from the
Lemovices; eight thousand each from the Pictones, Turoni, Parisii, and
Helvetii; five thousand each from the Suessiones, Ambiani,
Mediomatrici, Petrocorii, Nervii, Morini, and Nitiobriges; a like number
from the Aulerci Cenomani; four thousand from the Atrebates; three
each from the Veliocasses, Lexovii, and Aulerci Eburovices; two each from
the Rauraci and the Boii; thirty thousand in all from the states touching
the Ocean, commonly called by them Armoric, among whom are the
Curiosolites, Redones, Ambibarii, Caletes, Osismi, Veneti, Lemovices,
and Venelli. Of these the Bellovaci did not make up their quota, because
they declared that they would wage war with the Romans on their own
account and at their own direction, and would obey no man's command;
however, when Commius made request they sent two thousand men
with the rest, out of regard to their private relations with him.

[76] This Commius, as we have before mentioned,[41] had rendered
faithful and efficient service to Caesar in previous years in the expedition
to Britain. For these good offices Caesar had ordered his state to be
exempt from taxation, had restored its rights and laws, and had made the
Morini tributary to him. Yet so strong was the unanimity of Gaul as a
whole for the maintenance of their liberty and the recovery of their
ancient renown in war that no benefits, no memory of friendship could
influence them, and all devoted themselves with heart and strength to
the campaign before them. When eight thousand horsemen and about
two hundred and fifty thousand footmen had been collected, the force
was reviewed and a muster was taken in the country of the Aedui.
Officers were appointed, and the chief command was entrusted to
Commius the Atrebatian, Viridomarus and Eporedorix the Aeduans,
and Vercassivellaunus the Arvernian, a cousin of Vercingetorix. To them
were attached a staff selected from the states, by whose counsel the campaign was to be conducted. Full of spirit and confidence, all started for

---

[41] IV. 21, 35; V. 22.

Alesia; there was not a man of them all who thought the mere sight of so vast a host could be withstood, especially in a two-sided engagement, when there would be fighting with those who made a sortie from within the town, and outside the display of so vast an army of horse and foot.

[77] However, when the day on which they had expected reinforcements of their own folk was past, and they had exhausted all their corn, and knew not what was going on in the land of the Aedui, the Gauls besieged in Alesia called a council of war to consider what would be the issue of their own fortunes. Various opinions were expressed, one party voting for surrender, another for a sortie while their strength sufficed: but the speech of Critognatus should not, I think, be omitted, because of its remarkable and abominable cruelty. He was of high lineage among the Arverni, and considered to have great influence. "Of their opinion," he said, "who call a most disgraceful slavery by the name of surrender I purpose to say nothing; I hold that they should not be treated as citizens nor invited to the council. Let *my* business be with those who approve a sortie; and in their design, by your general agreement, there seems to remain a memory of ancient courage. This is faint-heartedness of yours, not courage, to be unable to endure want for a short space. It is easier to find men to fling themselves recklessly on death than men to endure pain patiently. And yet I might now have approved this view (so much weight with me has the authority of those who hold it) if I saw therein the loss of nothing but our life; but in making our decision we should have regard to the whole of Gaul, which we have aroused to our assistance. What, think ye, will be the spirit of our friends and kindred, when eighty thousand men[42] have been slain in one spot, if they are forced to fight out the issue almost over their very bodies? Refuse to rob of your support the men who for your deliverance have disregarded their own peril; forbear by folly, recklessness, or weak-mindedness of yours to lay prostrate, and subject to everlasting slavery, the whole of Gaul. Or do you doubt their faithfulness, their resolution, because they are not arrived to the day? What then? Do ye think that the Romans are daily engaged in those outer trenches for mere amusement? If it may not be that your resolve should be strengthened by messages from your friends, since every approach is blocked, yet take the Romans here to your witnesses that their coming draws nigh; and it is in fear thereof that they are busy in their works day and night. What, then, is my counsel? To do what our forefathers did in the war, in no wise equal to this, with the Cimbri and Teutones. They shut themselves into the towns, and under stress of a like scarcity sustained life on the bodies of those whose age showed them useless for war, and delivered not themselves to the enemy. And if we had not had a prece-

---

[42] *Cf.* ch. 71.

dent for this, I should still have judged it a most glorious thing for the sake of liberty to set such a one and to hand it down to posterity. For wherein was that war like this? The Cimbri devastated Gaul, they brought great disaster upon us, yet they departed at length from our borders and sought other countries, leaving us our rights, laws, lands, liberty. But the Romans—what else do they seek or desire than to follow where envy leads, to settle in the lands and states of men whose noble report and martial strength they have learnt, and to bind upon them a perpetual slavery? 'Tis in no other fashion they have waged wars. And if ye know not what is afoot among distant nations, look now on Gaul close at hand, which has been reduced to a province, with utter change of rights and laws, and crushed beneath the axes[43] in everlasting slavery."

[78] When opinions had been expressed they determined that those who by reason of health or age were useless for war should leave the town, and that every expedient should be tried before they had recourse to the counsel of Critognatus, resolving, however, to adopt that plan, if compelled by circumstances—that is to say, the delay of the reinforcements—rather than to submit to terms of surrender or of peace. The Mandubii, whose town had received them, were compelled to leave it with wives and children. When they reached the Roman lines they begged with tears and abject prayers to be received as slaves and helped with food. But Caesar posted sentries on the rampart and prevented their admission.

[79] Meanwhile Commius and the other leaders entrusted with the supreme command reached the neighbourhood of Alesia with all their force, and, seizing a hill outside,[44] halted not more than a mile from our entrenchments. The day after they brought their horsemen out of camp and filled the whole of that plain which we have described as extending for a length of three miles; their force of footmen they posted a little way back from the spot, on the higher ground. There was a bird's-eye view from the town of Alesia over the plain. At sight of these reinforcements the others hastened together with mutual congratulation, and all minds were stirred to joy. So they brought out their force and halted in front of the town; they covered over the nearest trench[45] with hurdles and filled it in with earth, and prepared for a sally and for every emergency.

[80] Caesar disposed the whole army on both faces of the entrenchments in such fashion that, if occasion should arise, each man could know and keep his proper station; then he ordered the cavalry to be brought out of camp and to engage. There was a view down from all the

---

[43] *i.e.* of the Roman lictors.
[44] On the S. W. of Alesia.
[45] The Roman trench on the W. of Alesia mentioned at the beginning of ch. 72.

camps, which occupied the top of the surrounding ridge, and all the troops were intently awaiting the issue of the fight. The Gauls had placed archers and light-armed skirmishers here and there among the horsemen to give immediate support to their comrades if driven back and to resist the charge of our cavalry. A number of men, wounded unexpectedly by these troops, began to withdraw from the fight. When the Gauls were confident that their own men were getting the better of the battle, and saw ours hard pressed by numbers, with shouts and yells on every side—those who were confined by the entrenchments as well as the others who had come up to their assistance—they sought to inspirit their countrymen. As the action was proceeding in sight of all, and no deed, of honour or dishonour, could escape notice, both sides were stirred to courage by desire of praise and fear of disgrace. The fight lasted, and the victory was doubtful, from noon almost to sunset; then the Germans in one part of the field massed their troops of horse, charged the enemy and routed them, and when they had been put to flight the archers were surrounded and slain. Likewise, from the other parts of the field, our troops pursued the retreating enemy right up to their camp, giving them no chance of rallying. But the Gauls who had come forth from Alesia, almost despairing of victory, sadly withdrew again into the town.

[81] After one day's interval, in the course of which they made a great number of hurdles, ladders, and grappling-hooks, the Gauls left camp silently at midnight and approached the entrenchments in the plain. Raising a sudden shout, to signify their coming to the besieged inside the town, they began to fling down the hurdles,[46] to dislodge our men from the rampart with slings, arrows, and stones, and to carry out everything else proper to an assault. At the same moment, hearing the shout, Vercingetorix gave his troops the signal by trumpet, and led them out of the town. Our troops, as on previous days, moved each to his appointed station in the entrenchments; with slings, one-pounders,[47] stakes set ready inside the works, and bullets,[48] they beat off the Gauls. As the darkness made it impossible to see far, many wounds were received on both sides.[49] A number of missiles were discharged by the artillery. Then Marcus Antonius and Gaius Trebonius, the lieutenant-generals to whom the defence of these sections had been allot-

---

[46] Into the trenches.

[47] Stones of a pound weight hurled by engines; or it is possible that the meaning here is: "with one-pounder slings."

[48] For use in slings.

[49] The general sequence is rather obscure. The missiles (of which many were discharged by the Roman artillery) flew more or less at venture, in the dark: casualties were numerous, but indecisive. But Antonius and Trebonius anticipated more serious fighting, and had reinforcements ready.

ted, withdrew troops from forts farther away, and sent them up to bring assistance wherever they remarked that our men were hard pressed.

[82] While the Gauls were some distance from the entrenchment they had more advantage from the quantity of their missiles; then, when they came up closer, they were soon caught unawares on the "spurs," or they sank into the pits and were impaled, or they were shot by artillery pikes[50] from the rampart and the turrets, and so perished on every side. Many a man was wounded, but the entrenchment was nowhere penetrated; and when daybreak drew nigh, fearing that they might be surrounded on their exposed flank by a sortie from the camps above them,[51] they retired to their comrades. Meanwhile the inner force brought out the appliances which had been prepared by Vercingetorix for a sortie, and filled in the nearer trenches;[52] but they lingered too long in the execution of the business, and, or ever they could get near the entrenchments, they learnt that their countrymen had withdrawn. So without success they returned to the town.

[83] Twice beaten back with great loss, the Gauls took counsel what to do. They called in men who knew the locality well, and from them they learnt the positions and the defences of the upper camps. On the north side there was a hill, which by reason of its huge circumference our troops had been unable to include within the works; they had been obliged to lay out the camp on the ground gently sloping, which put them almost at a disadvantage. This camp was held by Gaius Antistius Reginus and Gaius Caninius Rebilus, lieutenant-generals, with two legions. Having reconnoitred the locality by means of scouts, the commanders of the enemy chose out of the whole host sixty thousand men belonging to the states which had the greatest reputation for courage: they determined secretly together what should be done and in what fashion, and decided that the advance should take place at the moment when it was seen to be midday. In charge of this force they put Vercassivellaunus the Arvernian, one of the four commanders, a kinsman of Vercingetorix. He left camp in the first watch, and having almost completed his march just before dawn, he concealed himself behind the height and ordered his soldiers to rest after their night's work. When at last it was seen to be near midday he moved with speed on the camp above mentioned and at the same moment the horsemen began to advance towards the entrenchments in the plain, and the rest of the force to make a demonstration before the camp.

[84] When from the citadel of Alesia Vercingetorix observed his

---

[50] Heavy pikes fired from *ballistae* in wall or trench fighting.

[51] One of the main camps of the Roman legions, here referred to, lay on a height to the southward of Alesia: the other (referred to in ch. 83) on a height to the northward.

[52] See note 45, page 154.

countrymen, he moved out of the town, taking with him the hurdles, poles, mantlets, grappling-hooks, and all the other appliances prepared for the sally. The fight went on simultaneously in all places, and all expedients were attempted, with a rapid concentration on that section which was seen to be least strong. With lines so extensive the Roman army was strung out, and at several points defence proved difficult. The shouting which arose in rear of the fighting line did much to scare our troops, as they saw that the risk to themselves depended on the success of others;[53] for, as a rule, what is out of sight disturbs men's minds more seriously than what they see.

[85] Caesar found a suitable spot from which he could see what was proceeding in each quarter. To parties distressed he sent up supports. Both sides felt that this was the hour of all others in which it was proper to make their greatest effort. The Gauls utterly despaired of safety unless they could break through the lines; the Romans anticipated an end of all toils if they could hold their own. The hardest struggle occurred by the entrenchments on the hill, whither, as we have mentioned, Vercassivellaunus had been sent. The unfavourable downward slope of the ground had great effect. Some of the enemy discharged missiles, others moved up in close formation[54] under their shields; fresh men quickly replaced the exhausted. Earth cast by the whole body together over the entrenchments gave the Gauls a means of ascent and at the same time covered over the appliances which the Romans had concealed in the ground; and our troops had now neither arms nor strength enough.

[86] When Caesar learnt this, he sent Labienus with six cohorts to support them in their distress. He commanded him, if he could not hold his ground, to draw in the cohorts and fight his way out, but not to do so unless of necessity. He himself went up to the rest of the troops, and urged them not to give in to the strain, telling them that the fruit of all previous engagements depended upon that day and hour. The enemy on the inner side, despairing of success on the level ground, because of the size of the entrenchments, made an attempt to scale the precipitous parts, conveying thither the appliances they had prepared. They dislodged the defenders of the turrets by a swarm of missiles, filled in the trenches with earth and hurdles, tore down rampart and breastwork with grappling-hooks.

[87] Caesar first sent young Brutus with some cohorts, and then Gaius Fabius, lieutenant-general, with others; last of all, as the fight raged more fiercely, he himself brought up fresh troops to reinforce. The battle restored,

---

[53] *i.e.* that, if the line were broken elsewhere, they themselves would be in peril.

[54] In "tortoise" formation. See note 4, page 30.

and the enemy repulsed, he hastened to the quarter whither he had sent Labienus. He withdrew four cohorts from the nearest fort, and ordered part of the cavalry to follow him, part to go round the outer entrenchments and attack the enemy in rear. Labienus, finding that neither ramps nor trenches could resist the rush of the enemy, collected together forty cohorts, which had been withdrawn from the nearest posts and by chance presented themselves, and sent messengers to inform Caesar what he thought it proper to do. Caesar hurried on to take part in the action.

[88] His coming was known by the colour of his cloak,[55] which it was his habit to wear in action as a distinguishing mark; and the troops of cavalry and the cohorts which he had ordered to follow him were noticed, because from the upper levels these downward slopes and depressions were visible. Thereupon the enemy joined battle: a shout was raised on both sides, and taken up by an answering shout from the rampart and the whole of the entrenchments. Our troops discarded their pikes and got to work with their swords. Suddenly the cavalry was noticed in the rear; other cohorts drew near. The enemy turned to flee; the cavalry met them in flight, and a great slaughter ensued. Sedulius, commander and chief of the Lemovices, was killed; Vercassivellaunus the Arvernian was captured alive in the rout; seventy-four war-standards were brought in to Caesar; of the vast host few returned safe to camp. The others beheld from the town the slaughter and rout of their countrymen, and, in despair of safety, recalled their force from the entrenchments. Directly they heard what had happened the Gauls fled from their camp. And if the troops had not been worn out by frequent reinforcing and the whole day's effort, the entire force of the enemy could have been destroyed. The cavalry were sent off just after midnight and caught up the rearguard: a great number were taken and slain, the rest fled away into the different states.

[89] On the morrow Vercingetorix summoned a council, at which he stated that he had undertaken that campaign, not for his own occasions, but for the general liberty; and as they must yield to fortune he offered himself to them for whichever course they pleased—to give satisfaction to the Romans by his death, or to deliver him alive. Deputies were despatched to Caesar to treat of this matter. He ordered the arms to be delivered up, the chiefs to be brought out. He himself took his seat in the entrenchments in front of the camp: the leaders were brought out to him there. Vercingetorix was surrendered, arms were thrown down. Keeping back the Aedui and the Arverni, to see if through them he could recover their states, he distributed the rest of the prisoners, one apiece to each man throughout the army, by way of plunder.

---

[55] He wore the scarlet cloak *(paludamentum)* of a commander-in-chief.

[90] When these affairs were settled he started for the country of the Aedui and recovered the state. The Arverni sent deputies to him there who promised to carry out his commands: he required of them a great number of hostages. He sent the legions into cantonments. He restored some twenty thousand prisoners to the Aedui and the Arverni. He ordered Titus Labienus with two legions and cavalry to march off into the country of the Sequani, attaching Marcus Sempronius Rutilus to him. Gaius Fabius, the lieutenant-general, and Lucius Minucius Basilus he stationed with two legions in the country of the Remi, in order that they might suffer no damage from the neighbouring Bellovaci. Gaius Antistius Reginus he sent into the territory of the Ambivareti, Titus Sextius to the Bituriges, Gaius Caninius Rebilus to the Ruteni, with a legion apiece. Quintus Tullius Cicero and Publius Sulpicius he stationed at Cabillonum and Matisco, Aeduan towns near the Arar, to secure the corn-supply. He himself decided to winter at Bibracte. When the despatches of the campaign were published at Rome a public thanksgiving of twenty days was granted.

# BOOK VIII

*This book is the work of Aulus Hirtius, Consul with C. Vibius Pansa in 43 B.C.;*
*both fell in action that year, fighting against M. Antonius under the walls of*
*Mutina. A. Hirtius explains in his Preface here what is his purpose in adding an*
*eighth book to the seven of Caesar's commentaries.*

By your continual reproaches, Balbus,[1] which seemed to regard my daily
refusal not as a plea caused by difficulty, but as an evasion due to indo-
lence, I have been constrained to undertake a most difficult task. I have
tacked a supplement to the Commentaries of our great Caesar on the
operations in Gaul, as his previous and his subsequent writings did not
otherwise fit together; and his last work,[2] which was left unfinished from
the operations at Alexandria[3] onwards, I have completed as far as the
conclusion, not indeed of civil discord, of which we see no end, but of
Caesar's life. And I trust that those who will read it may understand how
unwillingly I have undertaken the task of writing this Commentary; for
so shall I the easier free myself from the charge of folly and of presumption for having intruded myself in the middle of Caesar's writings. For it
is universally agreed that nothing was ever so elaborately finished by others that is not surpassed by the refinement of these Commentaries. They
have been published that historians may not lack knowledge of those
great achievements; and so strong is the unanimous verdict of approval as
to make it appear that historians have been robbed of an opportunity
rather than enriched with one. Yet herein is our own admiration greater
than all other men's; the world knows how excellently, how faultlessly,

---

[1] Lucius Cornelius Balbus, a Spaniard from Gades, received the Roman citizenship from
Caesar, served as Caesar's *praefectus fabrum* (chief engineer) in Spain in 61 B.C., and
became afterwards Caesar's chief man of business. He was Consul in 40 B.C., the first for-
eigner to attain that distinction.
[2] i.e. the *de Bello Civili*.
[3] 48 and 47 B.C.

but we know also how easily, how speedily he completed his Commentaries. Caesar possessed not only the greatest facility and refinement of style, but also the surest skill in explaining his own plans. For myself, I had not the fortune ever to take part in the Alexandrian and the African campaign. It is true that those campaigns are partially known to me from the conversation of Caesar; but we listen in different fashion to events which fascinate us by their wonderful novelty, and to events which we are to state in evidence. Yet I doubt not that, in collecting every plea to excuse myself from comparison with Caesar, I incur a charge of presumption for imagining that there is anyone in whose judgment I can be set beside Caesar. Farewell.

[1] The whole of Gaul was now subdued, and Caesar, having been continuously engaged in war since the previous summer, desired to refresh his troops with a rest in cantonments after their great exertions. Reports came, however, that several states at once were considering fresh plans of campaign and forming conspiracies. The reason suggested for this movement was probable. All the Gauls, it was said, were aware that, on the one hand, it was impossible to make a stand against the Romans by the concentration of any number of men in one place, and that, on the other, if a number of states attacked them in separate places at the same time, the army of Rome was not likely to have strength or time or troops enough to deal with everything. Wherefore it was not proper for a particular state to refuse any trouble that might befall, if by such a respite the remainder could reclaim their liberty.

[2] Caesar did not wish to encourage the Gauls in this opinion: he therefore put Marcus Antonius, his quartermaster-general, in command of his own cantonments, and on the last day of December marched off himself, with an escort of cavalry, from the town of Bibracte to the quarters of the Thirteenth Legion, stationed in the country of the Bituriges not far from that of the Aedui, and he brigaded with it the Eleventh Legion, its next neighbour. Leaving two cohorts of each to guard the baggage, he led the rest of the army into the most fertile districts of the Bituriges, since, being the possessors of broad territories and numerous strongholds, they had proved more than a single legion in cantonments could restrain from warlike preparations and conspiracies.

[3] The sudden coming of Caesar brought the inevitable consequence on a folk dispersed and unprepared. They were tilling their farms without the least fear, and they were caught by the cavalry before they could flee for refuge into the strongholds. For even the ordinary sign of a hostile inroad (which is usually perceived by the wholesale burning of farm-buildings) had been omitted by Caesar's command, in order that his supply of forage and corn might not run short if he should wish to

advance further, nor the enemy be frightened by the conflagrations. The capture of many thousand persons struck terror into the Bituriges; and those who had been able in the first instance to escape from the coming of the Romans had fled for refuge into neighbouring states, trusting either to private relations or to political sympathy. In vain; for by means of forced marches Caesar appeared in every corner, giving no state a chance of thought for another's safety rather than for its own; and by this rapidity of action he contrived at once to keep friends loyal and to bring doubters by intimidation to terms of peace. The Bituriges saw that the clemency of Caesar opened the way for a return to his friendship, and that neighbouring states, without punishment of any kind, had given hostages and had been readmitted to protection; and the chance of such terms induced them to do likewise.

[4] In spite of winter days, the most difficult of marches, and cold weather beyond endurance, the troops had stuck most zealously to their work, and in reward for such effort and hardship Caesar promised them two hundred sesterces apiece, and as many thousand to each centurion, as a free gift in lieu of booty. Then he sent the legions back to cantonments, and himself returned on the fortieth day to Bibracte. While he was administering justice there the Bituriges sent deputies to him to seek help against the Carnutes who, as they complained, had made war upon them. On report of this, after a halt of no more than eighteen days in cantonments, he marched the Fourteenth and Sixth Legions from their cantonments on the Saône (these legions, as mentioned in the previous book of the Commentaries,[4] he had stationed there to keep the corn-supply clear); then, with the two legions, he started to punish the Carnutes.

[5] When report of the army reached the enemy, the influence of the disaster which had befallen the rest made itself felt. The Carnutes forsook the villages and the strongholds—in which they were living for protection against the winter, in mean buildings erected hastily to meet their need, for after their recent defeat[5] they had abandoned many of their strongholds—and fled in all directions. Caesar was unwilling that his troops should be subjected to the storms which break out in especial vehemence just at that time; so he pitched camp at Cenabum, the town of the Carnutes, and crowded the men partly into the dwellings of the Gauls, partly into huts built on to them with the thatch hastily collected for roofing the tents in winter. The cavalry, however, and auxiliary infantry were sent in all directions which the enemy were said to have taken, and not in vain, for as a rule our men returned with great store of

[4] VII. 90.
[5] See VII. 15.

booty. The Carnutes were overcome by the distress of winter and the fear of danger; they were driven out of their homes and durst make no no long stay in any place; nor when the storms were most severe could they get shelter in the protection of the woods. So they scattered abroad and dispersed among the neighbouring states, with the loss of a great part of their own folk.

[6] It was now the most troublesome season of the year, and Caesar, deeming it sufficient to scatter bands that were assembling so as to prevent any new outbreak of war, and feeling sure, so far as could reasonably be reckoned, that no war of first-rate importance could be stirred up until the summer season, stationed Gaius Trebonius, with the two legions of his own command, in cantonments at Cenabum. By frequent deputations from the Remi he was receiving information that the Bellovaci (who surpassed all the Gauls and Belgae in renown of war) and the neighbouring states were preparing armies under the leadership of Correus of the Bellovaci and Commius of the Atrebates, and concentrating the same. Their object was to make an incursion with all their host into the country of the Suessiones, who were tributaries of the Remi; and as Caesar deemed it important not only to his honour, but even to his security, that no disaster should come upon allies who had deserved exceedingly well of the Republic, he again called out the Eleventh Legion from cantonments. Further, he sent a despatch to Gaius Fabius bidding him bring his two legions into the country of the Suessiones, and summoned one of the two legions with Titus Labienus. Thus, so far as the situation of the cantonments allowed, and the tactics of the campaign required, he contrived, by continuous work on his own part, to lay the burden of expeditions on the legions in turn.

[7] When this force was collected, he marched for the country of the Bellovaci, and having pitched camp therein, he despatched troops of cavalry in all directions to catch any prisoners they could from whom he might learn the enemy's plans. The cavalry performed their duty, and reported that in the buildings a few persons had been found; and even these had not stayed behind to till the fields (for the emigration had been thorough everywhere), but had been sent back to act as spies. By inquiring of these as to where the main body of the Bellovaci was and what was their intention, he found out that all the Bellovaci able to bear arms had assembled in one place, and likewise the Ambiani, Aulerci, Caleti, Veliocasses, and Atrebates; that they had chosen for their camp high ground in a wood surrounded by a marsh, and had collected all the baggage in the more distant woods; that several chiefs were responsible for the war, but the rank and file were mostly under the orders of Correus, because they had perceived that he was the one to whom the name of the Roman people was most hateful. He further learnt that a few days

before Commius the Atrebatian had left their camp to bring up succours from the Germans, whose proximity was as imminent as their numbers were infinite. The Bellovaci, however, had determined, with the consent of all the chiefs and the utmost enthusiasm of the common folk, if Caesar, as was said, came with three legions, to offer battle, lest they might be compelled afterwards to fight it out with his whole army under conditions more miserable and severe. If Caesar brought up a larger force, they had determined to stand fast in the position they had chosen, while they tried, from ambuscades, to prevent the Romans from getting forage (which by reason of the time of year was both scanty and scattered), corn, and all other supplies.

[8] Upon this information, in regard to which most of the prisoners were in agreement, Caesar considered that the plans proposed were full of a prudence far removed from the recklessness of barbarians, and decided accordingly to make all possible efforts to induce the enemy, by contempt for the scanty numbers of the Romans, to come forth the more speedily to battle. For the truth was that he had the Seventh, Eighth, and Ninth Legions, real veterans of incomparable courage, and the Eleventh, a most promising corps of picked younger men: it was now on its eighth campaign, but in comparison with the rest had not yet won the same reputation for length of service and for courage. Accordingly, he summoned a council of war and set forth everything that had been reported to him; then he spoke encouragingly to the rank and file. To see if he could entice the enemy to a decisive battle by the appearance of only three legions, he arranged the order of the column as follows. The Seventh, Eighth, and Ninth were to march in front of all the baggage, and the Eleventh was to bring up the rear of the whole baggage-train (which, however, was but moderate, according to the custom on expeditions[6]), to prevent the enemy from catching a sight of greater numbers than they themselves had challenged. By this arrangement he formed the army almost in battle column,[7] and brought it within sight of the enemy before they expected it.

[9] When the Gauls (whose plans in all their self-confidence had been reported to Caesar) suddenly saw the legions in their formation advancing upon them in regular step as in line of battle,[8] they drew up their

---

[6] *i.e.* particular expeditions, apart from the main advance.

[7] Here (as in II. 19) the main body (three legions) marched in front of the baggage—possibly each legion in three columns—and the fourth legion formed the rearguard. The words used by A. Hirtius mean literally "rectangular column," *i.e.* a line of columns, in order of battle on a broad front, which could readily wheel or form into line of battle. *Cf* IV. 14.

[8] Or perhaps "formed as in line of battle."

force in front of their camp, but—either because they felt the risk of a struggle, or because of the suddenness of our arrival, or because they waited to see our plan—did not move from the higher ground. Anxious as he had been to fight, Caesar was surprised at the great number of the enemy, and set his camp over against that of the enemy, with a valley between, deep rather than extensive. He commanded the camp to be fortified with a twelve-foot rampart, a breastwork to be built on in proportion to the height of the same,[9] a double trench fifteen feet wide in each case to be dug with perpendicular sides, turrets three stories high to be set up at frequent intervals and connected by covered cross-bridges, having their front faces protected by a breastwork of wattles. His object was to hold the camp against the enemy by the double ditch and a double rank of defenders: one rank, posted on the bridges, from the greater safety afforded by height, could hurl its missiles with greater range and confidence; the other, posted on the actual rampart nearer the enemy, would be covered by the bridge from the showers of missiles. At the gateways he set doors and higher turrets.

[10] The object of this fortification was twofold. He hoped that the size of the works and the evidence of fear on his part would bring confidence into the minds of the natives, and he saw that whenever it was necessary to march farther afield for forage and corn the fortification of itself would make it possible to defend the camp with a small force. Meanwhile there were frequent encounters across the marsh[10] that lay between the two camps, for a few men would dash forward from either side; but sometimes our own Gallic or German auxiliaries would cross the marsh to pursue the enemy more fiercely, or in turn the enemy would push across it and force our troops to give ground. Moreover, in the daily expeditions for forage it happened—as was inevitable, when forage had to be collected from homesteads few and far apart—that scattered foraging parties were surrounded in troublesome places; and this occurrence, though causing our troops an insignificant loss in draught-animals and slaves, served nevertheless to arouse foolish fancies in the mind of the natives, the more so as Commius, who, as I have shown, had departed to fetch German auxiliaries, was now come with some horsemen. It is true they were no more in number than five hundred; nevertheless, the arrival of these Germans gave the natives something to rely on.

[11] Caesar remarked that for several days the enemy kept within their

---

[9] "The higher the rampart, the lower the breastwork that would be needed" (Reinhard); but the Latin seems to indicate that the breastwork was also of exceptional height.

[10] Perhaps these were encounters of archers "across the marsh," while those next mentioned were combats of close contact.

camp, which was fortified by the marsh and by its natural position, and that it could not be assaulted without an expensive action, nor the position enclosed by siege-works without a larger army than he had. Wherefore he sent a despatch to Trebonius to summon with all speed the Thirteenth Legion (which was wintering in the country of the Bituriges with Titus Sextius, lieutenant-general), and so with three legions to come to him by forced marches. He himself had called out a large number of horsemen belonging to the Remi, the Lingones, and other states; and he now sent these by turns to act as escort for the foraging parties and to resist sudden raids of the enemy.

[12] This happened daily, and at length the sameness of the duty began to diminish carefulness—the usual result of long continuance in one thing. Then the Bellovaci chose out a detachment of footmen, and, as they knew the daily stations of our cavalry piquets, set ambuscades about in wooded spots, and on the morrow sent thither horsemen also, first to lure on our men, and then, when they were surrounded, to attack them. As it chanced, the blow fell upon the Remi, to whom the performance of duty for that day had been allotted. When they suddenly remarked the enemy's horsemen, and in their superiority of numbers despised the scanty force, they pursued too eagerly and were surrounded by footmen on every side. They were more speedily thrown into confusion by this occurrence than is usually the case in a cavalry combat, and retired with the loss of Vertiscus, a chief of their state and commander of the horse. Though he could scarcely sit a horse by reason of age, yet, according to the custom of the Gauls, he had made no excuse of age in undertaking the command, and he had desired that no battle should take place without him. The spirit of the enemy was fired and excited by the success of the combat and the slaughter of a chief and commander of the Remi, and our own troops were taught by the disaster to search localities more carefully before they posted their piquets and to pursue a retiring enemy with more restraint.

[13] There was no interruption meanwhile of the daily combats in sight of both camps, which usually took place at the fords and passages over the marsh. In this sort of contest the Germans (whom Caesar had brought over the Rhine on purpose that they might fight intermingled with cavalry[11]) on one occasion crossed the marsh in a body with much resolution, cut down such few men as stood their ground, and stubbornly pursued the rest of the host. The result was a panic, not only of those whom they caught at close quarters or wounded at long range, but even of those who formed the regular reserve at a distance. It was a disgrace-

---

[11] See I. 48.

ful rout, which did not end until, after several times losing the advantage of position, the enemy reached once more their own camp, or in some cases were shamed into yet further flight. Their danger threw the whole force into such confusion that it was scarce possible to judge which was the greater—their arrogance after a trifling success, or their terror after a slight reverse.

[14] After several days spent in the same camp, the chiefs of the Bellovaci learnt that the legions with Gaius Trebonius, lieutenant-general, were come nearer; and fearing a siege like that of Alesia, they thought to send away at night all persons failing in years or strength, or unarmed, and the rest of the baggage along with them. While they were marshalling the crowded and disorderly column (for a great quantity of carts usually accompanies the Gauls, even when they are moving light), daybreak came upon them, and they drew up their force of armed men in front of their own camp, for fear that the Romans might essay to pursue them before their baggage-train had advanced to any distance. Caesar, however, considered that if they stood their ground they should not be attacked, owing to the steepness of the ascent, and yet that the legions should certainly be moved up close enough to make it impossible for the natives to withdraw from the spot without risk of an attack. Seeing, therefore, that camp was divided from camp by a troublesome marsh so difficult to cross that it could check the speed of a pursuit, and remarking that beyond the marsh the ridge, stretching almost to the enemy's camp, was cut off from the same by but a slight valley, he had gangways laid over the marsh, led the legions across, and speedily reached the highest plateau on the ridge, which was protected on its two sides by a downward slope. There he reformed the legions, and then reached the end of the ridge, where he posted his line of battle in a spot from which the missiles of the artillery could be discharged into the masses of the enemy.

[15] The natives relied on the natural strength of the position; and while they did not intend to decline battle, if perchance the Romans should try to mount the hill, they could not send their forces away gradually in detachments, for fear that, if so dispersed, they would be put to confusion. So they stood fast in line. Caesar noted their stubbornness, and forming up twenty cohorts, he measured out a camp on the spot and ordered it to be entrenched. The works finished, he set the legions in battle array before the rampart, and placed the cavalry, with chargers bridled, on outpost. The Bellovaci saw that the Romans were ready for pursuit, and feeling that they could not spend the night where they were, nor, indeed, remain longer without danger, they determined on the following plan of retirement. They had a very large quantity of straw bales and faggots in their camp; and passing these from hand to hand between them where they sat (for, as stated in former books of Caesar's

Commentaries, it is the custom of the Gauls to sit in line of battle), they piled them in front of their line, and at the end of the day they fired them simultaneously at a given signal. So a continuous flame suddenly covered the whole force from the sight of the Romans. When this occurred, the natives fled away at a most furious speed.

[16] Caesar could not observe the withdrawal of the enemy through the screen of fires, but, nevertheless, suspecting that the stratagem had been adopted with flight in view, he advanced the legions and despatched troops of cavalry in pursuit. He himself moved forward more slowly, fearing an ambuscade—in other words, that the enemy might perhaps try to hold their ground and to entice our troops on to unfavourable ground. The cavalry feared to enter the smoke and the thick belt of flame, and even if any more eager spirits entered therein, they scarce could make out the front part of their own horses; wherefore, in fear of an ambuscade, they gave the Bellovaci a free chance of retirement. So they fled, with as much of cunning as of fear, and with no loss; and proceeding no more than ten miles, they pitched camp in a strongly fenced place. Thence, often setting horsemen and foot in ambuscades, they wrought great havoc upon the Roman foraging parties.

[17] This happened somewhat frequently, and from a prisoner Caesar discovered that Correus, the chief of the Bellovaci, had chosen six thousand footmen and a thousand horse from the total number, to put them in ambuscade at the spot to which he suspected the Romans would be sending because of the store of corn and forage there. Upon information of this design Caesar brought out more legions than usual, and pushed forward cavalry, according to his practice of sending such as an escort for foraging parties,[12] and among them he put light-armed auxiliaries. He himself approached as near as possible with the legions.

[18] The enemy were set about in ambuscades. They had chosen for the despatch of the business a plain[13] extending no more than a mile in every direction, fenced every way by woods or by a most troublesome river: this plain they surrounded with a network of ambuscades. The enemy's design was found out, and our men, with hearts and hands all ready for fight—for with the legions supporting they had no idea of declining battle—reached the spot troop by troop. Their arrival led Correus to suppose that a chance of despatching the business was offered him; and showing himself first with a few men, he charged the nearest troops of cavalry. Our men stoutly withstood the onrush of the ambus-

---

[12] *e.g.* in ch. 11, *supra*.
[13] "On the southern bank of the Aisne, in the angle formed by its confluence with the Oise" (Rice Holmes).

caders without crowding together—and when such crowding occurs, as it generally does in cavalry combats, through a sense of fear, the mere numbers of the men engaged cause loss.

[19] Our troops of cavalry were thus posted in different places, and when scattered parties began one after another to engage, to prevent their comrades being outflanked, the rest of the enemy, while Correus was fighting, burst out of the woods. In different parts of the field a fierce struggle began; and as it tended to drag on indecisively, little by little there issued from the woods a formed body of footmen, which forced our cavalry to give way. But they were speedily supported by the light-armed infantry, which, as I have mentioned, had been sent on in front of the legions, and these, taking post between the troops of our cavalry, fought stoutly. For some time the battle was evenly contested; then, as was inevitable from the nature of the engagement, the troops which had withstood the first attack from the ambuscades began to get the better of it just because they had not suffered any damage from the ambuscaders through want of judgment.[14] Meanwhile the legions were drawing nearer, and frequent reports were being brought alike to our own side and to the enemy to the effect that the commander-in-chief was come with troops in order of battle. When they learnt this our men, relying on the support of the cohorts, fought most fiercely, for they feared that if they were too slow of execution they would be thought to have shared the glory of victory with the legions. The enemy's spirits fell, and by different roads they sought to flee. In vain; for they themselves were held fast by those difficulties of the locality, by which they had hoped to cut off the Romans. Still, beaten and broken as they were, and panic-stricken by the loss of more than half their number, they fled on, part by way of the woods, part by the river-side; yet even these fugitives were slain by the eager pursuit of our men. Meanwhile Correus, in no wise conquered by disaster, could not be induced to withdraw from the engagement and seek the woods, nor to surrender at our summons; nay, fighting most gallantly and wounding many men, he compelled the victors, in a frenzy of rage, to hurl their missiles against him.

[20] The business had been despatched after this fashion, and the traces of the combat were still fresh, when Caesar came on the scene. He supposed that the enemy were crushed by so dire a disaster, and that upon report thereof they would abandon their camping-ground, said to be not farther than eight miles, more or less, from the field of slaughter. He saw that his passage was impeded by the river, but, none the less, he led the army across and advanced. But when the Bellovaci and the rest

---

[14] e.g. by allowing themselves to be crowded together: cf. ch. 18.

of the states received suddenly among them the few fugitives, and those wounded, who by the help of the woods had escaped destruction, they recognized their disaster, seeing that all was against them, that Correus was slain, that their horsemen and the most gallant of their footmen were lost. And as they thought the Romans were coming upon them they suddenly summoned a conference by trumpet-call, and clamoured that deputies and hostages should be sent to Caesar.

[21] When this counsel was approved by all, Commius the Atrebatian escaped to the Germans from whom he had borrowed succours for that campaign. The rest at once sent deputies to Caesar, and besought him to be satisfied with a punishment of his enemy which, had he been able to inflict it without a battle while their strength was unimpaired, in his mercy and kindness he would assuredly never have inflicted. The power of the Bellovaci was crushed, they said, by the cavalry combat; many thousand chosen footmen had perished, scarcely had men escaped to tell of the slaughter. Nevertheless, for all the greatness of the disaster, the Bellovaci had gained one advantage by the combat, in the slaughter of Correus, who had originated the campaign and stirred up the people. For never during his lifetime had the council possessed so much power in the state as the untutored populace.

[22] To this petition of the deputies Caesar remarked that in the previous year the Bellovaci and the rest of the Gallic states had simultaneously engaged in war: the Bellovaci had stuck to their intention the most obstinately of all, and had not been brought to a right mind by the surrender of the rest. He was very well aware that it was easy enough to shift the blame of the offence on to the dead. But no one was so powerful that, if chiefs were reluctant, the council in opposition, and all good citizens adverse, he could excite and conduct a war by means of a feeble band of common folk. Nevertheless, he would be satisfied with the punishment which they had brought upon themselves.

[23] In the ensuing night the deputies reported his replies to their people, and the tale of hostages was made up. Deputies met hastily together from the rest of the states, which were watching to see how the Bellovaci fared. They gave hostages and did as commanded, with the exception of Commius, whom fear prevented from entrusting his personal safety to the honour of any man. The truth was that in the previous year, while Caesar was in Nearer Gaul administering justice, Titus Labienus, having discovered Commius to be tampering with the states and forming a conspiracy against Caesar, determined that his faithlessness might be suppressed without any breach of faith. And as he did not suppose that Commius would come to the camp on a summons, he did not wish to make him more cautious by any such attempt; he therefore sent Gaius Volusenus Quadratus to compass his execution on pretence of parley. He gave him a

party of centurions, chosen as fit for the purpose. When they were come to the parley, and, as agreed, Volusenus seized the hand of Commius, a centurion—unsteadied, it may be, by the strangeness of the task, or speedily prevented by the friends of Commius—could not despatch the man; however, with the first stroke he dealt him a severe blow on the head. Swords were drawn on both sides, but both thought not so much of fight as of flight, our own men because they believed that Commius had got a mortal wound, the Gauls because they knew it was an ambush, and feared more trouble than they saw. After this deed Commius, it was said, had resolved never to come within sight of any Roman.

[24] So the most warlike nations were subdued; and as he saw that there was no longer any state able to compass a war of resistance to himself—that not a few persons were moving out of the towns and fleeing away from the fields to avoid the dominion at their gates—Caesar determined to divide the army into several parts. Marcus Antonius, the quartermaster-general, with the Twelfth Legion he attached to his own force. Gaius Fabius, lieutenant-general, with five-and-twenty cohorts he sent to an entirely different part of Gaul, because he heard that certain states there were in arms, and believed that the two legions with Gaius Caninius Rebilus, the lieutenant-general in these parts, were not strong enough. Titus Labienus he summoned to join him, sending the Fifteenth Legion, however, which had been with Labienus in cantonments, to Italian Gaul[15] to protect the colonies of Roman citizens and to prevent the occurrence of a disaster, through a raid of barbarians, similar to that which had occurred the summer before to the men of Tergeste,[16] who had been overwhelmed by a sudden assault of Illyrian brigands. He himself moved off to devastate and plunder the country of Ambiorix; and, in despair of being able to bring the frightened fugitive into his power, he deemed it the best thing, out of regard for his own prestige, so completely to strip his territory of citizens, buildings, and cattle as to make Ambiorix hated by any of his subjects who might chance to survive, and to leave him no return to the state by reason of disasters so grievous.

[25] He despatched legions or auxiliaries into every part of the country of Ambiorix, wrought general devastation by slaughter, fire, and pillage, killed or captured a large number of persons. He then sent Labienus with two legions against the Treveri. This state, by reason of its proximity to Germany and its training in daily wars, differed little from the

---

[15] Literally "wearing the *toga*," *i.e.* enfranchised. The Cispadane part of Cisalpine Gaul had received Roman citizenship at the time of the Social War (90–89 B.C.); the Transpadane part received it in 49 B.C.
[16] Trieste.

Germans in its habits of barbarity, and never submitted to commands except under compulsion of an army.

[26] Meanwhile Gaius Caninius, lieutenant-general, had learnt by despatches and messages from Duratius that a great host of the enemy had assembled in the country of the Pictones. Duratius had remained throughout in amity with the Romans, though a certain part of his state had revolted. Caninius therefore pushed forward towards the town of Lemonum (Poitiers), and as he came near it he received more definite information from prisoners that Duratius was shut up in Lemonum and attacked by Dumnacus, chief of the Andes, with many thousand men. Not venturing to pit weak legions against the enemy, the Roman commander pitched camp in a fenced position. When Dumnacus learnt the approach of Caninius, he turned the whole of his force against the legions and prepared to assault the Roman camp. After spending several days on the assault, and failing, though with great loss of his men, to break down any part of the entrenchments, he returned again to the siege of Lemonum.

[27] Gaius Fabius, lieutenant-general, was readmitting several states to protection, with hostages to confirm the same, just at the moment when by a despatch from Gaius Caninius Rebilus he learnt what was happening in the country of the Pictones. Upon the information he started to render assistance to Duratius. But when Dumnacus learnt of the arrival of Fabius he despaired of safety, if he were to be compelled at one and the same time to withstand a Roman enemy outside and to keep an anxious watch upon the townsfolk; so he suddenly retired with his force from the place, thinking that he would not be really safe unless he marched his force across the river Loire, which by reason of its size had to be crossed by a bridge. Fabius was not yet come within sight of the enemy and had not joined forces with Caninius; nevertheless, on information derived from those who knew the character of the country, he believed that the enemy in panic would make for the spot for which they were actually making. So he pressed on with his force to the same bridge, and commanded the cavalry to advance to such a distance in front of the column as should make it possible, after such advance, to retire without fatiguing the horses to the same camp as himself. The Roman cavalry went in chase, according to their instructions, and attacked the column of Dumnacus, and as their assault was delivered upon panic-stricken fugitives in heavy marching order they slew many and got great spoil. So, their business well done, they retired to camp.

[28] The following night Fabius sent on the cavalry with instructions to fight and to delay the whole column till he himself should come up. And in order to carry out the operation in accordance with these instructions Quintus Atius Varus, commander of the cavalry, a soldier of

uncommon spirit and sagacity, after haranguing his men, caught up the enemy's column and, placing part of his troops of cavalry in suitable positions, with part engaged in combat. The enemy's cavalry fought with the greater boldness because their footmen were coming up in support, and the latter, halting their whole column, rendered assistance to their cavalry against ours. A fiercely contested combat ensued. Our cavalry despised an enemy they had beaten the day before, and, remembering that the legions were following up, were ashamed to yield and eager to finish the combat by themselves, so that they fought most gallantly against the footmen; while the enemy, believing, according to their information of the day before, that there were no more troops to come up, thought they had got a chance of exterminating our cavalry.

[29] As the fight went on for some time with the utmost keenness, Dumnacus was drawing up his line to furnish in due turn a support for his horsemen, when suddenly the legions in close order came into view of the enemy. At sight of them the troops of native horse were paralysed, the enemy's line was terror-struck; and throwing their baggage-column into confusion, with a great shout they scattered in every direction and betook themselves to flight. Then our own cavalry, who a moment before had been struggling most gallantly with a resisting foe, set up a great shout on every hand in the joyful excitement of victory and surrounded them as they retreated, and in that encounter they slew as long as their horses had strength to pursue and their hands to strike. So more than twelve thousand, armed men or men who had flung away their arms in the panic I have described, were slain, and the whole train of the baggage was captured.

[30] After the rout it became known that Drappes, a Senonian—who at the first outbreak of the revolt in Gaul had collected desperadoes from anywhere and everywhere, calling slaves to liberty, summoning exiles from every state, and harbouring brigands, and with these forces had cut off the baggage-trains and supplies of the Romans—with no more than two thousand men, collected from the rout, was making for the Province; and that Lucterius the Cadurcan, who (as we know from the preceding book[17] of the Commentaries) had desired to make an attack on the Province at the beginning of the Gallic revolt, had made common cause with him. Wherefore Caninius, the lieutenant-general, pressed on with two legions in pursuit of them to prevent the dire disgrace that must result, by loss or panic in the Province, from the acts of these desperate brigands.

[31] Gaius Fabius, with the rest of the army, marched off against the

---

[17] VII. 7.

Carnutes and the other states whose forces, as he knew, had been worsted in the battle which he had fought with Dumnacus. He had, indeed, no doubt that they would prove more submissive in view of the recent disaster, but felt that, if time and space were granted, they might be stirred up again on the provocation of Dumnacus. And on this occasion Fabius was attended by the most signal and speedy success in his recovery of the states. The Carnutes, who, though often harassed, had never made mention of peace, gave hostages and surrendered; and the other states situated in the most distant borders of Gaul, next the Ocean, the Armoric states so-called, were constrained by the example of the Carnutes to submit at once to orders when Fabius and the legions arrived. Dumnacus was driven out of his own country and compelled, in secret, solitary wanderings, to seek the uttermost parts of Gaul.

[32] But Drappes and his partner Lucterius, when they learnt that Caninius and the legions were at hand, conceived that with an army at their heels they could not enter the confines of the Province without certain destruction; and as they had no chance of ranging freely and committing acts of brigandage, they halted in the country of the Cadurci. Lucterius had wielded great power there among his own countrymen in earlier days when their fortunes were unimpaired, and a champion of revolution always exercised great influence among the natives. With his own and Drappes' forces he occupied Uxellodunum,[18] formerly a dependency of his, a town exceedingly well protected by its natural position, and he added the townsfolk to his force.

[33] Thither with all speed came Gaius Caninius. He noticed that every part of the town was protected by the most precipitous rocks, which, even if undefended, it was difficult for armed men to climb; but at the same time he saw that the townsfolk had great quantities of baggage, and that, if they tried to remove it in secret flight, they would be unable to escape not only the cavalry but even the legions. Accordingly he divided his cohorts into three detachments, and formed three camps on very high ground, from which he proceeded by degrees, according to the capacity of his troops, to run a rampart all round the town.

[34] When the townsfolk remarked this they were filled with anxiety, remembering the utter distress at Alesia; and fearing that a blockade might have similar result; and Lucterius most of all, having experienced that fate, admonished them to have a care for the corn-supply. By general consent, therefore, the two leaders determined to leave a part of their force there, and to set forth with a body of light-armed troops to get corn into the town. This plan being approved, Drappes and Lucterius the

[18] Puy d'Issolu.

following night left behind two thousand armed men and led the rest out of the town. In the space of a few days this party collected a great quantity of corn from the country of the Cadurci, some of whom were eager to assist them with a supply, while others were unable to prevent them from taking it; and several times they moved by night to attack our forts. Therefore Gaius Caninius delayed to make a ring of entrenchments all round the town, for fear he might not be able to defend the works when finished or might have to post weak detachments in a number of separate positions.

[35] Having collected great store of corn, Drappes and Lucterius established themselves not more than ten miles from the town, intending from this point to convey the corn into the town by degrees. The commanders divided the duties between them: Drappes stood fast with part of the force to guard the camp, Lucterius escorted the train of animals to the town. Having posted several detachments thereabout, he began about the tenth hour of the night to carry the corn into the town by narrow paths through the woods. The camp sentries noticed the noise thereof, and scouts, being sent out, reported what was afoot; so Caninius moved speedily with cohorts (which had stood to arms) from the nearest forts and attacked the corn-carriers just before dawn. They were panic-struck by the sudden blow, and fled helter-skelter to their own detachments. When our men saw it they dashed the more fiercely against the armed men, and suffered not one of the number to be taken alive. Lucterius fled away from the spot with a few followers, and did not return to the camp.

[36] After his success Caninius discovered from prisoners that a part of the force was with Drappes in camp not much more than twelve miles away. He ascertained this from several persons, and perceiving that if they were panic-stricken by the rout of one chief, the rest could easily be overwhelmed, he thought it a great piece of fortune that no one had escaped from the slaughter to the camp to bring news to Drappes of the disaster they had suffered. But, though he saw no danger in the attempt, he sent forward to the enemy's camp all the cavalry and the German infantry, the swiftest of troops, and, distributing one legion between the three camps, himself led off the other in light order. When he was come nearer the enemy, he learnt from the scouts he had sent forward that, according to the general rule of the natives, the higher ground had been abandoned and the camp brought down to the banks of the river; also that the Germans and cavalry had caught them altogether unawares when they swooped suddenly upon them, and had engaged. On this report he brought up the legion, armed and formed for action, and then suddenly, at a given signal, the upper ground was surrounded and captured. When this happened, the Germans and the cavalry, at sight of the standards of the line, fought with the utmost fury. The cohorts charged

at once from all sides, and as every man was killed or captured much booty fell into their hands. Drappes himself was captured in that engagement.

[37] After this brilliant success, with scarce a soldier wounded, Caninius returned to the blockade of the townsfolk; and now that he had exterminated the enemy outside, in fear of whom he had hitherto been prevented from breaking up his force into detachments[19] and surrounding the townsfolk with an entrenchment, he commanded siege-works to be carried out on every side. Next day Gaius Fabius joined him there with his own force and took a part of the town to blockade.

[38] Meanwhile Caesar left Marcus Antonius, quartermaster-general, with fifteen cohorts in the country of the Bellovaci, in order to give the Belgae no further chance of framing rebellious designs. He himself visited the rest of the states, making requisition of more hostages and quieting the general apprehension by words of encouragement. When he was come to the Carnutes, the state in which (as Caesar explained in the preceding book of his Commentaries[20]) the war had originated, he remarked that they were especially alarmed owing to their consciousness of guilt; and the more speedily to free the state from apprehension he demanded for punishment Gutruatus, the ringleader in that crime[21] and the instigator of the rebellion. And although the man would not trust himself even to his fellow-countrymen, all bestirred themselves speedily to seek him out and bring him to the camp. In opposition to his own natural inclination, Caesar was compelled to execute him by the troops who gathered in a mighty crowd, for they attributed to him all the dangers and losses of the war. He was therefore scourged to death and then decapitated.

[39] At this point Caesar learned by frequent despatches from Caninius what had been done with Drappes and Lucterius and what was the steadfast purpose of the townsfolk. And though he disregarded their small numbers, he judged nevertheless that their obstinacy must be visited with a severe punishment, for he feared that the Gauls as a whole might suppose that what had been lacking in them for resisting the Romans was not strength, but resolution; and that the rest of the states might follow this example and rely on any advantage offered by strong positions to reassert their liberty. All the Gauls were aware, as he knew, that there was one more summer season[22] in his term of office, and that, if they could hold out for that, they had no further danger to fear. And

---

[19] See ch. 34.
[20] VII. 3.
[21] The murders at Cenabum.
[22] *i.e.* the summer of 50 B.C. Caesar's term of office was to end on March 1, 49 B.C.

so, leaving Quintus Calenus, lieutenant-general, with the legions to follow after him by regular marches,[23] he himself with the whole of the
cavalry pressed on with all speed to join Caninius.

[40] He reached Uxellodunum altogether unexpected. He perceived
that the town was surrounded by siege-works and that the enemy had no
chance of retreat from an assault, and he had learnt from deserters that
the townsfolk were well supplied with a large quantity of corn; he began,
therefore, to try to cut off their water. A river ran through the bottom
of the valley which almost entirely surrounded the hill, and on the hill
was built the town of Uxellodunum, with a precipice on every side. The
lie of the ground prevented a diversion of the river, for its course at the
very base of the hill was such that it could nowhere be drawn off by sink-
ing trenches. But the townsfolk had a difficult and precipitous descent to
the river, so that our troops, without danger to life or limb, could prevent
them from either approaching the river or retiring up the steep ascent.
Caesar remarked this difficulty of theirs, and by posting archers and
slingers thereabouts, and, further, by placing artillery at certain points
opposite the easiest lines of descent, he sought to cut off the townsfolk
from the river-water.

[41] Subsequently the whole host of water-carriers assembled at one
spot, immediately under the town wall. A great spring of water gushed
out there, on the side where for an interval of about three hundred feet
there was a break in the circuit of the river. All the Romans wished that
the townsfolk could be cut off from this spring, but Caesar alone saw how
it could be done. He began, just opposite the place, to push up mantlets
against the hill and to build a ramp with great effort and continual fighting; for the townsfolk ran down from the higher ground and engaged
without risk at long range, wounding many men as they doggedly worked
upwards. However, our troops were not to be deterred from thrusting the
mantlets forward and from defeating the local difficulties by sheer labour
of engineering. At the same time they were pushing forward covered
mines from the mantlets to the head of the spring; and this kind of work
involved no risk, and could be done without suspicion on the part of the
enemy. The ramp was built up to a height of sixty feet, and upon it was
set a turret of ten stories, not, indeed, to reach the level of the walls, for
no siege-works could effect that, but to overtop the level of the spring.
When the artillery from the turret began to discharge missiles upon the
line of approach to the spring, and the townsfolk could not get water
without danger, not only cattle and beasts of burden, but even the great
host of the enemy, were like to die of thirst.

---

[23] *i.e.* not forced marches.

[42] Terror-struck by this trouble, the townsfolk filled tubs with grease, pitch, and shingles, and rolled them burning on to the works, at the same time engaging with the utmost ferocity in order that the danger of the fight might prevent the Romans from extinguishing the fire. A mighty flame suddenly shot forth in the midst of the works; for everything that was discharged over the escarpment was held up by the mantlets and the ramp, and set fire to the particular object which checked its course. On the other hand, our soldiers, though handicapped by the dangerous character of the fighting and by the disadvantage of position, none the less endured every difficulty in the most gallant spirit. For the action went on at a considerable height and in sight of our army, and great shouting arose on both sides. So each man, in as conspicuous a fashion as he could—the better to make his valour known and approved—faced alike the missiles of the enemy and the flames.

[43] Seeing not a few of his men wounded, Caesar ordered cohorts to climb the height from every side of the town and under pretence of attacking the walls to raise a shout all round. This action terrified the townsfolk, and in their uncertainty as to what was going on in the other quarters they recalled their men-at-arms from the attempt on the works and set them along the walls. So our men, when the fighting ceased, speedily extinguished or cut away the parts of the works which had caught fire. Although the townsfolk continued to resist stoutly, and stuck to their resolve, even when they had lost a great part of their number through thirst, at last by means of the mines the feeders of the spring were cut off and diverted. This caused the perpetual spring suddenly to dry up, and wrought such despair of deliverance in the townsfolk that they thought it due, not to the device of man, but to the act of God. And so necessity forced them to surrender.

[44] Caesar's clemency, as he knew, was familiar to all, and he did not fear that severer action on his part might seem due to natural cruelty; at the same time he could not see any successful issue to his plans if more of the enemy in different districts engaged in designs of this sort. He therefore considered that the rest must be deterred by an exemplary punishment; and so, while granting them their lives, he cut off the hands of all who had borne arms, to testify the more openly the penalty of evildoers. Drappes, taken prisoner by Caninius, as I have related, was so mortified at the indignity of bondage, or so fearful of yet more grievous punishment, that he abstained from food for a few days and so met his death. At the same time Lucterius, who escaped from the fight, as I described, came into the hands of Epasnactus, an Arvernian; for he had to change his quarters frequently and to entrust himself to the honour of many persons, as he felt that he could make no long stay anywhere without danger, conscious as he was how bitter an enemy he must have

in Caesar. And now Epasnactus the Arvernian, a devoted friend of the Roman people, put him in bonds without hesitation and brought him in to Caesar.

[45] Meanwhile, in the country of the Treveri, Labienus fought a cavalry combat with success, killing not a few of the Treveri and of the Germans, who never refused succours to any state against the Romans. Their chiefs he got into his power alive, among them Surus the Aeduan, a man of the highest distinction in courage as well as lineage, and the only Aeduan who had remained in arms up to that time.

[46] On report of this, Caesar saw that matters were going well in every part of Gaul, and he judged that in the campaigns of the previous summers Gaul had been conquered and subdued. But as he himself had never visited Aquitaine, though he had partially conquered it by the campaign of Publius Crassus, he started with two legions for that part of Gaul, to spend there the campaign season of his last summer.[24] And he carried out this work, like all others, with speed and success, for all the states of Aquitaine sent deputies to him and gave hostages. These affairs settled, he started for Narbonne with an escort of cavalry, despatching the army to winter quarters under command of the lieutenant-generals. Four legions he stationed in Belgium, with the generals Marcus Antonius, Gaius Trebonius, and Publius Vatinius; two he despatched into the country of the Aedui, whose influence he knew to be supreme in the whole of Gaul; two he stationed among the Turoni, on the borders of the Carnutes, to hold all that district next to the Ocean; the remaining two in the country of the Lemovices, not far from the Arverni, in order that no part of Gaul might be without an army. He himself stayed for a few days in the Province, and speedily passed through all the assize towns, investigated matters of public dispute, and assigned rewards to the meritorious; for he had the best possible chance of learning what had been the temper of each person in that revolt of all Gaul which he had withstood by the loyalty and the succours of that Province. This business despatched, he retired to the legions in Belgium and wintered at Nemetocenna.

[47] There he learnt that Commius the Atrebatian had had an encounter with the Roman cavalry. The truth was that Antonius had gone into cantonments, and the state of the Atrebates was loyal; but Commius, after the wound which I have related above,[25] had kept himself always in readiness for any rising in the interest of his fellow-countrymen, that when they sought a plan of campaign they might not lack a man to inspire and

---

[24] Or "the last part of the summer season" (the campaign season).
[25] Ch. 23.

to lead their arms. And now, when the state was in obedience to the Romans, with his own horsemen he supported himself and his followers by acts of brigandage, and by infesting the roads he cut off several trains of supplies which were being conveyed to the cantonments of the Romans.

[48] Gaius Volusenus Quadratus had been attached as cavalry commander to Antonius, to winter with him, and Antonius despatched him to pursue the enemy's horse. With the unique courage which he possessed Volusenus combined great hatred of Commius, so that he was the more willing to carry out this order. So he set ambuscades about, attacked the other's horsemen frequently, and won his actions. At last, in a fiercer struggle than usual, wherein Volusenus, in his desire to cut off Commius in person, had pursued him too persistently with a few followers, while Commius in furious flight had led Volusenus on too far, in his hatred of the Roman he suddenly called on the loyal assistance of his men not to leave unpunished the wounds inflicted on himself under pledge of faith,[26] then turned his horse and, leaving the rest, recklessly galloped at the Roman commander. All his horsemen did likewise, turning and pursuing our small party. Commius spurred on his horse and brought it abreast of the horse of Quadratus, pointed his lance, and with a mighty thrust pierced him in the middle of the thigh. When their commander was wounded our men at once stood fast, then turned their horses about and drove back the enemy. Upon this a number of the enemy were crushed and wounded by the strength of our onset, and some were ridden down in flight, some cut off. Their leader escaped this fate by the speed of his horse; but the Roman commander, so grievously wounded that he seemed likely to come within peril of his life, was carried back to camp. Commius, however, either because his wrath was appeased or because he had lost a great part of his following, sent deputies to Antonius and gave hostages to guarantee that he would report himself where Antonius should prescribe and submit to his commands. One concession he prayed might be granted to his fears—that he should not come into the sight of any Roman.[27] Judging that this demand proceeded from a legitimate fear, Antonius indulged his petition and accepted his hostages.

I am aware that Caesar has compiled a separate Commentary for each year; but I have deemed it unnecessary for me to do this, because the ensuing year, when Lucius Paulus and Gaius Marcellus were consuls,[28]

---

[26] See ch. 23.
[27] He had made this resolution after the first encounter.
[28] 50 b.c.

contains no operations on a large scale in Gaul. However, to leave no one in ignorance as to the positions of Caesar and his army at that time, I have decided to write a few remarks and add them to this Commentary.

[49] During his winter in Belgium Caesar had one definite purpose in view—to keep the states friendly, and to give hope or occasion of armed action to none. There was nothing, in fact, which he desired less than to have the definite necessity of a campaign imposed upon him on the eve of his quitting his province, for fear that, when he was about to lead his army south, he might leave behind a war which all Gaul could readily take up without immediate danger. Accordingly, by addressing the states in terms of honour, by bestowing ample presents upon the chiefs, by imposing no new burdens, he easily kept Gaul at peace after the exhaustion of so many defeats, under improved conditions of obedience.

[50] The winter season over, he varied his usual practice, travelling to Italy with all possible speed in order to address the boroughs and colonies to which he had already commended the candidature of his quartermaster-general, Marcus Antonius, for the priesthood.[29] He was glad to use his personal influence in the contest for an intimate friend of his own, whom he had sent on a little before to pursue his candidature; he was no less eager to do so in opposition to the powerful partisanship of the few who desired, by the defeat of Marcus Antonius, to upset the influence of Caesar when he should retire from his province. And although he had heard on the way that, before he could reach Italy, Antonius had been elected augur, he felt that he had no less legitimate reason for visiting the boroughs and colonies to thank them for affording Antonius their support in so large numbers, and at the same time to commend himself as a candidate for the office he sought for the following year. For his opponents were insolently boasting that Lucius Lentulus and Gaius Marcellus had been elected consuls[30] to despoil Caesar of every office and distinction, and that the consulship had been wrested from Servius Galba, though he had been far stronger in influence and votes alike, because he was intimately connected with Caesar by personal friendship and by service as his lieutenant-general.[31]

[51] The arrival of Caesar was welcomed by all the boroughs and colonies with honour and affection beyond all belief; for it was his first coming since the glorious campaign against a united Gaul. Nothing was omitted that wit

---

[29] He was a candidate for admission into the College of Augurs, election to which was, since the Lex Domitia of 105 B.C., in the hands of the people.

[30] For the year 49 B.C.

[31] *Cf.* III. 1.

could devise for the decoration of gates, roads, and every place where Caesar was to pass. The whole population, with the children, went forth to meet him, victims were sacrificed everywhere, festal couches, duly spread,[32] occupied market-places and temples, so as to anticipate, if possible, the joy of triumph so long, so very long expected.[33] Such was the magnificence shown by the richer folk, such the eagerness of the humbler sort.

[52] Having passed rapidly through all the districts of Italian[34] Gaul, Caesar returned with all speed to the army at Nemetocenna; he summoned the legions out of all the cantonments to the country of the Treveri, proceeded thither himself, and there reviewed the army. He put Titus Labienus in charge of Italian Gaul, that it might be won over to give stronger support to his candidature for the consulship. He himself marched as far as he deemed sufficient for change of stations, to keep the troops in health. In the course of his marches he frequently heard that Labienus was being tampered with[35] by his enemies, and he was informed that it was the aim of a few plotters to interpose a resolution[36] of the Senate and deprive him of some part of the army; nevertheless he believed nothing in regard to Labienus, nor could he be induced to take any action against the resolution of the Senate. For he judged that his cause was like to be easily gained if the votes of the conscript fathers were unrestrained. Indeed, Gaius Curio, tribune of the people,[37] had undertaken to defend the cause and the position of Caesar; and he had often promised[38] the Senate that, if any person suffered from apprehension of Caesar's arms, and as the armed tyranny of Pompeius was creating considerable alarm in the Forum, he would move that both leaders should give up arms and disband their armies. He held that by this means the state would be free and independent. And this was no mere promise, but he even tried to secure a decree by a division;[39] however, the consuls and

---

[32] There is an allusion here to *Lectisternium,* or feast of couches, when the images of the gods were laid on couches strewn with coverlets, and food was set before them.

[33] Or, "the rejoicing of a triumph so universally admired."

[34] See note on ch. 24 *supra.*

[35] In the next year he openly joined Pompeius.

[36] A proposal carried in the Senate, but vetoed by a Tribune, was known as *senatus auctoritas,* as distinguished from *senatus consultum.* It was often recorded, as a protest of one political party against the other.

[37] In 50 B.C.

[38] The whole sentence is very much involved. Note that Curio, now the spokesman of Caesar in the Senate, questions the apprehension caused by Caesar's arms, but he has no doubt of the alarm created by Pompeius' arms. Curio could not promise that both leaders would give up arms; but he did promise that he would move that they do so.

[39] A decree of the Senate was arrived at either by asking individual Senators for their opinions or "by a division." In the latter case, the Senators "divided" to opposite sides of the House.

the friends of Pompeius interposed to prevent it, and thus frustrated the attempt by delaying action.

[53] This testimony of the Senate as a whole was important, and consistent with their previous action. The year before, in the course of an attack on the position of Caesar, Marcellus had brought before the Senate prematurely, and in violation of a law of Pompeius and Crassus,[40] a motion touching the provinces of Caesar. Opinions were expressed, and when Marcellus, who coveted for himself any position to be secured from the feeling against Caesar, tried to divide the House, a crowded Senate passed over in support of the general negative.[41] These set-backs did not break the spirit of Caesar's enemies, but they prompted them to find more forcible arguments whereby the Senate would be compelled to approve what they themselves had resolved.

[54] Then a decree of the Senate was made that for the Parthian campaign one legion should be sent by Gnaeus Pompeius, a second by Gaius Caesar, and it was clear enough that the two legions were to be withdrawn from one man. For the First Legion, which he had sent to Caesar, as it had been raised from a levy in Caesar's province, Pompeius gave as one of his own. Caesar, though there was not the least doubt about the intention of his opponents, nevertheless sent the legion back to Pompeius, and on his own account ordered the Fifteenth, which he had kept in Nearer Gaul, to be handed over in accordance with the Senate's decree. In its stead he sent the Thirteenth Legion to Italy, to maintain the garrisons from which the Fifteenth was to be withdrawn. He himself arranged the cantonments for the army: he stationed Gaius Trebonius with three legions in Belgium, Gaius Fabius with the same number he moved into the country of the Aedui; for he thought that the safety of Gaul would best be assured if the Belgae, whose valour was greatest, and the Aedui, whose influence was strongest, were held in check by armies. He himself proceeded to Italy.

[55] When he was come thither he learnt that through the action of the consul Gaius Marcellus the two legions sent back by himself, which in accordance with the Senate's decree ought to have been marched off for the Parthian campaign, had been handed over to Gnaeus Pompeius and kept in Italy. This action left no doubt in any man's mind what was afoot against Caesar; still, Caesar determined to submit to anything so long as some hope was left to him of a constitutional settlement rather than an appeal to arms. He pressed . . .[42]

---

[40] The law prolonged Caesar's command for five years, from 1 March, 54 B.C., to 1 March, 49.

[41] See note 39, page 182.

[42] Apparently not many words have been lost here. A sentence or so would suffice to bring the reader to the opening words of *The Civil Wars*.

# INDEX I—PERSONS

# INDEX II—TRIBES

*[A modern name is given in parentheses, e.g. Ambiani (cf. Amiens), where it appears to be derived from, or connected with, the Latin designation.]*

189

# INDEX III—GEOGRAPHY

[*Present names of towns, rivers, etc. are given in parentheses.*]

193

# INDEX IV—SUBJECTS